LPF

LOCOS POR EL FÚTBOL

# 7

# Un regate habilidoso
### Frauke Nahrgang

Ilustración
**Betina Gotzen-Beek**

Traducción
**Frank Schleper**

EDELVIVES

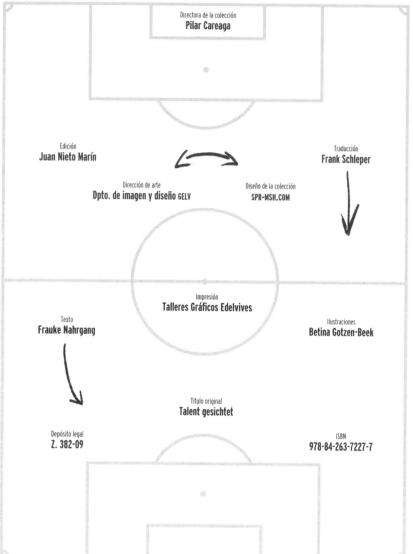

Directora de la colección
**Pilar Careaga**

Edición
**Juan Nieto Marín**

Traducción
**Frank Schleper**

Dirección de arte
**Dpto. de imagen y diseño GELV**

Diseño de la colección
**SPR-MSH.COM**

Impresión
**Talleres Gráficos Edelvives**

Texto
**Frauke Nahrgang**

Ilustraciones
**Betina Gotzen-Beek**

Título original
**Talent gesichtet**

Depósito legal
**Z. 382-09**

ISBN
**978-84-263-7227-7**

© Bertelsmann Jugendbuch Verlag,
división del grupo editorial Random House GmbH,
München, Germany, 2007
Negociado a través de Ute Körner Literary Agent, S. L., Barcelona

© De esta edición: Editorial Luis Vives, 2009
Carretera de Madrid, km. 315,700
50012 Zaragoza
teléfono: 913 344 883
www.edelvives.es

 Talleres Gráficos Edelvives (50012 Zaragoza)
Certificados ISO 9001
Printed in Spain

# Los Lobos

Niko    Catrina    Frank

Mehmet    Peter

# Jugadores más importantes

| | | |
|---|---|---|
| **Catrina** | Lobos: defensa | 5º colegio Bosel |
| **Frank** | Lobos: delantero | 5º col. Campo de los Espíritus |
| **Mark** | Tigres: defensa | 5º col. Campo de los Espíritus |
| **Mehmet** | Lobos: portero | 5º col. Campo de los Espíritus |
| **Niko** | Lobos: capitán | 5º col. Campo de los Espíritus |
| **Olli** | Lobos: delantero | 5º colegio Morsen |
| **Orhan** | Lobos: benjamín | 3º col. Campo de los Espíritus |
| **Peter** | Lobos: defensa | 5º col. Campo de los Espíritus |
| **Ralf** | Tigres: portero | 5º colegio Morsen |
| **Serkan** | Lobos: delantero | 5º col. Campo de los Espíritus |

## 01

# Los Lobos son inseparables

—¡GOL! ¡GOL! ¡GOL! ¡GOL! ¡GOOOOOL!

Aliviado, Frank levanta el puño. Acaba de marcar en el último minuto del partido. Los Lobos van ganando 5 a 0. Claro que, si no hubiera marcado, habrían ganado igual. Pero Frank no quería quedarse sin «su» gol. ¿Que es igual quién marque siempre que sea alguien de los Lobos? Vale, de acuerdo, pero siempre es mejor si uno consigue marcar. Aunque sea en el último segundo.

—¡Pura casualidad! —dice el defensa contrario que vuelve a pegarse a Frank.

Es un chico desagradable que le ha parado muchos tiros a puerta, especialmente en el segundo tiempo.

—¡Hasta mi abuela lo habría metido! —añade con muy mal gesto.

—¿De verdad? —contesta Catrina—. Entonces deberíais incorporar a tu abuela al equipo inmediatamente. ¡Para no perder siempre!

Con decisión, como buena defensa que es, separa a su amigo del jugador contrario para que el resto de los Lobos pueda llegar hasta Frank y celebrar el gol. En un momento, la avalancha humana llega y se lo lleva.

¡Una victoria contundente! ¡Menos mal! Ahora que había llegado la primavera y la vuelta a la Liga, los Lobos tenían grandes esperanzas. Por fin podían salir del pabellón de fútbol y volver al campo. El fútbol sala no está mal, especialmente si has conseguido ganar el torneo escolar,

tal y como lo hicieron Frank y sus amigos. Pero cualquier futbolista de verdad sabe que no se siente a gusto en un lugar cerrado.

El auténtico fútbol se juega al aire libre. Sin embargo, la vuelta a la Liga no ha empezado nada bien para los Lobos: sólo una victoria muy ajustada y unos cuantos empates sin gloria. No obstante, con la victoria de hoy contra el Neunhain, las cosas han cambiado. Además, con este resultado se ha saldado el mal resultado del partido de ida en otoño. Por eso, a Frank le da igual que el defensa del equipo contrario tenga razón en el fondo: no ha sido precisamente un gol muy bonito. El balón le ha caído delante de los pies y Frank sólo ha tenido que empujarlo hacia dentro.

Es verdad que una abuela del Neunhain podría haber hecho lo mismo si hubiera estado en el segundo palo. Pero allí no estaba ella, sino un delantero buenísimo con un olfato de gol muy desarrollado. Y, por eso, ahora sus compañeros están casi ahogando a Frank, y no a la abuela.

—¡Guaaay, Frank! —grita Rebeca en el momento en el que el árbitro pita el final del partido, y se lanza corriendo hacia él.

¡Qué vergüenza! Todo el mundo está mirando. A Niko y a Peter se les escapa una sonrisa de oreja a oreja. Sin perder un segundo, Frank se agacha y se ata los cordones de las botas. Menos mal, Rebeca pasa de largo y da un abrazo a Catrina. ¡Ha tenido suerte!

—¡Habéis jugado como nunca! —exagera Rebeca en su entusiasmo.

En realidad, ella no entiende mucho de fútbol. No hacía nada que este deporte y todos los que lo practicaban la echaban para atrás. Pero esto cambió radicalmente cuando conoció a Frank. Ahora es una auténtica hincha de los Lobos. Todos los amigos dicen que este cambio sólo se debe a Frank. ¡Menuda tontería! Lo que pasa es que Rebeca por fin ha entrado en razón y se ha dado cuenta de que no se puede vivir sin el fútbol. Además, con la loba Catrina ha encontrado a su primer amiga, su única amiga de verdad. Por eso viene ahora a ver los partidos. No tiene nada que ver con Frank.

—Debo irme —dice Rebeca con pena—. Mi madre quiere llevarme al cine. ¡Hasta luego!

Después de unos metros, se da la vuelta y pega un grito:

—¡Nos vemos en clase el lunes!

—Me temo que sí —dice Frank con ironía.

Sus compañeros se ríen, pero Catrina se lo reprocha con la mirada.

—A mí me cae muy bien —añade con voz seria.

En realidad, a Frank también. Rebeca puede ser muy pesada porque no deja de hablar y es una sabelotodo, pero luego es muy simpática. Y, además, siempre está dispuesta a ayudar. Más de una vez, ha sacado de apuros a Frank y sus amigos.

Pero no importa. Los chicos son muy rápidos en hacerse ideas raras. Como que Frank está enamorado y esas cosas. Por eso le conviene no hacer mucho caso a Rebeca.

En el pasillo de los vestuarios, los Lobos se vuelven a encontrar con los jugadores del Neunhain. Parece que han batido el récord en cambiarse deprisa porque ya están saliendo. Nadie dice ni mu. Incluso el defensa bocazas que marcaba a Frank sólo le lanza una mirada despectiva antes de cerrar la puerta de salida con un portazo.

¡Sí, señor! El adversario se ha quedado sin palabras. ¡Como debe ser! Ahora ya puede empezar la fiesta en el vestuario de los Lobos.

—¡Vaya paliza que les hemos dado! —dice con orgullo Mehmet, el portero, y brinda con sus compañeros.

—¡Por la victoria!

Todos brindan con entusiasmo. El líquido de los refrescos se vierte y forma una mezcla pegajosa en el suelo, pero a nadie le importa.

—Esta victoria ha sido megaimportante, especialmente por la diferencia de goles —anuncia Niko, el capitán del equipo, como si fuera un jugador de la Liga profesional en una entrevista en la tele—. Nos sube la moral para el miércoles.

El miércoles: el próximo partido de la Copa. Los Lobos están a punto de alcanzar su mayor triunfo. Habían empezado el torneo como un equipo sin pretesiones y ahora ya están en semifinales. Y si ganan este partido… ¡Ya pueden soñar!

Pero Peter, uno de los defensas, no pierde el tiempo soñando. Para él, todo está ya decidido. Levanta las manos para pedir silencio. Después, pega un grito como si estuviera en el fondo sur de un campo de fútbol:

—¿Quién va a ganar la Copa?

—¡Los Lobos! —responden todos a la vez.

Peter se pega una mano en la oreja como si estuviera sordo.

—¿Quién? —repite la pregunta.

—¡Los Lobos, los Lobos!

—Si ganamos, los Tigres se morirán de envidia —comenta Niko sonriendo—. ¿Os acordáis de cómo los eliminamos?

¡Desde luego que sí! Un día así no será olvidado jamás por un Lobo. En octavos, los Lobos eliminaron a los Tigres, el odiado rival que había ganado la Copa varios años seguidos. Fue la gran sorpresa de la temporada.

Después, los Lobos ganaron al Senberg, y ahora les toca jugar contra el Steinheim.

—¡Los vamos a arrollar! —chilla Orhan.

En su entusiasmo, el hermano menor de Mehmet se olvida de que en realidad juega con los benjamines de los Lobos, y que sólo entra en el equipo de los mayores en contadas situaciones excepcionales. Pero eso no le quita la alegría.

Frank acaricia el pelo al enano.

—¡La Copa será nuestra! —dice con optimismo—. Porque tenemos espíritu de equipo. Ya sabéis: «Once amigos, un solo corazón…».

—Hablando de canciones —añade Catrina con alegría—: tengo una nueva que viene que ni pintada.

—¡Ay, no!

—¡No nos hagas esto!

Catrina se hace la sorda. Se sube a un banco, levanta una botella como si fuera un micrófono y empieza a cantar:

—*Los Lobos son inseparables, un Lobo nunca está solo…*

—Preferiría estarlo, la verdad —se queja Niko.

Su reacción no es extraña. La voz de Catrina suena a serrucho oxidado. Pero eso no quita las ganas de cantar a la chica. Sus canciones favoritas son los himnos de fútbol. Y, desgraciadamente, su repertorio es inagotable.

—*…porque lo que más les gusta es ayudarse uno al otro.*

—¡Ay, cómo duele!

—¡Falta! ¡Agresión contra los oídos!

—¡Árbitro, tarjeta roja!

Las críticas sólo la animan más:

—*Los Lobos son inseparables…*

¿Inseparables? Como Catrina siga, la amistad correrá peligro. Frank debe hacer algo. ¡Y rápido!

# Como en la Edad Media

## 02

—¡Chicos, dejadla cantar! —dice Frank intentando aplicar una estrategia nueva—. Se lo merece porque ha jugado estupendamente.

Sus amigos no dan crédito, pero Catrina muerde el cebo.

—¿Qué has dicho? —pregunta intrigada.

Niko entiende el plan de Frank.

—¡Es cierto! —dice—. Si hemos ganado es sólo gracias a Catrina.

—¡Pero qué dices! —exclama ella, ahora tímida, mientras se aclara la garganta, lo que significa el fin definitivo para la canción.

Niko lanza una sonrisa a Frank y levanta el pulgar, como diciendo: «Un truco estupendo».

Pero, en realidad, no todo es un truco para callar a Catrina. La verdad es que ella ha jugado superbien. Tal vez incluso haya sido la mejor de todo el equipo. Durante el primer tiempo, nada les salió bien a los Lobos. Jugaban como si tuvieran miedo de algo. En dos ocasiones, fue Catrina la que despejó el balón en el último momento. En este sentido, sí que hay que agradecerle a ella que el Neunhain no se pusiera delante en el marcador. Luego, en el descanso, fue también Catrina la que les soltó un sermón de lo lindo. Incluso Norbert, el entrenador, se quedó callado. Así que los Lobos se animaron y empezaron el segundo tiempo con la moral alta. Después, ella dejó en bandeja el primer gol. Hizo un regate en su propio campo, dio un pase largo a Niko y éste hizo una pared con Frank, que marcó. El tanto supuso un alivio para los Lobos y una gran sorpresa para el Neunhain. El resto fue sólo un juego de niños.

—Es cierto —insiste Frank—. Sin ti no habríamos ganado.

—No seas pelota —contesta Catrina, que se sonroja y disimula buscando algo en su bolsa.

Durante unos segundos, se hace un silencio que demuestra la satisfacción del equipo.

Después, es Peter quien toma la palabra:

—Me dan pena todos los que no son Lobos.

—A mí también —confirma Frank con convicción.

No hace ni un año que lleva la camiseta verde y amarilla del equipo. El verano pasado sus padres se separaron y Frank se vino aquí con su madre desde Asdorf. Al principio se sentía muy solo, pero al poco tiempo entró en el equipo de fútbol y, desde entonces, los compañeros se han convertido en sus amigos incondicionales.

—Lástima que no vayamos a poder jugar juntos siempre —dice Peter de repente.

Todos lo miran asombrados.

—Pero, ¿qué dices?

—¡Lobos ahora, Lobos para siempre!

—Bueno, ahora sí —contesta Peter—, pero luego… —Se pone colorado y se calla.

Vaya, recapacita Frank, su amigo tiene razón. No es la primera vez que lo piensa.

—Se refiere a cuando seamos profesionales y juguemos en diferentes equipos.

En el caso de Frank, ya hace mucho que se decidió por uno: el Hamburgo; ése es el equipo de sus sueños. En cuanto lo llamen, firmará…

—Yo jugaré en el Fenerbahçe —dice Orhan.

Mehmet, su hermano, pone los ojos en blanco y dice en voz baja:

—Sí, seguro. Como limpiabotas, supongo.

—Fenerbahçe, Bayern, Arsenal… da igual. Lo malo es que algún día nos tengamos que separar —opina Niko.

O tal vez no. Está claro que Frank no podrá llevarse a todos sus amigos al Hamburgo, pero igual a Niko sí. Un centrocampista como él, con sus fantásticos pases largos, es justo lo que necesita un delantero con hambre de gol como Frank. A la hora de negociar su contrato no podrá dejar de mencionar a su amigo. Eso sí, los demás tendrán que buscarse su propio equipo. Pero hay una forma de conservar la amistad:

—¡Vamos a jugar todos juntos en la selección!

—¡Eso es! ¡Claro que sí! Nos veremos en todas las concentraciones.

—Y durante las Eurocopas y los Mundiales.

—¡Seremos campeones de Europa!

—¡Ganaremos a todos los países! —dice Orhan con su optimismo indestructible.

—¡Chócala! —invita Niko a Frank, levantando la mano.

Pero antes de chocar la del amigo, Frank baja la suya en el último momento. ¡Catrina! Sus fantásticos planes de futuro no la incluyen.

—¿Por qué me miras así? —pregunta la amiga, desconfiada.

—Porque…

«¡Madre mía! ¿Es que no se le ha ocurrido nunca?».

—¿Qué? —insiste Catrina.

—Pues, porque eres chica.

—Sí, toda la vida, ¿y?

—Bueno, es que…

Frank no sabe cómo decirlo. ¿Por qué tenía que salir el tema ahora?

—Por la selección. Para entonces, ya habrás dejado el fútbol…

—¿CÓMO? —se enfada Catrina—. ¡No dejaré nunca el fútbol! ¡JAMÁS!

—Claro que no —intenta interceder Niko—. Frank se refiere a que sólo podremos jugar juntos hasta cuando cumplamos quince años. Después tendrás que ir a un equipo de chicas.

—¡Fútbol femenino! —se ríe Peter y hace como si bostezara para expresar su opinión sobre este tipo de deporte.

—Tienes toda la razón, es superaburrido.

—Claro, por que no regatean de verdad.

—Están hechas de azúcar.

—Técnicamente, las chicas juegan en otro planeta.

—El fútbol lo inventaron los chicos.

—Por eso el fútbol femenino no tiene espectadores. No tiene gancho.

—¿Ah, no? —bufa Catrina con desprecio—. Me parece que os habéis quedado en la Edad Media.

Con rabia, mete sus cosas en la bolsa y sale corriendo del vestuario, dando un portazo que hace vibrar las ventanas. Los chicos se estremecen del susto.

—¿Por qué se ha enfadado? —pregunta Mehmet.

—No sabe aceptar la verdad —dice Niko.

En ese momento, entra Norbert.

—¡Qué raro! —dice asombrado—. Me acabo de cruzar con Catrina en el pasillo, y casi me tira al suelo. ¿Qué le ha pasado?

—¡Chicas! —responde Peter soltando un suspiro—. ¡A veces se ponen así de tontas!

¿Tonta, Catrina? Puede que la hermana mayor de Peter se ponga tonta a veces, pero no Catrina. Su reacción tiene otro motivo. Si Peter se hubiera

acabado de enterar de que no
podría jugar al fútbol en el futuro, y que lo único que
podría hacer iba a ser pasarse la pelota con unas tipas
medio cojas, se enfadaría también.

# Un gol perfecto...
# en propia puerta

## 03

—¡Un gran partido! —dice el abuelo de Frank de camino a casa.

—Mmh.

Antes, cuando Frank vivía aún en Asdorf, para el abuelo no existía nada más que la bolera. El fútbol le daba totalmente igual. Pero desde que viven juntos, el abuelo ha cambiado mucho. Cuando los Lobos encontraron un nuevo delantero, Frank, ganaron también un hincha fiel.

—¡Tu gol ha sido fantástico!

—Mmh.

Frank suele dar clases teóricas al abuelo: cuando ven juntos los programas de fútbol en la tele, le explica las reglas y le señala las jugadas especiales. Ahora

23

mismo, sin embargo, no le apetece explicar las diferencias entre una buena jugada y un gol oportuno. Ahora está pensando en otra cosa.

¿Le durará el enfado a Catrina hasta el miércoles? No sería nada bueno para el partido de semifinales. Para clasificarse, hace falta la máxima concentración de cada uno de los jugadores. Si estás triste, no lo das todo. ¡Y no pueden prescindir de Catrina! Hoy mismo se ha visto claramente lo importante que es para el equipo. ¡Es indispensable para los Lobos! A ver si se le pasa en sólo cuatro días. Ha sido un golpe muy duro.

Al llegar a casa, un coche aparcado en la acera distrae a Frank.

—¡Papá!

¡Qué gran sorpresa! Frank corre los últimos metros, pero no hay nadie dentro. ¡Qué raro! Normalmente su padre le espera sentado al volante. ¿Habrá entrado? Frank mira preocupado al abuelo.

Su padre nunca le ha caído bien al abuelo. Y cuando los padres de Frank se separaron, fue peor aún. Desde entonces, su padre no ha vuelto a entrar en casa. Una vez, incluso, el abuelo le cerró la puerta en las narices. Eso sí, desde que coincidieron en la final del campeonato de fútbol sala y celebraron juntos la victoria de los Lobos, la cosa ha mejorado un poco, pero siguen sin ser precisamente amigos.

Parece que el abuelo saber leer el pensamiento de Frank.

—No te preocupes —dice dándole un suave codazo—. No voy a comerme a tu padre.

Sus padres están hablando en el salón. ¡Eso sí que hace tiempo que Frank no lo ha visto! En Asdorf, sólo había discusiones.

—¡Papá! —grita Frank—. ¿Cómo es que no me has avisado? ¡Por qué no has ido a ver el partido? ¡Hemos ganado! Podríamos haber…

—¡Vaya forma de saludar! —se ríe su padre—. No te enfades conmigo. Tenemos mucho tiempo porque me quedo hasta mañana. Ahora voy a buscar un hotel para pasar la noche.

El abuelo mueve el cuello como si tuviera que tragarse un trozo enorme de comida.

—Bueno… —tartamudea—, por mí…, quiero decir… —Y vuelve a tragar saliva—. También puedes dormir aquí.

—¡Qué guay! —grita Frank y da un abrazo al abuelo—. ¡Puedes dormir conmigo! ¡Gracias, abuelito!

El abuelo se suelta con una sonrisa.

—Ya te había dicho que no me iba a comer a tu padre —susurra—. Pero sólo si ahora me dejáis cenar tranquilo.

Más tarde, Frank y su padre dan un largo paseo. El hombre le habla de Asdorf, del SV, de Tom y de sus otros antiguos amigos. Frank los echa mucho de menos. Pero, ¿quiere decir eso que le gustaría volver? Es difícil saberlo. Si lo hiciese, podría ver a su padre más a menudo. Eso estaría bien. Y podrían ir a Hamburgo, al estadio. No está lejos de Asdorf. Pero, entonces, ¿qué pasaría con su nuevo equipo y con sus nuevos amigos?

Frank decide pensar en otra cosa. De todas formas, no es muy probable que vuelva a Asdorf. Su madre ha dicho que entre ella y su padre ya no hay nada, y que sería mejor no perder el tiempo pensando en ese tema.

—¡Deberías venir a vernos más a menudo! —dice Frank.

—Ése es precisamente mi plan —afirma su padre.

El domingo, poco después de comer, tocan el timbre. Son Mehmet y Orhan, los hermanos que viven al lado de Frank.

—¿Qué haces? ¿No estás listo? —Mehmet le pregunta impaciente.

¡Madre mía! Normalmente su amigo es el chico más tranquilo que uno pueda imaginarse. A esta hora suele estar tumbado en el sofá viendo la tele. Casi siempre es Frank el que tiene que insistir para que Mehmet se levante. Su lema es «No agotarse». Y justo hoy ha tenido que hacer una excepción. Justo hoy, cuando está aquí su padre y quieren aprovechar cada minuto para estar juntos. Por otro lado, el partido que juegan los domingos es uno de los mejores momentos de toda la semana, una cosa que uno no debería perderse.

Indeciso, Frank mira hacia el salón. Su padre se asoma y saluda a los amigos de su hijo.

—Anda, vete con ellos —dice—. En cuanto haya terminado con el café, me voy a tener que poner en marcha.

Frank no se lo piensa dos veces, agarra las botas y sale corriendo.

El campo de fútbol no está muy lejos. «Bienvenido al Club Deportivo de los Lobos», puede leerse en el arco de madera de la entrada. A pesar de este simpático saludo, hoy la puerta está cerrada. El primer equipo del club ha preferido jugar su partido de Liga en el campo de césped, en el polideportivo municipal. Mucho mejor, así Frank y sus amigos tienen todo el campo para ellos solos. El que sea de tierra batida, donde cada falta se paga con sangre, y no de césped, sólo asusta a los blandengues que estén acostumbrados a la hierba, pero no a un auténtico Lobo. Y con la puerta cerrada no pasa nada tampoco. Todos saben que a pocos metros hay un agujero en la valla. El vigilante no lo ha visto porque está tapado por arbustos. Y ninguno de los Lobos se lo va a decir.

—¡Hola, chicos! —les saluda el señor Jahn, que vive enfrente.

Con mucho cuidado, está limpiando sus queridos enanos de jardín que «defienden» el césped delantero de su casa.

—¿Vais a entrenar hoy también? —pregunta con una sonrisa.

—Los verdaderos deportistas no deben dormirse en los laureles —responde Frank.

El señor Jahn se ríe. Es curioso cómo ha cambiado este anciano. Hace sólo unos meses decía que el ruido del campo de fútbol era insoportable. Y cada vez que los chicos entrenaban fuera del horario oficial, no tardaba ni un segundo en llamar por teléfono al presidente del club y quejarse. Desde entonces, afortunadamente, el señor Jahn y los Lobos han hecho

las paces. Ahora ya no hay ningún obstáculo para disfrutar de un buen domingo de fútbol.

Sin perder el tiempo, los tres pasan por el agujero. En el campo, Niko, Peter, Serkan y Hendrik se están pasando el balón.

—¿Y Catrina? —saluda Niko a los recién llegados.

¡Madre mía! ¡Catrina! Inmediatamente Frank se acuerda de lo que pasó el sábado durante la celebración de la victoria. Con la visita de su padre se había olvidado por completo del asunto.

—¿No ha venido? —dice a pesar de que la pregunta sobra.

—¿Tú la ves? —contesta Niko nervioso, arqueando las cejas.

—Ya vendrá —añade Mehmet, pensando que, igual que él, cualquiera puede retrasarse.

Catrina, no. Hasta ahora, a pesar de que vive en la otra punta de la ciudad, no se ha retrasado ni una sola vez.

En ese momento, hay un ruido entre los arbustos. Todos se dan la vuelta para mirar. Pero es Eddy.

—Lo siento —dice jadeando—. He tenido que pasar por casa de mi abuela.

—Vamos a empezar —decide Niko.

Rápidamente se forman dos equipos. Como siempre, Mehmet es el portero de ambos.

Pero sin Catrina no es lo mismo. Una y otra vez, Frank mira hacia el agujero de la valla, pero nada.

Niko tampoco está muy concentrado. Por segunda vez falla un centro.

—¿Estás dormido? —se queja Peter.

Niko ni siquiera intenta recuperar el balón.

—Me gustaría saber dónde está —gruñe.

—Seguirá enfadada —dice Orhan.

—Todos nos ponemos de mal humor alguna vez —comenta Peter—. Pero, ¿tanto tiempo? No tiene gracia.

No suele pasarle —añade Mehmet, frunciendo el ceño.

—Además, no tiene ningún motivo —dice Niko.

—O tal vez sí —le contradice Frank.

Todos lo miran sorprendidos.

—Ayer se dio cuenta de que su carrera futbolística va a acabar pronto —explica Frank—, y que nunca podrá ser una profesional.

La evidencia de sus palabras hace callar a todos.

—Sería un golpe durísimo para cualquiera —dice Peter suspirando.

—Para mí no —replica Hendrik.

Todos lo miran, y el chico se pone rojo.

—Bueno, quiero decir —se explica—, que no voy a ser jugador de fútbol. Quiero ser, ejem, científico espacial.

En fin, hay gustos para todo. Pero, la verdad, Hendrik es un caso un tanto raro. En los entrenamientos es el más aplicado, pero en los partidos todo lo contrario. Por eso se queda casi siempre en el banquillo. Y parece no importarle nada. Las pocas veces que llega a jugar en serio se pone supernervioso. Es decir, Hendrik no parece estar hecho para ser un jugador profesional. Catrina, sin embargo, sí.

—Juega tan bien como nosotros —resume sus pensamientos Frank—, pero jamás podrá ser profesional. Seguro que acabará en un trabajo superaburrido, como peluquera, maestra o algo así.

—¡Pobre Catrina!

—Tampoco puede ganar la Eurocopa —se da cuenta Peter.

—Pero no es culpa nuestra, ¿verdad? —pregunta Niko, un poco inseguro—; que sea chica, quiero decir.

—Ni que la Federación sea tan carca y no deje jugar a las chicas —añade Mehmet.

—Claro que no —dice Frank suspirando—. Pero a lo mejor se lo podríamos haber dicho de forma más suave.

—Y no cuatro días antes de las semifinales de la Copa —apunta Niko.

¡Desde luego! Si Catrina sigue enfadada hasta el miércoles, los Lobos habrán marcado un gol perfecto, pero en propia puerta.

# ¡Qué potra!

## 04

El lunes por la mañana, Frank y sus amigos se acercan al campo de fútbol en el patio del recreo. No hay nada mejor para que empiecen a funcionar las neuronas que un buen partidillo antes de clase. Sin embargo, en la esquina les está esperando un obstáculo: Rebeca.

—¡Ay, no! —se queja Peter—. Seguro que quiere contarnos toda la película. Mejor nos piramos.

Pero ya es tarde. Rebeca los ha visto.

—Tapaos los oídos —recomienda Niko en voz baja.

Curiosamente, hoy no hace falta taparse nada. Rebeca acaba rápido.

—Menudos futbolistas de pacotilla —les saluda con ironía, y les da la espalda.

A los pocos metros, sin embargo, se le ocurre otra cosa y se da la vuelta:

—Por cierto, que lo sepáis: Catrina jugará en la Liga de fútbol profesional antes que cualquiera de vosotros.

Con estas enigmáticas palabras, se pierde entre la muchedumbre del patio.

Los amigos se miran asombrados.

—¿Futbolistas de pacotilla? —repite Niko perplejo—. ¿Qué habrá querido decir con eso?

—¡Futbolistas de pacotilla! ¡Ja, ja! ¡Qué bueno! —se ríe Mark, que ha oído a Rebeca.

Se queda mirando a los Lobos con ganas de pelea, pero los chicos no le prestan atención.

—¡Quién hubiera dicho que la empollona sabe tanto de fútbol! —sigue provocandoles Mark, pero de nuevo no hay reacción alguna.

Derrotado, se da la vuelta y se marcha.

Mark está en la misma clase de Frank y sus amigos, y también juega al fútbol, pero no con los Lobos, sino con sus archienemigos los Tigres, el equipo del sur de la ciudad. Cualquier auténtico Tigre mira con absoluto desdén a los Lobos y, por otro lado, cualquier Lobo odia visceralmente a los Tigres.

En otro momento, a Frank y sus compañeros no les habría importado montar una buena bronca. La rivalidad entre los dos equipos es un aliciente más de los derbis, y hay que mantenerla todo lo posible, pero hoy los Lobos están pensando en otra cosa.

—¿Habéis caído en la cuenta de por qué Catrina no fue al campo ayer? —pregunta Niko preocupado—. Estaba con Rebeca.

Le habrá contado cualquier cosa sobre nosotros.

—¡Un montón de mentiras!

¡Vaya plan! Si Catrina no jugó al fútbol con sus amigos para poder compartir sus penas con Rebeca, la situación es aún mucho más seria de lo que los chicos habían pensado.

—Deberíamos hablar con ella para que entre en razón —propone Mehmet.

—No va a ser fácil —dice Peter, que tiene mucha experiencia con su hermana mayor—: es una chica.

—Da igual —añade Niko—. Puede que tenga razón para estar enfadada, pero el partido del miércoles es más importante que cualquier cosa.

—Podríamos pedirle perdón —plantea Frank.

—Eso debería hacerlo la Federación de fútbol profesional, y no nosotros —dice Niko.

—Sí, claro. Estoy viendo al presidente de la Federación —se ríe Peter—: reconoce sus errores y ofrece la mano a Catrina.

—Por eso. Será más rápido que hagamos nosotros algo —dice Frank.

—¡Pero no tenemos la culpa! —insiste Niko.

—No importa. Hacemos como si la tuviéramos —opina Mehmet—. Reconocer nuestra culpa y mostrarnos arrepentidos, eso funciona muy bien con las chicas. Lo vi el otro día en una peli.

—Una de esas románticas, seguro —se queja Niko—. Pero, en fin, ¿por qué no intentarlo? Esta misma tarde, en el entrenamiento.


—El consumo medio de agua de un hogar de cuatro personas es de…

La señorita Pirosky, la profe, intenta que se concentren en el tema de la clase.

Frank se esconde detrás del libro de texto para pensar con tranquilidad en sus cosas, que son mucho más importantes que el consumo de agua.

Catrina no está nada contenta. Eso es seguro. A Frank le gustaría ayudarla. No sólo por el partido de la Copa, sino también por todo lo que Catrina ha hecho por él. Si no fuera por Catrina, Frank no jugaría con los Lobos. Nada más llegar a la ciudad, Frank consiguió que todos los futbolistas se enfadaran con él. Si Catrina no hubiera aparecido para actuar como mediadora, su carrera futbolística ya habría acabado para siempre. Por eso le debe una. Si hay suerte, esta misma tarde harán las paces y, de este modo, podrán jugar el partido del miércoles con tranquilidad. Pero, ¿qué pasará después? Unas cuantas palabras bonitas no cambiarán toda la situación. El fin de la carrera de Catrina parece seguro. ¿O habrá alguna solución?

¿Qué era lo que había dicho Rebeca? ¿Catrina jugará en la Liga profesional? ¿Será que Rebeca solicitará a la Federación de fútbol un permiso especial para su amiga con el que pueda jugar con los profesionales? Es cierto que Rebeca sabe hablar muy bien y es muy convincente. Lo ha demostrado más de una vez. Pero, ¿conseguirá convencer a los jefes de la Federación? No parece muy probable. ¡Qué pena!

—¿Frank?

La señorita Pirosky lo mira expectante. Pero Frank no tiene ni idea de lo que la profe ha preguntado. Le pasa con frecuencia, y no suele ser ningún problema porque está sentado al lado de Rebeca, que es una estudiante ejemplar que siempre sabe las respuestas, y se las susurra al oído.

Pero hoy no. Lástima. Hoy Rebeca tiene la nariz metida en el libro y no hace ni caso a Frank.

La que sí le presta atención es la señorita Pirosky. Le suelta un sermón acerca de no distraerse en clase. ¡Como si no tuviera ya bastantes problemas!

—Igual no viene hoy tampoco —dice Orhan de camino al entrenamiento por la tarde.

Afortunadamente, se ha equivocado. Catrina ya ha llegado. Está haciendo malabares con el balón detrás de la portería.

Ahora llegan también Peter y Niko. Frank les hace una señal.

—¡Vamos!

Catrina golpea el balón con las rodillas. Para este ejercicio necesita la máxima concentración.

—Catrina, queríamos decirte una cosa…

—Diecisiete, dieciocho…

—¡Catrina!

El balón se le cae al suelo.

—¡Mierda! —se queja la chica—. ¿Por qué me interrumpís? Estaba a punto de batir mi récord.

—Catrina, queríamos pedirte perdón.

—Bueno, no es para tanto. Voy a intentarlo otra vez. Veinticinco veces sin que toque el suelo.

Deja a los chicos solos para recuperar el balón.

Ellos se miran asombrados.

—Está totalmente normal, ¿no? —pregunta Niko.

—Sí, eso parece.

—Así, sin más, sin disculpas ni nada.

—Parece como si no hubiera que lamentar daños irreparables —dice Mehmet aliviado.

El único que no se fía aún es Frank. Durante todo el entrenamiento no deja de observar a Catrina. Pero no nota nada raro. La defensa de los Lobos está igual de entregada que siempre. Incluso, a lo mejor, un poco más si cabe. Más tarde, en el partidillo de defensas contra delanteros, Catrina aplica su temida zancadilla y manda a Frank de viaje más allá de la línea de banda.

—¡Catrina, eso ha sido falta! —le avisa Norbert.

—Sólo he tocado el balón —contesta con su excusa de siempre.

Aliviado, Frank se frota el muslo dolorido. Ahora está seguro de que Catrina ha superado su decepción y que es nuevamente la de siempre. Al final, parece que los Lobos han tenido potra.

# ¡El talento está aquí!

## 05

¡Miércoles! ¡Por fin ha llegado el día de las semifina
les! El fin de semana juegan todos los equipos, pero
entre semana sólo pueden hacerlo los que se lo mere-
cen. ¡Hay tensión en el ambiente!

El microbús del club lleva al equipo de Los Lobos
al pueblo de su siguiente rival, el Steinheim. No va a
ser nada fácil. Los jugadores de este equipo son muy
altos y fuertes, y ya les complicaron bastante las cosas
a los Lobos durante el campeonato de fútbol sala.
Entonces, el primer partido lo ganaron los Lobos con
algo de suerte, pero en la vuelta sufrieron una terrible
derrota.

Pero todo eso ya es historia. En el camino hasta las
semifinales, los Lobos han ganado a equipos mucho

más difíciles. Por eso, hoy da lo mismo que el rival se llame Steinheim o Real Madrid. Sea como sea, los Lobos van a triunfar.

—¡Victoria! ¡A domicilio! —canta Niko con entusiasmo, y los demás se unen a él.

—¡VICTORIA! ¡A DOMICILIO!

Eso es, hoy hay que ganar a domicilio. En la Copa no hay partidos de ida y vuelta. El lema es: «todo o nada». La eliminatoria se decide en un solo día, y los Lobos están convencidos de que hoy se lo van a llevar todo.

A través de la luna trasera, Frank saluda a su abuelo que va en su propio coche, siguiendo al microbús. Aunque quedaban asientos en el coche del abuelo, Frank ha preferido viajar con sus compañeros porque se siente más a gusto y fomenta el espíritu de equipo. Por eso, al abuelo sólo le acompañan Orhan y Rebeca. Parece ser que Rebeca, igual que Catrina, ya ha perdonado a los chicos del equipo. En el colegio, ha vuelto a hablar sin parar y esta tarde, antes de salir, ha estado más nerviosa que nunca. Seguro que ahora le está dando la lata al abuelo. Menos mal que parece no importarle nada. El abuelo sonríe y levanta el pulgar. ¡Qué suerte que las tonterías del sábado ya estén olvidadas!

Norbert lleva el microbús por un camino de tierra lleno de baches.

—¡Madre mía! Pero, ¿dónde estamos? —se queja Peter—. ¿Venimos aquí a jugar al fútbol o a ordeñar vacas?

Parece que iba a añadir otra cosa, pero en ese momento llegan al campo de fútbol. A partir de ahora, el lema debe ser: «¡plena concentración!».

Los del Steinheim ya están en el césped, vestidos de rojo, haciendo ejercicios de calentamiento.

—Creo que han crecido más aún —dice Mehmet.

—¿No tendréis miedo? —pregunta Catrina.

—¡Qué va!

—¡Para nada!

—Menos mal —añade Catrina contenta—. Da igual que sean altos o bajitos. No podemos permitir que nos asusten.

Está claro: si los Lobos quieren ganar la Copa, tienen que enfrentarse al adversario sin miedo.

Frank está con los ejercicios de calentamiento cuando se da cuenta de que no se ha quitado el reloj. Es un regalo de Navidad de su padre y le gusta mucho, pero ya se sabe: a los árbitros no les hacen gracia ni los relojes ni las pulseras ni nada. Debería haberlo dejado en la taquilla del vestuario, pero seguro que ya lo han cerrado con llave. Menos mal que ha venido el abuelo. Con él, el reloj va a estar más seguro que en la caja fuerte de un banco.

Frank corre hacia la banda y le da el reloj. El abuelo lo recoge sin dejar de hablar. ¿Con quién? Un señor bajito y gordo. No parece nada interesante. Aunque Rebeca lo está mirando como si fuera Don Importante en persona. ¡Qué más da! Ya se sabe que Rebeca está siempre exagerando. Aburrido, Frank se da la vuelta para volver al campo. En este momento, escucha la voz del señor gordo:

—Y, entonces, ¿dónde está el prometedor talento?

«¿TALENTO?».

Frank clava los talones en el suelo para frenar. Se queda helado y se gira para mirar al señor. ¡No puede ser! Hace años que sueña con la visita de un cazatalentos y, ahora, sin previo aviso, ha aparecido. ¡Qué locura!

«¡Aquí! —le apetecería gritar—. ¡El talento está aquí!». Pero justo en ese mismo instante, se queda sin voz.

¡Conque es el gordo! ¿Quién lo hubiera dicho? Pero, claro, ¿por qué no? Es mucho mejor si no tiene su profesión escrita en la frente. Hay muchos jugadores que se pondrían nerviosos si supieran que los están observando. Se pondrían supertensos, cuando lo importante es jugar con naturalidad.

—Ejem…, bueno…, yo…

Parece que tiene un nudo en la lengua.

Antes de conseguir desatársela, Frank escucha el grito impaciente de Niko:

—¡Qué pasa, tío! Si estás cansado antes de empezar, más vale que juegue Orhan por ti.

—¡Ay, sí! —chilla el enano, encantado—. ¿Quieres que juegue yo?

—De eso nada —gruñe Frank.

Faltaría más. Mira por última vez al señor gordo, y hace un *sprint* hasta el centro del césped, aunque le siguen flaqueando un poco las piernas. Lástima que no haya podido hablar personalmente con el cazatalentos. Pero da igual. Tendrá que llamar su atención jugando. En realidad, las cosas hay que demostrarlas en el campo, y un gol dice más que mil palabras.

Los Lobos están corriendo en fila india. Frank se pone detrás de Peter, pero es incapaz de concentrarse. ¿Qué está pasando entre el público? Ahora Rebeca está hablando con el señor. A ver si no es muy pesada. Pero no, el cazatalentos se ríe y le da una palmadita en el hombro a la chica. Parece ser que Rebeca le cae simpática. ¡Estupendo! A ver si también le habla bien de Frank.

—¡Qué pasa! ¿Estás dormido?

Frank no se ha dado cuenta de que todos han dado la vuelta, y ha chocado de bruces contra Peter. ¡Qué vergüenza! Frank sólo espera que Rebeca haya distraído al señor,  y que éste no haya visto su torpeza.

Nada más empezar el partido, Frank pone toda la carne en el asador. Va a toda máquina mientras los demás siguen arrancando. Estaría bien lograr un golpe de efecto al principio para que el cazatalentos se enterase de a quién tiene que mirar. Entonces, abriría su libreta —porque todos los cazatalentos llevan libreta— y apuntaría el 20, el número de la camiseta de Frank, con un signo de exclamación al lado.

Durante un segundo, Frank se permite mirar hacia el público. El gordo tiene las dos manos metidas en los bolsillos. Claro, hasta ahora no hubo nada interesante que apuntar.

—¡Qué haces, Frank!

Asustado, Frank se da la vuelta. A su lado, el balón cruza la línea de banda. Menos mal que el hombre sigue con la libreta guardada.

Los Lobos atacan de nuevo. ¡Atención y concentración! Catrina lleva el balón. Frank se ofrece por la banda izquierda. Agita la mano. Grita. Por fin, Catrina da el pase, pero hacia el centro. Allí hay demasiados defensas y los contrarios se hacen con el esférico.

—¡Oye, estaba totalmente…! —grita Frank, pero no termina la frase.

Seguramente, a los cazatalentos no les gustan los quejicas. No son buenos para la moral del equipo.

Otro ataque de los Lobos. Eddy pasa el cuero a Niko. Niko a Frank. Tiene espacio. Va hacia arriba. ¡Qué sensación! Mariposas en la tripa, ¡qué ilusión! Ya falta poco. No, en este instante no hay que mirar al público. Después, tal vez, durante la celebración del gol, cuando sus amigos le feliciten. Uno de los altos defensas del Steinheim se le acerca. ¡Que venga! Frank está preparado. ¡Cuidado! Ahora va a emplear el truco brasileño. Frank retrasa el balón y lo pasa por detrás con su talón. El defensa se queda con las ganas. Pero Frank también. Otro defensa, el número seis, un chico gordito, despeja la pelota con fuerza —de manera nada brasileña—, y cae a los pies del nueve, que inicia rápidamente el contraataque. Menos mal que Catrina está atenta.

—¿Por qué regateas tanto? —se queja Peter.

Su compañero no debería ser tan quejica. No es bueno para la moral del equipo.

De nuevo ataca el equipo contrario. Pero el disparo es flojo. Mehmet no tiene problemas. Rápidamente, pasa el cuero a Catrina, que hace un pase largo a Frank. Otra vez hacia arriba. Allí están los defensas, el alto y el gordo. Esta vez no va a haber trucos. A regañadientes, Frank se despide del balón y centra. ¡Qué bueno! Exactamente a la cabeza de Olli. ¡Sólo tiene que meterlo! ¡Ay, no! ¡Qué rabia! Frank le da una patada al césped. ¡Cómo es posible no aprovechar un centro tan bueno! El esférico se ha marchado por encima del larguero. Por varios metros. ¡Qué lástima! Ahora ya nadie se acuerda de lo bueno que era el pase.

No importa. Ya está. Hay que seguir. Lo importante es que los Lobos están jugando bien. No hay duda. Sólo falta el resultado. El punto sobre la i. A ver, a lo mejor esta vez. Otro pase largo, a la espalda de los defensas rojos. Parecen gallinas asustadas. Antes de que puedan reestablecer el orden, Frank ya ha entrado en el área. Uno contra uno. El portero sale hacia él. No le servirá de nada. Frank sólo tiene que encajar el balón. Muy fácil. Demasiado fácil, tal vez. Un delantero con talento aquí debería hacer algo especial. Una vaselina, por ejemplo. Eso es. Primero engañar al meta y luego tirarle por encima el balón.

¡Sí, señor! Frank ya levanta los brazos. Pero el portero también. Extiende las manos y agarra la pelota con las puntas de los dedos. ¡No puede ser! Totalmente atónito, Frank baja los brazos. Si el señor gordo está buscando a un portero de primera, ya puede dejar de hacerlo.

—¿Por qué no juegas raso, tío? —se queja Niko.

Porque sí. ¡Que no se meta!

Y otro ataque buenísimo de los Lobos. Frank hace la pared con Niko y dispara. ¡Qué fuerte! El portero ya está batido, pero esta vez le ayuda el palo. De allí, el balón se marcha afuera. Entre el público se oyen murmullos. Algún tímido aplauso. ¿Qué más? El señor gordo está hablando por el móvil. ¿Será que no tiene libreta? ¿Será que llama directamente a los presidentes de los clubes de la Liga profesional?

El abuelo saluda con la mano. ¡Qué bochorno! Frank ya no es ningún bebé. Rápidamente, gira la cabeza y se concentra en el partido. Al poco rato, el árbitro pita el final del primer tiempo.

—Está claro que estamos dominando —resume Peter en el vestuario.

—Pero no se nota en el marcador —se queja Catrina.

—Si no marcamos pronto, podríamos arrepentirnos —añade Niko.

—Tenemos que presionar más, y crear muchas oportunidades de gol —exige Norbert—. Por eso vamos a hacer el primer cambio. Serkan, ¿estás listo?

—Desde luego —responde encantado.

Serkan: otro delantero. Entonces, ¿a quién va a sustituir Norbert? ¿No será…? Por favor, hoy no…

—Vamos a ir a por todas —anuncia el entrenador—. Con tres delanteros. Así vamos a doblegar al Steinheim.

¿Tres delanteros? ¿Será buena idea? Igual se van a pisar los pies unos a otros. Pero da igual. Lo importante es que Frank sigue en el campo.

Boris, el defensa adelantado, se va al banquillo. No le hace ninguna gracia. Enfadado, tira sus espinilleras en la bolsa.

—En la final vuelves a jugar —intenta consolarle Catrina—. Hoy me encargo yo de tu parte.

Es totalmente capaz. Puede defender por dos. Menos mal que es una chica. Si no, el cazatalentos podría quedarse deslumbrado por ella.

Cuando todos están a punto de salir del vestuario, Norbert se dirige a Frank.

—Oye, ¿qué te pasa hoy? —pregunta preocupado—. Me parece que no estás muy centrado.

¿Sabrá el entrenador que hay un cazatalentos entre el público? No parece muy probable porque, si no, ya habría hablado con él. ¿Debería Frank decírselo? No, mejor después.

—¿Te pasa algo? —insiste Norbert.

—No, nada —responde Frank.

Pero el entrenador no parece estar convencido.

—Escucha.

—¿Sí?

—En el segundo tiempo, no chupes tanto.

—Vale, de acuerdo.

Con prisa, Frank sigue a los demás.

# ¡Qué hipócritas!

## 06

—Jonas, ocúpate del veinte.

Frank se queda encantado con esta instrucción del entrenador del Steinheim. ¿Lo habrá oído también el cazatalentos? Un marcaje especial es un honor que sólo se concede a jugadores extraordinarios.

En cuanto se reanuda el partido, el chico gordito con el seis se pega a Frank. ¡Así que éste es Jonas! Pues, qué bien, será fácil dejarlo atrás.

Pero, ¡de fácil, nada! Jonas es mucho más rápido de lo que parece, y no se aparta ni un ápice de Frank. A éste no le hace ninguna gracia. Seguro que queda en ridículo si no consigue dejar atrás a un chico tan gordito.

En la otra banda, Serkan tiene todo el espacio que quiere. Los rojos no parecen haberse dado cuenta de su presencia. Ahora, una vez más, pasa por las filas rojas sin demasiados problemas. Frank se ofrece, intenta apartarse del seis, pero el gordito no lo deja solo ni un segundo. Con semejante sombra, es imposible que le pasen el balón.

Serkan sigue avanzando. Mete un pase largo en el área. Olli salta, acerca la cabeza al balón y lo cuela en la red.

Frank tendría que alegrarse, pero le cuesta levantar los brazos. ¿Cómo era aquello de «es igual quién marque, siempre que sea alguien de los Lobos». Pero, ¿da lo mismo cuando hay un cazatalentos entre el público? Seguro que ahora se ha fijado en Serkan. ¡El comodín que ha preparado el primer gol! Eso sí que impresiona. ¿Y qué pasa con Olli? En vez de aprovechar el centro buenísimo de Frank del primer tiempo, acierta ahora. ¡Qué mala suerte!

Una vez más, Niko inicia un ataque de los Lobos con un pase largo hacia la banda izquierda. Pero como siempre, el gordito está atento y, encima, ahora le ayuda el alto. No hay forma de pasar.

¿Cómo había dicho Norbert en el descanso? ¿Ser menos egoísta? ¡Qué gracia! Ahora mismo está prácticamente fuera del partido. Los rojos tienen la banda izquierda cerrada, y Frank se estampa una y otra vez contra el muro. Casi toda la acción se desarrolla ahora por el lado derecho, y los actores son otros. Como Catrina, por ejemplo. En este instante, manda hacia arriba a Olli. El delantero esquiva a varios defensas que se quedan parados como los enanos de jardín del señor Jahn. El portero duda, da unos pasos hacia delante, se para y mueve los brazos extendidos como si quisiera cazar moscas. No se parece en nada al portero de primera de antes. Olli no tiene ningún problema para meter el balón en la portería y marcar el 0 a 2.

Los Lobos van ganando. Frank se mete en la piña que se ha formado alrededor de Olli. De lo contrario, parecería como si no formara parte del equipo.

El público también lo está celebrando, al menos los hinchas de los Lobos. El señor gordo aplaude. Seguro que le ha impresionado el doble goleador. No sabe que Olli es un caracol, un oportunista del área, un paralítico. Es como si, de repente, le hubieran salido alas. Sólo puede haber una explicación: se ha enterado de quién es el señor gordo, y quiere impresionarlo. ¡Menudo chulo!

Pero, un momento: ¿cómo puede saberlo?

Sólo cabe una posibilidad: Rebeca. Ha hablado con el señor, y en el descanso se lo ha dicho a Catrina. Frank se imagina el cuchicheo: «Catrina, escucha, ¿te has enterado de lo último…? Es tu gran oportunidad. Demuéstrale de lo que eres capaz». La pobre Rebeca no se ha enterado de que su amiga no tiene futuro en el fútbol.

Catrina lo sabe todo, y se lo ha dicho a los demás. Por eso los Lobos han mejorado tanto en el segundo tiempo. Todos quieren convencer al cazatalentos.

Pero, ¿por qué Catrina no ha dicho nada a Frank? ¿Ni Niko? ¿Ni Mehmet? Porque quieren hacerle el vacío. Quieren pasar de él hasta el momento en el que llegue el gran éxito. Probablemente, en secreto, se están riendo de él porque está corriendo por el campo como un memo. Y Frank que pensaba que eran sus amigos. ¿Uno para todos y todos para uno? ¡Mentira cochina! Pero vale, si las cosas son así, Frank ya no tiene que preocuparse por nadie más que por él mismo.

Fuera del campo, el señor gordo está dando la mano al abuelo. Parece que se está despidiendo. Si Frank quiere llamar su atención, debe darse prisa. Y si sus compañeros de banda pasan de él, tendrá que meterse por el centro. No le va a resultar difícil actuar como Olli. Deberá simplemente esperar en el área hasta que llegue su oportunidad.

En el borde del área, el balón le cae delante de los pies. Ahora o nunca, no puede titubear. Frank se gira con rapidez y chuta. ¡Demasiado fuerte! El disparo sale del campo.

Poco tiempo después, los Lobos marcan el tercer tanto. Un tiro de Niko desde fuera del área decide definitivamente el partido. El Steinheim se rinde. Decepcionado, también el defensa gordito deja de marcar a Frank. Es la oportunidad que había esperado. Con una espectacular chilena, mete el balón por la escuadra. ¡Qué golazo! Desgraciadamente, ya no sirve de nada. El cazatalentos se ha marchado.

Cuando termina el partido, Frank sigue a los demás hacia los vestuarios, totalmente desilusionado. Sin embargo, todos se muestran supercontentos. Peter gruñe como un cerdo para expresar su alegría. Catrina chilla como una loca por la misma razón. Niko se sube a uno de los bancos y da saltitos que sacuden toda la sala.

Mehmet intenta duchar a Olli con su botella de refresco, pero éste se agacha con rapidez y el líquido pegajoso da a Frank en toda la cara.

—¡Idiota! —grita enfadado.

Mehmet se traga el resto del refresco y eructa con alegría.

—No te pongas así —contesta tranquilamente—. No pasa nada.

—¿Que no pasa nada? —se cabrea Frank—. Lo has hecho a propósito.

Sus compañeros van a pensar que está de mal humor por la ducha del refresco.

—No te preocupes —dice Peter con picardía—. Es bueno para la piel.

—Pues mete la cabeza dentro de un barril —resopla Frank.

—¡No vais a pelearos en un día como hoy! —intenta intermediar Catrina.

¡Qué bonito! La carrera profesional de Frank acaba de fastidiarse. A nadie parece importarle que se eche a perder su talento. Un verdadero profesional tiene que rendir lo máximo siempre. Y justamente hoy Frank ha jugado como un suplente. Así, sólo puede esperar a jugar en la Liga Regional cuando sea mayor. ¿Qué dirá su padre? Siempre han imaginado que jugaría en el Hamburgo. Este sueño se ha acabado.

—¿Y esa cara? —le pregunta Mehmet—. ¿No te has enterado? ¡Estamos en la final, tío! ¡En la FI-NAL!

¿Y qué? ¿Para qué sirve eso? ¡La final de los aficionados! El fútbol de verdad se juega en otra parte.

—¿De la Copa Regional? ¡Bah! —dice Frank poniendo cara de asco—. Menudo mérito. ¿O creéis que en la final los cazatalentos van a hacer cola?

—¿Cazatalentos? —pregunta Niko frunciendo el ceño—. ¿De qué estás hablando?

—Lo sabes perfectamente —bufa Frank.

Sin decir ni una palabra más, mete sus cosas en la bolsa y sale corriendo. Totalmente deprimido, se esconde en el asiento de atrás del coche del abuelo.

Puede que viajar en el microbús del club sea bueno para el espíritu de equipo, pero ahora mismo esos hipócritas le importan un pepino.

Al día siguiente, Frank llega al colegio más temprano que nunca. El patio de recreo está vacío. No hay ni alumnos ni profes. Ni siquiera la señorita Pestum está patrullando. Con un gruñido de enfado, la tripa de Frank le indica que tiene hambre. Con las prisas, no ha tenido tiempo de desayunar, pero tenía que salir antes que otras veces de casa para no coincidir en el camino con Mehmet y Orhan. No le apetecía escuchar ni las preguntas cotillas ni los consejos bienintencionados de los hermanos. Y seguro que los dos también prefieren ir solos. Después del espectáculo que ha dado el día anterior, seguro que los Lobos ya no quieren saber nada de él.

De repente, como si se hubieran teletransportado, aparecen sus amigos.

—¿Qué, tío? ¿Ya estás mejor? —le saluda Niko.

A Frank le encantaría estar mejor. Olvidarse de todo y hacer las paces, pero está demasiado decepcionado. Le habían decepcionado los demás, pero sobre todo él mismo. Nota que se le está formando un nudo en la garganta del tamaño de un balón de fútbol. ¡Ahora no puede echarse a llorar!

—¡Dejadme en paz! —dice en voz baja.

En ese momento aparece la señorita Pestum para vigilar el patio. Enseguida se fija en los Lobos y se acerca deprisa.

—¿Algún problema? —pregunta desconfiada.

¿Problema? ¡Si sólo fuera uno! Pero una profesora que no tiene ni idea de fútbol ni de jugadores no puede ayudar.

—¿Os pasa algo? —insiste la señorita.

—No.

—Todo bien.

Pero a la Pestum no se la convence así de rápido. Echa una mirada a Frank como si fuera inspectora de policía. Después, se aleja de los chicos.

—Oye, Frank —dice Niko con voz preocupada—. No sé qué te pasa. Pero cuando quieras hablar, ya sabes dónde estamos.

Se da la vuelta y Mehmet y Peter le siguen.

Sólo Orhan se queda con él.

—Mal de amores, ¿verdad? —dice el pequeño y le da una palmadita en el brazo a Frank—. No te preocupes, se te pasará.

Sin esperar una respuesta, sale corriendo detrás de los otros. Como está siempre enamorado de alguna chica, Orham se ha convertido en un verdadero experto en temas de amor. Pero en este caso, desgraciadamente, está equivocado.

¿Mal de amores? Ojalá. No, los problemas de Frank son mucho más graves.

# La confesión del abuelo

## 07

— ¿No te gusta la comida? —pregunta el abuelo preocupado.

Frank no se había dado ni cuenta de que sólo estaba haciendo dibujos en el puré de patatas con el tenedor.

—Lo siento, pero no me sale tan bien como a tu madre.

En realidad, eso no es cierto. Siempre que la madre de Frank está trabajando, el abuelo prepara la comida, y lo hace estupendamente.

—Qué va, está muy rico —contesta Frank y, para demostrárselo, se corta un gran trozo de salchicha y se lo mete en la boca.

Sin embargo, tiene la sensación de que allí se hace cada vez más grande y que no va a conseguir tragárselo. Pero la culpa no la tiene la comida del abuelo, sino el partido de Copa, que le quita el hambre. Siempre había soñado con ser descubierto algún día. Pero, ¿cuántas veces un cazatalentos asiste a un partido de los benjamines? ¡Casi nunca! Si aparece uno, es una suerte enorme. Como si te tocara el Gordo de Navidad. Es una oportunidad que hay que aprovechar cuando se presenta. Pero Frank fracasó. ¿Porque los demás le hicieron el vacío? ¡Tonterías! Fue precisamente él quien se enteró antes que nadie de la misión del señor gordo. Y a partir de ese momento, fue como si los Lobos dejasen de existir para Frank. Quería destacar por encima de todos. Por eso se comportó como un idiota y jugó fatal, de forma arrogante y egoísta. No le habrá gustado nada al cazatalentos. El fútbol es un deporte que se practica en equipo. Ningún club necesita a un luchador que no cuenta con su equipo, ni siquiera el HSV de Hamburgo.

¿Realmente sus amigos se habían enterado de la presencia del cazatalentos? Ayer, Frank estaba convencido de ello, pero hoy ya no está tan seguro. Olli, el delantero con olfato de goleador, ha metido muchos goles, incluso cuando nadie lo estaba observando. Y Niko, el organizador del juego en el mediocampo, ha dado muchos pases decisivos para el resultado final en un montón de partidos. ¿Y Serkan? Juega siempre como una máquina, especialmente si ha pasado todo el primer tiempo en el banquillo. En Steinheim, los Lobos sencillamente jugaron bien, y probablemente eso no tenga nada que ver con el cazatalentos. Es decir, Frank ha sido injusto con sus amigos.

Pero eso es sólo el menos grave de sus problemas. De alguna manera, conseguirá arreglarlo. Hablará con Niko y los demás, y le perdonarán. El verdadero problema es el cazatalentos. Alguien debería hablar con él e interceder a favor de Frank. «Sabe usted, el veinte habrá tenido un mal día. Normalmente, juega mucho mejor…».

¿Quién podría conocer a ese hombre? ¿A lo mejor el abuelo? Ayer no paró de hablar con él. ¿No podría hacerlo una vez más?

Frank se inclina sobre el plato y corta la salchicha. De repente, como si no tuviera importancia, pregunta al abuelo:

—Por cierto, ¿quién era ese señor con el que hablaste ayer?

De repente, el anciano se pone a toser durante un buen rato. Parece ser un auténtico ataque de tos.

Cuando por fin se recupera, se dedica de nuevo a comer.

—Ya sabes a quién me refiero. Ayer, durante el partido. El gordo. Estabais uno al lado del otro. Os despedisteis con un apretón de manos.

—Ejem…, no me acuerdo…, ejem…, no sé…

Desesperado, el abuelo prefiere callarse. Nunca ha sabido mentir bien. Pero, ¿por qué lo está haciendo ahora? Nunca ha habido secretos entre ambos. ¡Qué extraño!

—Venga, abuelito, a mí me lo puedes decir —insiste Frank cambiando de estrategia—. Y, además, ya lo sé.

—¡Pero yo no te he dicho nada! —se le escapa al abuelo.

—No, claro que no —lo tranquiliza Frank.

Por fin, el hombre se rinde:

—Bueno, total, si ya lo sabes…

—Claro —responde Frank mirándolo con expectación.

—Pero no se lo puedes decir a nadie. De momento, es un secreto.

—Lo prometo.

—Vale. Pues el señor se llama Lichting.

De nuevo, el abuelo se calla como si no quisiera soltar más información.

—¿Y entonces? —insiste Frank.

—El señor Lichting es entrenador.

Claro. Justo lo que Frank había pensado.

—Estaba observando a Catrina.

—¿QUÉ? ¿A CATRINA?

—¡Shh! —exclama el abuelo apoyando el dedo en la boca.

Sin poder evitarlo, Frank baja la voz:

—Pero, abuelo, Catrina es una chica.

—Efectivamente. Por eso se interesa por ella. El señor Lichting es el entrenador de la selección regional de chicas.

—¿Una selección de chicas?

Frank sacude la cabeza, asombrado. Es la primera noticia que tiene.

—Eso es —continúa el abuelo con entusiasmo—. Parece una cosa estupenda. Me dijo que dos de sus antiguas jugadoras están hoy en la Liga profesional. ¿Sabías que hay una Liga profesional femenina?

—Mmh, claro —masculla Frank.

¡Ojalá el abuelo no le pregunte por el nombre de sus equipos! Menos mal que sigue hablando.

—Catrina va a jugar en la selección regional. El señor Lichting dice que tiene mucho talento.

El abuelo habla con tanto entusiamo que parece como si él mismo hubiera descubierto a Catrina. ¡Vaya! ¡Menuda noticia!

—Entonces, ¿el señor Lichting es un cazatalentos de chicas? —pregunta Frank para estar totalmente seguro.

—Sí. Supongo que podría llamarse así.

Frank se siente tan aliviado que le entran ganas de reír. Pero no quiere que el abuelo piense que se ha vuelto loco. Había creído que con el mal juego de ayer se había fastidiado la gran oportunidad de su vida, pero no es así. Un cazatalentos para chicas jamás se habría fijado en él, aunque hubiera jugado como el mejor delantero del mundo. Su gran oportunidad, el Gordo de Navidad, puede llegar todavía. A partir de ahora, no volverá a hacer el imbécil.

¡Catrina en la selección regional! ¿Quién lo hubiera dicho? Frank cree que se lo merece. Es una defensa de primera y, además, una buena amiga.

Pero a Frank le queda aún una duda.

—¿Y por qué es un secreto? ¡Una jugadora de los Lobos en la selección regional! Es una gran noticia. Todo el mundo debería enterarse. Sobre todo, los Tigres. Imagínate la cara que pondrían.

—No, no puede ser —dice el abuelo y baja de nuevo la voz—. El señor Lichting ha tenido también otra idea más. Cree que Catrina podría jugar la próxima temporada en un equipo de chicas, pero quiere que se lo piense tranquilamente, sin presión. Piensa que, si todo el mundo se entera, intentarán influir en su decisión.

—¿Catrina cambiará de equipo? —pregunta Frank asustado—. ¿Dices que se quiere ir de los Lobos?

—Lichting dice que sí, a un equipo con futuro —responde el abuelo, como si quisiera defender al señor gordo.

Ahora Frank se enfada de verdad.

—Necesitamos a Catrina —grita—. Díselo al señor Importante. Sólo por ser un cazatalentos cree que se puede permitir cualquier cosa. Si no deja en paz a Catrina, se arrepentirá.

—No debería haberte dicho nada —dice el abuelo preocupado—. Pero como ya lo sabías…

Frank aparta su plato y sale corriendo.

—¡Recuerda! —exclama el abuelo—. ¡Ni una palabra de todo esto! ¡A nadie!

Pero Frank ya ha cogido el teléfono.

—¿Niko? Soy yo.

—¿Estás mejor ya? —pregunta el amigo, en vez de saludar.

—¿Mejor? Todo lo contrario. Estoy a punto de estallar. No vas a creer lo que acabo de oír.

## 08

# Demasiada casualidad

El miércoles suele ser el día del entrenamiento para los Lobos, pero, como esta semana han jugado el partido de Copa, Norbert los ha convocado para el jueves.

—¡Ala, chicos! —los anima dando unas palmadas—. Hoy vamos a tener un entrenamiento suave. Empezaremos con los regates.

—¡Sí, hombre! —se queja Mehmet en voz baja.

Al portero cualquier esfuerzo le molesta, y le dan igual las preocupaciones de Norbert por la condición física de los Lobos.

—Falta Catrina —dice Mehmet en voz más alta.

Norbert niega con un gesto de la mano.

—Hoy no la vamos a esperar. La pobrecilla tiene que ir al dentista.

—No me extraña —se ríe Peter—. Se habrá roto los piños de tanto cantar mal.

Frank y Niko intercambian una mirada. ¡Conque al dentista! ¡Ja! Menuda excusa. Catrina tendrá su primer entrenamiento con la selección de las chicas. Frank puede imaginar sus conversaciones: «¿Has jugado con chicos? ¡Qué horror! Mejor que juegues con nosotras, somos mucho más simpáticas...».

¡Estúpidas! Y, encima, por culpa de sus nuevas compañeras Catrina ha mentido al entrenador y da plantón a sus amigos.

—Frank, un poco más de energía, por favor. No te duermas —le pega un grito Norbert.

¡Conque suave! Enfadado, Frank va a toda máquina, pasando los pivotes que marcan el recorrido del ejercicio.

Llega el momento del descanso. Norbert aprovecha para hablar a los Lobos del partido de ayer.

—¡Chicos! ¡Me dejasteis impresionado!

Bueno, depende. Frank, avergonzado, prefiere mirar al suelo, pero el entrenador no se da cuenta.

—Frank —añade—, en el segundo tiempo mejoraste mucho. A veces, incluso, te marcaban tres defensas a la vez. Eso hizo que los otros tuvieran más espacio y enseguida pudimos meter gol.

¿En serio? Entonces, Frank sí que puso su granito de arena en la victoria del equipo. Con tanto cazatalentos, ni se había enterado.

—Y ahora estamos en la final —continúa Norbert—. Pero no quiero que os durmáis en los laureles. El sábado jugamos el partido de liga contra el Tiefen. Hay que darlo todo y estar concentrados, si queremos hacer algo. Así que vamos a seguir con los tiros a puerta.

Eso sí que le gusta a Mehmet. El meta se levanta rápido para colocarse entre los palos, pero Niko lo agarra del brazo.

—Luego tenemos que hablar de una cosa —le dice en voz baja.

—¿Qué pasa? —se interesa Peter.

—¡Chicos! ¡No estamos aquí para cotillear! —les pega un grito Norbert.

—¡Luego! —dice Niko, que agarra uno de los balones y ocupa la posición en el borde del área.

Una vez terminado el entrenamiento, los amigos se reúnen en la entrada del campo.

—¡Dispara! —dice Peter.

—¡Y rápido! —se impacienta Mehmet—. Me muero de hambre.

—Se te van a quitar las ganas, ya verás —profetiza Niko.

En ese preciso momento, sale Norbert del vestuario.

—¿Reunión secreta sin el técnico? —bromea.

—No, sólo un poco de estrategia para el partido del sábado —responde Niko.

—Pero no os entretengáis. Si no llegáis a casa pronto, vuestros padres se preocuparan… Nos vemos.

Se despide y va silbando hacia el coche.

Niko espera hasta que el entrenador ya no pueda oírlos.

—Es por Catrina —dice finalmente en voz baja—. Parece que va a dejar los Lobos —añade y mira expectante a sus amigos.

Éstos, sin embargo, no están muy impresionados.

—¡Tonterías!

—¿Catrina? Imposible.

—¿De dónde sacas eso?

Niko mira a Frank y le pide ayuda:

—¡Cuéntaselo tú!

Y, ante el asombro general, Frank habla a los demás del señor Lichting. Aunque, eso sí, la parte en que había estado a punto de hacer el ridículo se la calla. Pero cuando se trata de explicar los planes oscuros del cazatalentos, no olvida ningún detalle.

—Pretende llevársela a un equipo de chicas —dice para concluir.

—¡No lo creo! —contesta Peter—. ¿Catrina en un club de té? ¡Jamás!

Frank no está tan seguro.

—De club de té, nada. El gordo dice que es un equipo con futuro.

—¿Cómo? —pregunta Peter incrédulo—. ¿Un equipo de chicas con futuro? ¿Qué diablos significa eso?

—Significa que…, es decir… ¡Mierda! ¡Qué más da!

No da igual —dice de repente Hendrik.

Claro, ¡quién si no iba a hablar! Como no se levantó del banquillo, estuvo al lado del gordo durante casi todo el partido.

—Venga, suéltalo ya —le anima Frank.

—El señor Lichting dice que el equipo ese podría subir a Segunda División Femenina —explica Hendrik.

¡Segunda División! ¡Menuda noticia! Los chicos se quedan sin habla.

—¡Segunda División! —repite Niko con respeto, recuperando la voz antes que nadie.

—¿Una liga de verdad? —pregunta Peter, incrédulo—. Pensaba que las mujeres sólo hacían tonterías con el balón para pasar el rato.

—De eso, nada —continúa Hendrik—. El señor Lichting dice que el fútbol femenino está creciendo un montón. ¿Sabíais que la selección femenina alemana ya ha ganado la Eurocopa y el Mundial?

Lo dice muy orgulloso, como si él mismo hubiera ganado esos títulos.

—¿El Mundial?

—¡Madre mía! Creo que había oído algo, pero…

—¡Quién lo hubiera dicho!

—¿Os acordáis de lo que dijimos el otro día sobre el fútbol femenino? —pregunta Niko avergonzado.

—Fueron sólo tonterías —reconoce Frank.

—Pero da igual —contesta Mehmet con decisión—. Aun así, ese tío no tiene ningún derecho a llevarse a Catrina de nuestro equipo.

—En realidad, no es ésa su intención —defiende Hendrik al cazatalentos—. Al contrario, dice que Catrina debería pensárselo, y mucho. Seguir jugando en un equipo de chicos puede tener también sus ventajas. Es que…

—Catrina tiene que quedarse con nosotros —lo interrumpe Mehmet—. Sin ella, nuestra defensa no vale para nada. No me apetece que me metan goles, uno tras otro, en todos los partidos.

—¿Cómo? ¿Qué pasa? ¿Yo no existo? —pregunta Peter, el otro defensa.

—Claro que sí, y menos mal —lo consuela Frank.

Lo último que el equipo necesita ahora es que se peleen entre ellos.

—Pero el equipo necesita a más de un defensa —continúa.

—Es cierto, y yo necesito a Catrina —le da la razón Peter, otra vez contento—. Tiene que quedarse.

—Y no sólo por la defensa —añade Orhan en voz baja—. También por…, porque… ¡No quiero que se vaya!

El enano ha resumido la situación mejor que nadie. ¿Los Lobos sin Catrina? Sería impensable.

—Tenemos que encontrar la manera de evitarlo —decide Frank.

—Pero ¿cómo? —pregunta Niko—. Estamos hablando de la Segunda División. Me parece que nos queda un poco grande.

Durante un rato, todos se callan.

—No hay mal que por bien no venga —rompe el silencio Serkan, pero con poca convicción—: al menos, ya no nos romperá los huesos en los entrenamientos.

—Ni los tímpanos —dice Peter e imita la voz de serrucho de Catrina—: *«Los Lobos son inseparables»*.

Luego escupe al suelo con rabia.

—¡Menuda letra! —añade Niko con amargura—. ¡Todo mentira!

—No sé —murmulla Orhan—. A mí me gustaba…

El enano está pensando muy concentrado.

—¡Ya lo tengo! —grita de golpe—. ¡Norbert! Tiene que prohibirle que se vaya.

Niko lo devuelve a la realidad:

—Olvídate de eso. Cuando termine la temporada, está libre para marcharse donde quiera.

—Desgraciadamente —afirma Frank—, así son las cosas.

De repente, suena el móvil de Peter. Mira la pantalla y cancela la llamada.

—Mi madre —explica sin ganas—. Querrá que vaya a casa.

—En fin, ya está todo dicho —concluye Niko, agarra su bolsa como si fuera a cámara lenta y se da la vuelta para marcharse con Peter.

—Venga, vámonos —Mehmet le mete prisa a Frank—. ¿O quieres que echemos raíces aquí?

—Espera.

Hendrik ya está montando en la bici, cuando Frank se dirige a él:

—Oye, ¿qué es lo que contabas que había dicho el gordo? ¿Qué ventajas tiene jugar en un equipo de chicos como el nuestro?

—Según él, si el equipo de chicos es bueno, una defensa de primera puede aprender a ser dura.

¡Aprender a ser dura! Frank se frota la pierna que ya ha sentido las patadas de Catrina más de una vez. No, aprender a ser dura ya no le hace falta a Catrina. Para eso no va a necesitar ni a Frank ni a sus amigos. ¡Qué pena!

Frank está tirado en el sofá jugando con el mando a distancia. De repente, suena el teléfono. ¿Será Niko? ¿Habrá tenido una idea con la que convencer a Catrina para que se quede? ¡Menos mal que el capitán de los Lobos tiene buenas ideas para resolver situaciones difíciles incluso fuera del campo!

Frank se levanta para ir al pasillo donde está el teléfono, pero el abuelo ha sido más rápido. Ya está alargando la mano para levantarlo, aunque Frank se mete en medio y lo empuja hacia atrás. Juego brusco al límite de lo reglamentario. Menos mal que no hay ningún árbitro a la vista.

—Perdona, abuelo —dice el chico y se lleva el auricular al oído—. ¿Niko?

¡No! ¡Se ha equivocado! ¡Es su padre!

—Ah, vaya, eres tú.

—Pero bueno. ¿Qué tipo de saludo es ése? ¿Estás de mal humor?

—No. Bueno, sí. Es por Catrina.

—Anda. No sabía que Catrina y tú…

—¡Jo, papá! —Frank pone los ojos en blanco. Parece que los adultos sólo piensan en el amor y

cosas del mismo estilo en vez de
concentrarse en los problemas
de verdad.

—No es eso, sino que durante el último partido de Copa un
cazatalentos se ha fijado en Catrina.

—Pues, estupendo, ¿no? —
opina su padre—. Igual se hace
famosa en la Liga profesional. El fútbol femenino está
creciendo mucho. La selección de Alemania ya…

—… ha ganado la Eurocopa y el Mundial —le
interrumpe Frank.

Parece ser que todo el mundo estaba enterado, a
excepción de los Lobos. ¡Menuda vergüenza! Pero el
padre de Frank no se da cuenta de lo apurado que
está su hijo.

—Entonces, ¿dónde está el problema? —insiste.

—En que probablemente Catrina se vaya a jugar a
un equipo de chicas.

—¿Catrina? No creo. Su sitio está con los Lobos.

—Pues díselo tú, papá.

—Vosotros se lo tenéis que decir. O, mejor aún, tenéis
que demostrárselo. Seguro que conseguís convencerla.

—Lo dudo —dice Frank soltando un suspiro—. Creo que ya hemos perdido esta ronda de negociaciones.

Su padre se queda callado.

—¿Has dicho que la descubrió un cazatalentos? —pregunta por fin.

—Sí.

—¿Y cómo es que ha ido a vuestro partido de Copa?

En eso Frank no había pensado.

—Por casualidad, supongo.

—¿Casualidad? No sé. Es como si te tocara el Gordo de Navidad. Llevo años comprando décimos y no me ha tocado nunca.

Y Frank lleva años jugando al fútbol y no ha sido descubierto. ¿Será verdad que fue casualidad? ¿O puede haber otra explicación? No, sólo hay una.

—Catrina ha tenido suerte.

—Bueno, puede —dice su padre, y Frank casi puede oír cómo sacude la cabeza.

Es evidente que no está nada convencido.

# Los Lobos en lo alto de la tabla...

## 09

A la mañana siguiente, Mark está en el patio del colegio. Cerca hay unos cuantos jugadores de los Tigres, todos unos niñatos de un curso inferior. Mejor ni mirarlos. Pero cuando Mark ve a Frank y sus amigos, se dibuja una sonrisa cruel en su cara. Es evidente que tiene ganas de provocar. Incluso el árbitro más ciego se daría cuenta.

—¡Eh, chicos! —grita con falsa alegría—. ¿Queréis oír un chiste? ¿Qué hay que hacer para que los Lobos estén en lo alto de la tabla? Pues, muy sencillo: ¡poner la tabla al revés!

De acuerdo. Ha llegado el momento de tener una buena pelea. La última fue hace años luz. Eso sí, no por tan poca cosa, claro. Aunque, bueno, los niñatos de los Tigres se están riendo con Mark. ¡Como siempre! Los Tigres no tienen ni dos dedos de frente. Pero un auténtico Lobo no se deja provocar con tanta facilidad.

—Ja, ja —dice Niko con voz aburrida.

Peter sólo se encoge de hombros.

Mehmet hace como si tuviera ganas de bostezar.

Pero Mark no se rinde aún.

—Por cierto, ¿sabéis quién va a ganar la Liga Regional esta temporada?

Desgraciadamente, sí, y a ningún Lobo le agrada mucho. Parece ser que, un año más, los campeones van a ser los Tigres. Los Lobos no han tenido mucha suerte en la Liga. Demasiadas lesiones y sanciones. Además, Frank se perdió los primeros partidos de ida porque vivía todavía en Asdorf. Y los primeros partidos después del invierno no han ido tampoco muy bien. No, hay que ser realistas. Las posibilidades de quitar el título a los Tigres son tan remotas que habría que buscarlas con catalejos.

Es mejor no perder energía dándole vueltas. Más vale atacar de nuevo la próxima temporada. Frank jugará desde el principio, y entonces triunfarán los Lobos.

Frank jugará, pero Catrina no. Ella estará con las Gallinas con Futuro, y los Lobos jamás volverán a ser como antes… ¡Qué pena!

—¿Y quién ganará la Copa? —pregunta ahora Niko con la misma ironía que antes utilizó Mark.

—¿Copa? —el Tigre pronuncia la palabra como si le diera asco—. Te refieres al premio de consolación para perdedores, ¿no? Pero no vais a conseguir ni eso. En la final, os van a dar una paliza.

Niko frunce el ceño, y Peter y Mehmet empiezan a prepararse.

—¡Ten cuidado con lo que dices, chaval!

La pelea está a punto de estallar. Encantados, los enanos del equipo de los Tigres se esconden detrás de su compañero alto.

—No lloréis, chicos —insiste Mark—. No todos pueden jugar en un buen equipo como el nuestro.

¿Buen equipo? No le falta razón. ¿Estaría Catrina pensando en cambiar de equipo si estuviera jugando con los Tigres? Tal vez no. Si estás en el equipo que más ligas ha ganado, no hace falta dar un empujón a tu carrera.

—¿Los Tigres? ¡Qué asco! Antes dejaríamos de jugar al fútbol.

—Más os vale. Sólo sois unos aficionados sin talento alguno.

La cosa se calienta y está a punto de estallar. Ahora es cuestión de segundos.

Peter se saca las manos del bolsillo. Mehmet deja la mochila en el suelo.

Ni siquiera Orhan se quiere perder la pelea:

—¡Los Lobos molan mucho más que los Tigres!

Mark sacude la cabeza como si le diera pena:

—Un poquitín retrasado, el pobre —se ríe—. Con suerte, los Reyes Magos os lo cambiarán por un jugador de verdad.

Mehmet tiene mucha paciencia, pero si hay algo que no aguanta es que insulten a su hermanito. Y mucho menos si el insulto viene de un Tigre. Está a punto de agarrar a Mark, pero en ese momento reacciona Frank.

Se pone entre Mark y su amigo, y grita:

—Mark, ¡eres un fenómeno!

El Tigre entrecierra los ojos y mira con desconfianza a Frank, pero el Lobo le mantiene la mirada con una sonrisa.

—¿Qué tonterías dices, tío? —pregunta Mark por fin.

—Sólo quería darte las gracias. Si no hubiera sido por ti…

Mark está acostumbrado a oír los insultos de los Lobos, pero tanta amabilidad le pone nervioso.

—¿Las gracias? ¿De qué estás hablando? —Mira a su alrededor por si esto es una trampa, pero, al no ver nada, intenta quitar importancia al asunto—: me parece que te falta un tornillo.

Hace una señal a sus seguidores y se marchan.

—¡Jo, tío! —exclama Mehmet decepcionado—. Esta vez habría acabado con él si no te hubieras metido —le reprocha a Frank.

—«Si no hubiera sido por ti…» —imita Niko a Frank, enfadado—. ¿A qué venía esto?

—¿No os dais cuenta? —pregunta Frank con auténtica alegría—. Mark nos acaba de decir cómo podemos conseguir que Catrina se quede.

—¿Qué?

—No ha dicho nada de Catrina.

—No, no directamente —reconoce Frank—, pero me ha dado una idea con lo del buen equipo. ¿Lo captáis? Si conseguimos el doblete, ya sabéis, la Liga y la Copa…

—Ya sé lo que quiere decir doblete —contesta Niko poniendo los ojos en blanco—. Lo que no sé es qué tiene esto que ver con Catrina.

¡Madre mía! Hoy están más cortos que nunca.

—¿El doblete es algo muy especial? ¿O no? —insiste Frank.

—Claro que sí.

—Desde luego.

—Por eso tenemos que ganar las dos cosas. Por Catrina. Y luego le diremos…, ejem, le diremos que…

—¿Qué tal si le decimos que somos un equipo de chicas y que llegaremos muy lejos en el fútbol femenino? —propone Peter con ironía.

De un momento a otro, el entusiasmo de Frank se desvanece. Peter tiene toda la razón. Incluso si los Lobos ganasen más títulos que el Bayern de Múnich, no habría forma de competir con un equipo de Segunda División. Su idea ha sido estúpida. Es una lástima que por eso se hayan perdido la pelea con el chulo de los Tigres.

—No sé, tal vez tengas razón —le apoya de repente Mehmet—. Si ganamos la Liga y la Copa seremos un equipo importante. Entonces no será tan fácil dejarnos.

Niko se pone a dar vueltas a un mechón de pelo hasta que le sobresale de la cabeza como una antena.

—¿Por qué no? —admite—. Mientras no tengamos una idea mejor…

A Orhan le gusta también el plan.

—¡Campeones de Liga! ¡Claro! Es lo que siempre he querido ser.

Pero Peter sigue mostrándose escéptico:

—La Copa, vale. Pero, ¿ganar la Liga? Igual ya es un poco tarde.

—No digas eso —protesta Niko con gran entusiasmo—. Matemáticamente, todo es posible. —Las *mates* no son precisamente su fuerte, pero la tabla de la Liga se la sabe de memoria—. Si a partir de ahora conseguimos todos los puntos, podríamos lograrlo. ¡Pero sólo si nos quedamos con todos!

—¡Nada de empates!

—¿Sólo victorias?

—¡Sólo victorias!

—¡Guay! Así me gusta —dice Mehmet frotándose las manos—. Me encantan las finales.

—Y la primera, mañana, contra el Tiefen.

Tiefen… No es precisamente un equipo bueno. En la primera vuelta de la Liga, los Lobos no se anduvieron por las ramas y ganaron por un contundente 5 a 1. Pero, aparte del partido contra el Tiefen, aún les esperan otros equipos bastante difíciles. Y el más duro será el de la última jornada, contra los mismísimos Tigres. ¿Sólo victorias? No parece muy probable que lo consigan, pero hay alguna posibilidad y justo es eso lo que hace al fútbol interesante. Además, hay un refrán entre los jugadores que dice: «si te queda alguna posibilidad, ¡aprovéchala!». Frank está decidido.

—¿De acuerdo, Peter? —insiste.

El amigo se encoge de hombros.

—Vale, tío —contesta—. Habrá que intentarlo al menos.

—Y a ver si el año que viene no esperamos hasta el último momento —reflexiona Niko—. Empezaremos fuerte y decidiremos el campeonato mucho antes.

—Eso es, a partir de ahora los Lobos se van a dedicar a coleccionar títulos.

—Y de la envidia los Tigres se van a poner tan verdes como sus camisetas.

—Y las chicas tendrán que buscar otra defensa.

—¡Eso es! —se ríe Frank y choca los cinco con sus amigos.

Si alguien quiere llevarse a Catrina y romper el muro defensivo de los Lobos, no se quedarán mirando sin hacer nada.

En ese momento llega Rebeca.

—¿Qué estáis haciendo? —cotillea.

¡Típico! Las cosas que más le interesan son siempre las que menos le conciernen.

—Son cosas de fútbol —responde Niko con frialdad—. No lo vas a entender.

—Tal vez mejor que vosotros —dice Rebeca con voz provocadora.

—No me digas.

—Pues sí. Y os vais a enterar.

—Sí, Rebeca, ¡la nueva estrella en el cielo del fútbol!

—Y que juegue con el equipo de los Tigres, por favor —se ríe Peter—. Para que pierdan seguro.

# La «final»

—Hay que tener cuidado con el cuatro. Es superpeligroso. Estaba en todos los contraataques. ¿Y os acordáis del siete, de cómo apareció un par de veces frente a la portería? Y tened mucho cuidado con los saques de falta porque…

—Oye, Frank, ¿por qué no te callas? —se queja Mehmet—. Llevas más de una hora diciendo tonterías. ¿Cómo quieres que me concentre?

¿Una hora? ¡Qué exagerado! Como mucho lleva cinco minutos. Y es más, Frank no dice tonterías sino que da consejos muy útiles. El portero debería agradecérselo.

Los chicos llegan al campo de Los Lobos. Desde allí, el microbús del club los llevará a Tiefen, a jugar la

101

primera de las «finales». Si hoy no ganan, tendrán
que olvidarse del título. Y con él, de Catrina. Este partido va a decidir su destino.

—No te pongas nervioso —intenta animar Orhan
a su amigo—. Los del Tiefen no son buenos.

—No estoy nervioso —contesta Frank bufando—. No estoy nada nervioso. ¡ESTOY MUY TRANQUILO!

Orhan se asusta. En ese momento, llega Catrina en bici.

—¿A qué vienen esos gritos? —pregunta.

Frank nota un brillo metálico en la boca de su amiga. En un momento, sus nervios han desaparecido.

—Pero si tienes aparato —dice aliviado.

—No me digas —responde Catrina con ironía—. No me había dado cuenta.

—Entonces, ¿fuiste al dentista?

¡Qué va! Lo compré en las rebajas. ¿A qué viene tanta pregunta?

—No, nada —intenta disimular Frank.

Catrina no lo entendería. Lo importante es que había dicho la verdad. El jueves no había ido a ver a su nuevo equipo de chicas. Realmente había ido al dentista. ¡Es una buena señal!

Catrina se encoge de hombros.

—Como quieras…

En la casa que hay justo enfrente del campo se abre una ventana.

—¡Hola, chicos! —grita el señor Jahn—. ¿Cómo va eso? ¿Tenéis un partido importante?

Catrina y los chicos se acercan a la valla.

—Todos los partidos son importantes —explica Catrina.

—Espero que ganéis —les desea el hombre.

El abuelo de Frank acaba de aparcar su coche. En el camino, ha recogido a Rebeca. Los dos se acercan al grupo.

—Seguro que todo ira bien. Y si hay problemas, ponéis a jugar también al abuelo —bromea el señor Jahn.

—Será mejor que no —se ríe éste—. Últimamente no he entrenado mucho.

—Además, se ocupa de otra tarea superimportante —añade Frank—: es el chófer de la afición.

Ahora llega el microbús del club, con Norbert al volante. Éste baja la ventanilla.

—Me acaba de llamar Olli —dice el entrenador—. No va a llegar a tiempo.

—¡Vaya! —se queja Niko—. Olli siempre llega tarde.

En realidad, el delantero no tiene la culpa. Vive lejos, en otro pueblo, depende de su madre para que lo lleve en coche y a ella no le interesa mucho el fútbol. Siempre tiene que hacer miles de recados en el camino. Por eso, Olli a veces llega en el último momento.

—¿Qué hacemos? —pregunta Catrina con preocupación.

—Vamos a esperar un poco —dice Norbert enco-giéndose de hombros—. Eso sí, si tarda mucho vamos a tener un problemilla.

—Olli no puede faltar —comenta Mehmet—. El año pasado marcó dos goles contra el Tiefen.

—Ya llegará —dice Frank en voz baja.

¿Y qué si no llega a tiempo? Al menos, no habría dudas sobre la alineación: Frank jugaría esta primera «final» superimportante desde el primer segundo, sería uno de los dos delanteros.

—No hay problema —dice Rebeca de repente—. Podéis salir ahora con el microbús, y tu abuelo y yo nos quedamos esperando a Olli.

A Norbert le parece buena idea.

—¿Haría eso por nosotros?

—Claro que sí —afirma el abuelo.

—Entonces, sobra un sitio en el microbús —dice Orhan entusiasmado, que sube y se busca un asiento junto a la ventanilla.

—Vámonos —exclama Norbert—. Cuanto antes lleguemos a Tiefen, mejor.

Una vez en el campo del contrincante, los chicos empiezan con los ejercicios de calentamiento.

—Espero que Olli llegue pronto —dice Catrina preocupada.

Pero cuando los dos equipos entran en el campo, el delantero sigue sin aparecer. ¡Lástima! Aunque eso puede dar igual. Los Lobos siguen siendo muy peligrosos con sus otros dos delanteros.

Después de que el árbitro tira la moneda al aire, los del Tiefen, hoy con camiseta verde, son los que eligen el campo en el que quieren empezar a jugar.

—Así al menos han ganado algo hoy —dice Niko riéndose en voz baja.

Frank sonríe. Ésa será la única victoria del Tiefen. Los Lobos tienen que presionar desde el primer momento para no dar ninguna posibilidad al rival.

Desgraciadamente, los verdes no están de acuerdo. Nada más empezar el partido, uno de ellos intercepta el balón y lo tira fuera. Saque de banda, y a empezar de nuevo. Frank se ve rodeado de jugadores verdes y tiene que pasar la pelota hacia atrás. Menos mal que Catrina está atenta, la recibe y se la tira a Niko, que hace un pase largo a Serkan. ¡Bien! Pero de nuevo el Tiefen le roba el balón.

¡Pero bueno! ¿Qué pasa hoy?

Parece que el equipo contrario ha cambiado de estrategia desde el último partido del año pasado. Su

106

defensa es imbatible, y cualquier intento de ataque de los Lobos es cortado de raíz. Como sigan así, el partido va a ser difícil. No importa, incluso el muro defensivo más fuerte debe de tener algún hueco. Sólo hay que buscarlo con tranquilidad. Y una vez que los Lobos se pongan por delante en el marcador, los verdes tendrán que abrirse. Y entonces habrá más sitio para hacer buenas jugadas.

Pero todavía no. El balón no se mueve con facilidad. El Tiefen corta siempre. El partido se rompe. No se ve un buen fútbol. La defensa de los Lobos se aburre. Sólo dos o tres veces los verdes se acercan tímidamente, pero sin peligro de verdad. Catrina y sus compañeros no tienen ningún problema.

El primer tiempo se está acabando. Los Lobos aumentan la presión. Hasta ahora, Frank ha llegado dos veces hasta la línea de fondo, desde donde ha centrado. Aún no ha habido suerte, pero los defensas del Tiefen se están empezando a cansar. ¡Hay que seguir! Es sólo cuestión de tiempo.

De repente, Serkan tropieza y pierde el balón. Uno de los verdes da un pase largo al número cuatro. Catrina se acerca corriendo. En el mismo momento, ambos jugadores tocan el esférico con fuerza. El balón

sale disparado y, con un grito, Catrina se cae al suelo.
Asustado, Frank se acerca a ella.

—No he… No ha sido a propósito —tartamudea el
cuatro, pálido.

Catrina se frota el tobillo.

—No ha sido culpa tuya —lo tranquiliza—. Ha
sido un encontronazo y yo… —le muestra el aparato
de los dientes— me he llevado la peor parte.

Apoyada en el hombro de Norbert, sale del campo
de juego. Poco tiempo después, el árbitro pita el final del primer tiempo.

—¡Qué rollo! —bufa Niko en el vestuario—. Lo
que hacen éstos no es fútbol. Parece que ni siquiera
buscan marcar.

—¡Cuidado! —le contradice Catrina, que tiene el pie en alto, cubierto de cubitos de hielo.

Afortunadamente, no es nada grave, sólo una pequeña contusión. Aun así, no se va a perder el segundo tiempo.

—Tenéis que tener mucho cuidado atrás. Pero hasta ahora lo habéis hecho muy bien —les anima Norbert—. No perdáis la paciencia. El gol va a caer, seguro. Y a Catrina la va a sustituir...

—¡Olli! —grita Hendrik.

El chico parece estar aliviado.

¡Olli ha llegado! Ahora que la alineación ya no es ningún problema, Frank se alegra también de que haya venido. Tal vez su olfato de goleador sea la llave que consiga abrir la puerta del muro del Tiefen.

—¡Mi madre! —bufa Olli—. Quería a toda costa...

—Será mejor que hagas unos cuantos ejercicios para entrar en calor —le interrumpe Norbert—. Luego nos lo cuentas.

—No hace falta. Estoy que ardo de rabia. Creo que voy a estallar.

—Mejor metes por lo menos un par de goles —le propone Frank—. Verás lo rápido que se te pasa la rabia.

# Después del partido

## 11

Los Lobos empiezan el segundo tiempo con tres delanteros. Pero el partido no cambia nada: ellos atacan y el Tiefen despeja. Ni siquiera Olli encuentra el hueco.

Poco a poco, a Frank y sus amigos se les acaba el tiempo. ¿Paciencia? A Norbert le resulta fácil decirlo. No se ha enterado de lo importante que es realmente este partido. En una verdadera final, un empate a cero no sirve de nada. Para un equipo de verdad, con ganas de ser campeón, eso es muy poco. Hace falta una victoria, ¡y ya! Nadie se va a conformar con quedarse atrás.

Sólo Mehmet está en el campo de los Lobos. Todos los demás jugadores se amontonan cerca del área del Tiefen, como si fuera el primer día de las rebajas.

Frank tiene el balón. Dos de los verdes le cierran el camino. No pasa nada, es la hora de Olli. Frank le hace un pase, pero se queda corto. Un jugador del Tiefen mete la punta de la bota y el balón cae a otro de los verdes. Un pase, otro pase. De repente, lo recibe el cuatro, y éste se marcha hacia arriba. Ya está pasando la línea central.

¡Catrina! ¡CATRINA!

Pero Catrina está entre el público. Grita y gesticula, pero no puede ayudar.

Mehmet sale de la portería, decidido a parar al cuatro. Da un salto, pero el otro lo esquiva y mete el balón en la red con toda la tranquilidad del mundo.

¡No puede ser! El resultado no se corresponde con lo que ha pasado en el campo hasta ese momento. ¡Una sola oportunidad para el Tiefen, y ahora van ganando! ¡No es justo! ¡Es cruel!

Pero no hay tiempo para lamentarse. Aún queda partido para poner las cosas en su sitio. Hay que dar la vuelta al marcador. Sólo eso.

Sin embargo, el gol ha dejado su marca en los Lobos. La defensa ha perdido su seguridad. Ahora parecen estar distraídos. Peter falla un pase sencillo y el Tiefen reacciona rápido de nuevo. Otro contraataque, esta vez tres contra tres, y el número siete lo culmina con una vaselina que sorprende a Mehmet y lo deja sin posibilidad alguna. Se acabó.

Los Lobos están destrozados, mientras que el Tiefen se anima cada vez más. Con una combinación bien hecha —esta vez no es un contraataque— consiguen incluso el 3 a 0. Pero eso no es todo. Poco antes del final, Mehmet se contagia con la inseguridad de sus compañeros y un remate sin peligro alguno se cuela entre sus manos.

El pitido final es un alivio para los Lobos. Frank se deja caer al suelo. Siente que tiene la cabeza vacía.

Alguien lo sacude, pero Frank no tiene ganas de prestarle atención.

—Ven, levántate —insiste Niko—, ¿o quieres quedarte aquí tumbado?

¿Y por qué no? Da lo mismo. Finalmente, Frank se levanta y se arrastra detrás de sus amigos hacia los vestuarios. En el camino, pasan por delante de los jugadores del Tiefen que siguen celebrando la victoria.

—¡Qué locos! —gruñe Niko—. ¡Ni que hubieran ganado la Eurocopa!

—¿Qué os había advertido en el descanso? —les echa la bronca Catrina, apoyándose en Rebeca—. ¡Son muy peligrosos! ¡Siempre! Os había avisado, pero habéis caído en su trampa como principiantes.

No será para tanto. Catrina pronto dejará de aguantar a esos «principiantes». Olvidará rápidamente la vergüenza de esta derrota y dará la espalda a los Lobos. Nadie se lo tomará a mal. La futura jugadora de la selección no debe quedarse en este equipillo de aficionados. Necesita otro tipo de retos. Si Frank pudiese, se marcharía con ella. Pero desgraciadamente, es sólo un chico.

En el vestuario reina un ambiente de funeral. Nadie dice nada. Normal. Tenían una pequeñísima posibilidad de hacerse campeones, y no la han aprovechado.

De repente, Rebeca se aclara la voz.

—Escuchad todos —dice en voz alta—. Catrina tiene que deciros una cosa.

Los chicos se miran unos a otros. Parece que ha llegado el temido momento.

—Acabemos cuanto antes —murmura Niko.

—Bueno, ejem, es que… —tartamudea Catrina—. Quieren que…, puedo…, bueno, si quisiera, podría…

Rebeca no aguanta más.

—A partir de ahora, Catrina juega en la selección regional —la interrumpe con orgullo—. Pero hay más. Venga, Catrina, suéltalo ya.

—He recibido una oferta de un equipo de chicas —dice Catrina, haciendo de tripas corazón.

El vestuario se queda en un silencio absoluto. Sólo Orhan está jadeando como si le faltara el aire. Rebeca está tan contenta como si hubiera encontrado ella misma el nuevo equipo para su amiga. ¿Qué se cree? Frank la había tratado demasiado bien hasta ahora, pero eso se ha acabado. Y dejará de sentarse al lado de ella en el cole. El mismo lunes se buscará otro sitio.

—Claro que es una oportunidad buenísima —continúa Catrina—. Pero significaría tener que dejar a los Lobos, y por eso...

Frank está a punto de estallar. ¿Para qué tanta ceremonia? Sería mejor que dijese claramente que los Lobos ya no le importan un pimiento.

—... he tardado tanto en decidirme. En serio.

Enfadado, Frank mete la ropa dentro de su bolsa. No cree ni una palabra. ¡Qué hipócrita!

—Incluso hoy al mediodía todavía no sabía qué hacer. Luego he visto lo mal que habéis jugado en el segundo tiempo, y me he dado cuenta...

¡Hasta aquí hemos llegado! Frank no aguanta más, y mucho menos si ahora Catrina se pone a insultar a su equipo. Agarra la bolsa y se levanta.

—… de que no puedo dejaros solos. Pues eso, ya está.

Frank se deja caer de nuevo sobre el banco de madera. ¿Que no puede dejarnos solos? ¿Qué quiere decir con eso? Desconcertado, mira a sus amigos para buscar ayuda. Pero todos se encogen de hombros, y sus miradas le dicen que tampoco han entendido nada.

Rebeca mira a todos en silencio, con los brazos cruzados.

El primero que vuelve en sí es Niko.

—¿Quieres decir que…, que no quieres…?

—¡Que sí! —dice Catrina sonriendo, mostrando su aparato dental nuevo—. Me iré, pero no ahora.

¿Que no se va a marchar? ¿No ahora? ¿Quiere decir que se va a quedar otra temporada?

—El señor Lichting dice que podría empezar a jugar con las chicas incluso dentro de tres o cuatro años —continúa explicando Catrina—. Y por eso me

quedo con vosotros hasta entonces. Me necesitáis más que ellas. Eso ha quedado muy, pero muy claro hoy.

¡No puede ser!

«Demostradle que la necesitáis», había dicho papá. Pero, ¿eso significaba que debíamos correr por el césped como gallinas asustadas? Y ahora resulta que esa «antiestrategia» ha sido precisamente la salvación. Catrina no se va a marchar. ¡Aún! Al principio habían hecho todo lo posible para ganar, pero ahora está claro que, si lo hubieran conseguido, habrían perdido a Catrina. Al final, ¡la derrota ha sido la solución!

¡Tres años! ¡O tal vez cuatro! Es muchísimo. Para entonces, ya serán casi adultos. Hasta ese momento pueden pasar tantas cosas... Tal vez algún cazatalentos encuentre el camino hasta los Lobos. Y a lo mejor Frank entonces recibirá la llamada del Hamburgo que tanto desea. Pero ya habrá tiempo para pensar en todo eso. Ahora mismo hay temas más urgentes. Por ejemplo, la Copa. Y la ganarán los Lobos, eso está claro. Y la próxima temporada atacarán de nuevo todos juntos. Con Catrina. Y entonces harán el doblete. ¿Y por qué no? Con la mejor alineación, todo es posible.

—Oye, ¿no te has enterado? —pregunta Niko dándo un codazo fuerte a Frank para que vuelva a la realidad.

Los Lobos lo están celebrando como si hubieran ganado.

En ese momento entra Norbert.

—¿Qué pasa aquí? —pregunta asombrado—. ¿Es que el Tiefen ha sido sancionado y nos han dado los puntos a nosotros?

—Mucho mejor —grita Frank entusiasmado—. Gracias a nuestro malísimo juego hemos conseguido frustrar un intento de fichaje.

—¿Intento de fichaje? —Norbert frunce el ceño—. ¿Cómo es que no sabía nada de eso?

—Porque no queríamos preocuparte —explica Niko.

—Y porque hemos podido controlar la situación nosotros solos —añade Mehmet convencido.

—Vale. Me alegro. Y ahora, daos prisa, por favor. Tenemos que irnos.

Durante todo el viaje de vuelta, hay buen ambiente en el microbús.

—¡Escuchad todos! —chilla Orhan, que se ha colado allí a pesar de que Olli ha subido también—. ¡Atención! Entonces, no ha sido todo mentira.

—¿Mentira? —pregunta Niko—. ¿De qué estás hablando?

—De los buenos amigos —explica Orhan con entusiasmo—. De que son inseparables, y todo eso.

—¡Cállate! —susurra Mehmet y se lleva un dedo a los labios.

Pero ya es tarde. Catrina ya se ha enterado y empieza a cantar:

—*Los Lobos son inseparables, un Lobo nunca está solo...*

—Tal vez sí que deberíamos habernos esforzado más para ganar al Tiefen —susurra Peter poniendo cara de sufrimiento—. Así cantaría pronto en otro lado.

—*... Porque lo que más les gusta, es ayudarse uno al otro.*

—Es el castigo de haber jugado tan mal —dice Niko y se tapa los oídos con los puños—: ¡otros cuatro años de tortura!

A Catrina le da igual. Encantada de la vida, repite la estrofa:

—*Los Lobos son inseparables, un Lobo nunca está solo...*

—No sé, a mí me gusta —dice Orhan—. Tiene algo...

El enano tiene toda la razón. Claro que la voz de Catrina no es precisamente bonita, pero lo importante es la letra. Es la pura verdad. No importa dónde vayan a jugar los Lobos en el futuro —en qué equipos, en la selección masculina o en la femenina, o si vuelan por el espacio sin jugar, como Hendrik—, lo importante es que seguirán siendo amigos. Todo lo demás da igual.

Con convicción, Frank se une a la canción:

—… *Porque lo que más les gusta, es ayudarse uno al otro.*

# Planes de futuro

## 12

¡Por fin llega el recreo! Con la ayuda de un partidito de fútbol, los Lobos quieren olvidarse del estrés del colegio. Pero una vez más, primero tienen que deshacerse de Rebeca. Esta chica se pega a Niko más que un defensa pesado a un delantero peligroso, y sólo porque pretende ayudarle con los problemas de la última clase de *mates*.

—Entonces, si tu corazón late mil veces en un cuarto de hora, ¿cuánto tiempo ha pasado si late…?

—Rebeca, estamos en el recreo.

—¿Y qué? —insiste ella—. El corazón late también durante el recreo. Entonces, ¿cuánto tiempo…?

En ese momento, los Lobos reciben la ayuda involuntaria de uno de los Tigres. Es el pesado de Mark quien interrumpe el acoso de Rebeca.

—¿Qué pasa? ¿Volvisteis a perder el sábado, no? —pregunta.

—Todo lo contrario —contesta Niko.

—Ganamos —confirma Frank.

—Pero..., si nos lo contó todo nuestro entrenador —insiste Mark, aunque ya mucho menos seguro de lo que dice—. Nos dijo que el Tiefen había ganado por 4 a 0.

—Se habrá confundido —explica Peter con una sonrisa amable—. Pobrecillo.

—Ejem, bueno, es posible —dice Mark—. Da lo mismo. Hasta luego.

Rápidamente se da la vuelta para marcharse.

—¡Eso es! —exclama Niko levantando el puño de la victoria—. Lobos contra Tigres, 1 a 0.

—¡Bien! —dice Frank—. Si nos mantenemos unidos, podemos ganar a cualquiera, a los Tigres, a los cazatalentos…

—¿Qué cazatalentos? —pregunta Rebeca como si no lo supiera.

—Ese gordo, ya sabes, el que apareció por casualidad en el partido de Copa la otra semana.

—Primero, el señor Lichting —corrige Rebeca— no está gordo. No mucho, quiero decir. Y segundo —añade con una sonrisa conspiradora—, no apareció por casualidad.

—Ah, ¿no?

—¿Por casualidad no?

—Pero ¿qué dices?

—Muy sencillo: lo había llamado yo.

—¿Tú?

—No puede ser.

—Desde luego que sí.

Durante unos segundos, Rebeca disfruta con el asombro de sus amigos. Luego se dispone a explicárselo todo:

—No habíais tratado muy bien a Catrina. Habíais dicho un montón de tonterías: eso de que las chicas no pueden ser profesionales y todo lo demás. Estaba muy deprimida, y por eso le dije: ¡no les hagas caso! No saben nada.

Rebeca se interrumpe para lanzar una mirada triunfadora a su público antes de seguir:

—Le prometí que me encargaría personalmente —estira la cabeza— de su carrera profesional. En realidad, fue superfácil. Me pasé por la Delegación de Deportes, y pregunté por los nombres de la gente más famosa del mundillo del fútbol femenino. Me dieron el teléfono de Lichting y de unos cuantos más. Lo llamé enseguida para decirle que conocía a una chica con muchísimo talento. Estaba muy interesado. Decía que era especialmente difícil encontrar a una buena defensa. Y por eso fue a ver el partido.

Mientras iba hablando Rebeca, a Niko se le iba cambiando el color de la cara. Primero, de blanco a rosado incrédulo, y luego a rojo oscuro de rabia. Por fin explotó:

—Pero, ¿te has vuelto loca? ¿Cómo se te ocurre meterte en nuestras cosas? Te juro que si Catrina se hubiera marchado de los Lobos…

Peter y Mehmet secundan la bronca de Niko afirmando con la cabeza y haciendo algunos breves comentarios.

Frank no les presta mucha atención. ¡Conque había sido Rebeca quien había encontrado al cazatalentos! ¡A un auténtico cazatalentos! Es decir, ¡el Gordo de Navidad! El premio que no le toca a casi nadie. Pero Rebeca no esperó a que llegase por casualidad, sino que lo buscó directamente. ¡Cómo mola!

Rebeca tiene los brazos cruzados y espera pacientemente a que Niko se quede sin aliento. Luego vuelve a las matemáticas como si no hubiera pasado nada.

—Decía que tu corazón late mil veces por cada cuarto de hora. ¿Cuánto tiempo…?

En ese momento suena la campana.

—Vale, entonces seguimos en el siguiente recreo —se despide de los chicos sin darse por vencida.

—Oye, tío —dice Niko a Frank agitando la mano delante de sus ojos—. ¿Hay alguien en casa?

—¿Cómo? —se sobresalta.

Niko lo mira desconfiado.

—¿Por qué no le has dicho nada a Rebeca? —pregunta—. La has contemplado como si fuera una santa.

De forma inoportuna, Frank se pone colorado. ¡Mierda!

—Porque está enamorado de esa pesada —responde Peter en su lugar—. Ya lo sabíais.

—Tonterías —se enfada Frank.

Quiere seguir hablando para darles más explicaciones, para que de una vez por todas le dejen en paz, pero de repente se le ocurre otra cosa: ¡que piensen lo que quieran! Incluso puede ser una ventaja para él si se equivocan de esta manera.

En realidad, lo que ocurre es algo muy diferente. Frank está pensando que más adelante, dentro de tres o cuatro años, pedirá a Rebeca que sea su agente. No tiene nada que ver con el amor y esas cosas. Se trata exclusivamente de fútbol. Y es que el que quiera llegar lejos en el mundillo de este deporte, necesita a alguien que se ocupe de su carrera profesional. No basta con tener talento. Ese talento necesita ser descubierto. Y desgraciadamente, eso ocurre muy pocas veces. Por eso, hay que hacer algo más que esperar, hay que buscar la suerte. Tener a una agente lista como Rebeca sería estupendo. Si ella se ocupa de todo, seguro que el Hamburgo fichará a Frank. Y mientras tanto, es mejor que los demás no sepan nada de todo eso. Si no, querrán que Rebeca sea también su agente. Y si ella tiene que colocar a todo el mundo, no tendrá el tiempo suficiente para ocuparse debidamente de la carrera de Frank.

—¿Enamorado? —dice de repente y se encoge de hombros como si no le importara—. Si tú lo dices.

No, definitivamente no tiene ganas de aclarar el asunto. Al menos, de momento. Tendrá tiempo para ello cuando haya firmado con el Hamburgo.

# Apuntes del abuelo de Frank

**Copa:** competición que va enfrentando a los equipos de dos en dos, en partidos super-emocionantes, que se juegan en sus respectivos campos. Se van eliminando hasta que llegan a la final, que se juega en un campo neutral con miles de seguidores cantando y animándoles.

**Derbi:** partido entre dos equipos que son rivales acérrimos. ¡Cuidado con los hinchas!

**Liga:** competición en la que juegan todos los equipos contra todos. ¡Es larguíííísima! Gana el equipo que consigue más puntos.

**Palomita:** gran salto del portero, estirando a tope el cuerpo y los brazos, para parar o despejar el balón. ¡Como si quisiera volar!

**Pared:** pases combinados entre dos jugadores que avanzan pasándose el balón y rebasando a sus rivales, que se quedan con dos palmos de narices.

**Chilena:** salto increíble, que dan los superhombres, de espaldas a la dirección del balón, moviendo las piernas como una tijera, para rematar o despejar el balón.

**Túnel:** regate en plan chulo. El balón pasa por debajo de las piernas de un jugador y el que lo ha realizado recupera el balón a la espalda del otro.

**Vaselina:** tiro a portería que hace un jugador por encima de otro. Si mete gol, el puenteado se tira de los pelos.

# Índice

# LOCOS POR EL FÚTBOL

Frauke Nahrgang | Betina Gotzen-Beek

Los compañeros del nuevo colegio de Frank juegan
en dos equipos: los Lobos o los Tigres. Y son camaradas
o rivales, según que los partidos que disputen sean
de Copa, de Liga o el Torneo Escolar. Pero, sobre todo,
son amigos y se enfrentan juntos a los retos
que les plantean su situación familiar y personal.

### 1 > Un buen fichaje

Frank va a vivir con su abuelo
cuando se separan sus padres.
Su pasión por el fútbol le llevará a jugar
con los Lobos y a integrarse con rapidez
en la vida de su nuevo colegio.

### 2 > Una dura temporada

Niko, el capitán de los Lobos,
está muy raro y pasa del equipo. Sus
amigos deberán resolver el problema
antes del gran derbi. Finalmente la
empollona Rebeca encontrará la solución.

Una serie que destaca
lo mejor que tiene el fútbol:
la solidaridad, la ayuda
mutua y la no discriminación
ni de sexos ni de etnias
entre los deportistas.

### 3 > ¡Vamos por la Copa!

En el torneo escolar, Frank y Niko tienen
que enfrentarse a su compañera de los Lobos,
Catrina, y jugar junto con su rival de los
Tigres, Mark. Y descubrirán que el trabajo
en equipo es el germen de la amistad.

### 4 > Se busca delantero

Al incorporarse el delantero Olli al equipo,
el entrenador manda a Frank al banquillo.
Éste opta por marcharse a vivir
con su padre. La pesada Rebeca
conseguirá que cambie de decisión.

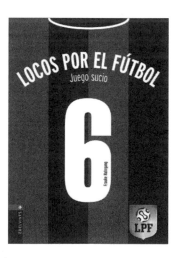

### 5 > Un balón con efecto

Un jardín repleto de enanitos y un viejo
cascarrabias complicarán el entrenamiento
de Frank y el equipo de los Lobos para
el nuevo Campeonato de fútbol sala.

### 6 > Juego sucio

Durante el Campeonato de fútbol sala,
Orhan, el hermano pequeño del portero
de los Lobos, es víctima del chantaje de
uno de los jugadores de los Tigres.

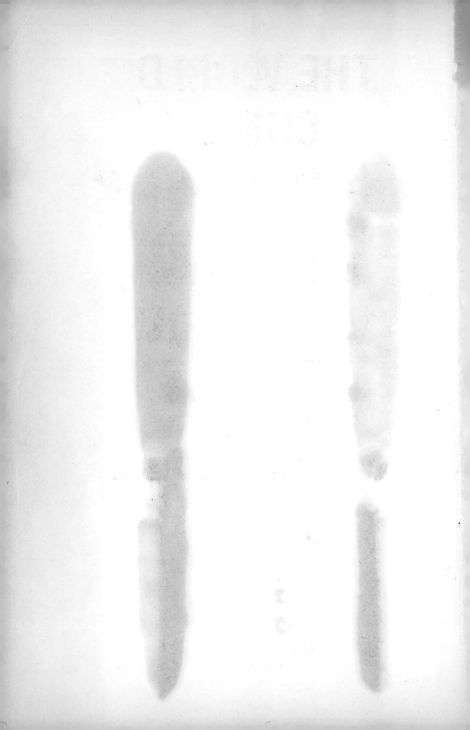

# THE WORLD CHESS CHAMPIONSHIP

## KORCHNOI vs. KARPOV

by

RAYMOND KEENE

The Inside Story of the Match

SIMON & SCHUSTER
NEW YORK

Library of Congress Cataloging in Publication Data

Keene, Raymond D.
    World chess championship : Korchnoi vs. Karpov.

    1. Chess--Tournaments.  2. Korchnoi, Viktor, 1931–
3. Karpov, Anatolii Evgen'evich, 1951–    I. Title.
GV1455.G388    794.1'57    78-16067
ISBN 0-671-24647-X
ISBN 0-671-24648-8 pbk.

## SYMBOLS

| | |
|---|---|
| + | Check |
| ! | Good move |
| !! | Excellent move |
| ? | Bad move |
| ?? | Losing move |

# CONTENTS

# Part I

## 1

# THE UNREAL WORLD— AN INTRODUCTION TO THE WORLD CHAMPIONSHIP 1978

On 18th July in Baguio City in the Philippines the first game was played in the 1978 World Chess Championship.

There has not been a title fight for six years, not, in fact, since the notorious Spassky-Fischer encounter at Reykjavik in 1972, which finally broke the Soviet monopoly dating from 1948. Fischer's case was curious. After becoming World Champion in the most highly publicised chess match of all time, he simply stopped playing, and his three-year reign was marred by total absence of any chess activity on his part. When he also showed no willingness to defend his title after the stipulated three-year period, Anatoly Karpov of the USSR (winner of the 1974 Candidates' tournament) was declared World Champion by default.

To most observers Fischer's conduct was, at best, dereliction of duty to the public and, at worst, insane, yet Fischer's withdrawal was comprehensible in one sense: having once scaled the peak of an intellectual Everest there is a certain psychological reluctance — even a mental block — against performing the feat a second time. Fischer seems to have regarded himself as 'World Champion', and saw no necessity to prove this fact again. Those World Champions of the past who have descended from Olympus to defend their hard-won titles have, by eventually losing to the most worthy challenger, ultimately compromised their reputations, however infinitesimally. By total withdrawal Fischer, like his compatriot Morphy, preserved a mythical nimbus of invincibility. But achievement cannot be allowed to stagnate. If one rests on one's laurels for too long, they wither and perish. The world has passed Fischer by, an isolated figure on his lonely summit, while the centre of attention has shifted inexorably towards those who are actively involved in the struggle — Karpov and Korchnoi.

Anatoly Karpov and Victor Korchnoi could hardly form a greater contrast. Karpov is a model Soviet citizen, a golden boy of the establishment, who, at 27 years of age, has enjoyed an unbroken and brilliant path of success without a single serious setback. Korchnoi, at 47, has reached the top by a more lengthy and arduous method, having qualified for the Candidates' tournament on no less than five occasions, but nearly always faltered at the final hurdle. But what differentiates him most sharply from Karpov is his attitude to the Soviet state. Half Jewish and always prone to rebellious sentiments and contentious statements,

Korchnoi went the whole hog in 1976 and defected from the USSR, alleging that the state was interfering with his professional career. In spite of the upheaval in his personal affairs, Korchnoi's defection was the occasion of a marvellous upsurge in his play, as can be seen from the fact that he won the 1977 Candidates' with relative ease, disposing of three of his former Soviet colleagues (Petrosian, Polugayevsky and Spassky) en route.

There can be no doubt that the match in Baguio is a contest between the two foremost active Grandmasters of the day. The evidence of their respective tournament and match performances is given in chapters 2 and 3, while the most recent Elo calculations for the two put Karpov at 2720 and Korchnoi at 2704. The Elo rating is a statistical method of determining a player's current strength: 2200 on the scale indicates a Master; 2400 plus should represent the International Master level, while at 2500 Grandmaster territory begins. A player who reaches 2600 should be thinking in terms of qualifying for the Candidates' tournament, while 2700 (a rare distinction) reveals a player of World Championship class. The latest figures prove that both Karpov and Korchnoi are within this narrow band, while the third highest rated player, Spassky, is well below at 2648.

These Eleusinian numerals are deeply symbolic. Existence for top chessplayers has a strange, hermetic quality, which ignores common certitudes and practicalities, concentrating instead on the achievement of success in a highly abstract field. Karpov is a slight figure with a high-pitched voice. He only seems to live when he is at the chessboard, and even there the signs of animation are subdued, but in a very quiet way he is enormously self-confident. There is even one theory which suggests that his self-confidence is the product of hypnosis — hence his ability to play so quickly (see chapter 7). But this is pure speculation!

Korchnoi has a restless streak. His defection from the USSR caused a splash, but he has changed countries twice since then (Holland to Germany to Switzerland) and no one has noticed. He often laments his education in the USSR, but in comparison with Karpov he seems to be a polymath. He has written one book *Chess is My Life* — an inflammatory document and a must for all students of chess current affairs. While playing chess Korchnoi too lives in a world of his own construction. His absolute concentration is aided by deafness which helps him to exclude the external world from his inner consciousness.

## Why Baguio?

Why indeed? The Philippines, remote from the centres of western chess life, with its highly spectacular form of personal government in the flamboyant shape of President Marcos, seems an exotic venue for a World Chess Championship. But we should not forget that Manila had first option on the Fischer-Karpov match which did not take place!

For 1978 four realistic bids (prize fund of over 1 million Swiss Francs each) were made to FIDE (the World Chess Federation): Graz (Austria), Hamburg (W. Germany), Tilburg (Holland) and Baguio. Korchnoi's preferences were for Graz, Baguio, Tilburg and Hamburg, in that order, while Karpov put Hamburg first, left second place blank, Baguio third and Graz fourth. FIDE President Euwe then decided on Baguio, and rejected a subsequent offer from Graz and Hamburg to share the match. Karpov is said to have reacted badly to this news. Apparently he only included the Philippines on his list as a political move to exclude Holland, which was Korchnoi's domicile for one year after his defection. Probably he also harbours bad dreams about Manila 1976, one of his worst results as World Champion.

In what follows of Part I, I will attempt to give enough background information for the reader to form his own opinion as to the stature of Karpov and Korchnoi in the historical context of the World Championship, and also to form his own judgement as to their relative merits and respective chances of success. In the section on style I have sought to underline features which may aid appreciation of the games from Baguio.

# 2

# KARPOV'S PLAYING RECORD

## TOURNAMENTS

| | | Place | + | = | − |
|---|---|---|---|---|---|
| 1966 | USSR Junior Championship | | 4 | 4 | 1 |
| | Masters v. Candidate Masters | | 5 | 10 | 0 |
| | Scandinavia Juniors-USSR Juniors | bd. 6 | 1 | 1 | 0 |
| 1966/7 | Trinec | 1st | 9 | 4 | 0 |
| 1967 | RSFSR Spartakiad | | 3 | 1 | 1 |
| | USSR Junior Championship, ½ Final | 5 | 3 | 1 | 3 |
| 1967/8 | Groningen | 1st | 6 | 8 | 0 |
| 1968 | USSR—Yugoslavia | bd. 12 | 3 | 1 | 0 |
| | USSR Juniors—Scandinavia Juniors | bd. 2 | 0 | 1 | 1 |
| | Moscow University Championship | 1st | 7 | 6 | 0 |
| | 6th USSR Team Championship | bd. 6 | 9 | 2 | 0 |
| 1969 | Leningrad Match-Tournament | 1st | 5 | 5 | 2 |
| | USSR Juniors—Yugoslavia Juniors | bd. 3 | 2 | 2 | 0 |
| | USSR Armed Forces Team Championship | bd. 2 | 5 | 1 | 1 |
| | World Junior Championship, Stockholm | 1st | 12 | 5 | 0 |
| | Hungary—RSFSR, Budapest | | 0 | 2 | 2 |
| 1970 | USSR Armed Forces Team Ch. zonal | | 3 | 3 | 0 |
| | RSFSR Championship, Kuibyshev | 1st | 8 | 9 | 0 |
| | Caracas | 4-6 | 8 | 7 | 2 |
| | USSR Armed Forces Team Championship | | 2 | 3 | 1 |
| | 38th USSR Championship, Riga | 5-7 | 5 | 14 | 2 |
| 1971 | 39th USSR Ch. Daugavpils ½ Final | 1st | 9 | 8 | 0 |
| | Student Olympiad, Mayaguez | bd. 3 | 7 | 1 | 0 |
| | USSR Team Ch. Rostov-on-Don | bd. 6 | 6 | 1 | 0 |
| | USSR Armed Forces Team Championship | bd. 1 | 2 | 4 | 1 |
| | Leningrad University Team Ch. | | 4 | 0 | 0 |
| | 39th USSR Ch. Leningrad | 4 | 7 | 12 | 2 |
| | Alekhine Memorial, Moscow | 1-2 | 5 | 12 | 0 |
| 1971/2 | Hastings | 1-2 | 8 | 6 | 1 |
| 1972 | USSR Olympiad, Moscow | bd. 2 | 4 | 3 | 2 |
| | Student Olympiad, Graz | bd. 1 | 5 | 4 | 0 |
| | Skopje Olympiad | 1st res. | 12 | 2 | 1 |
| | San Antonio | 1-3 | 7 | 7 | 1 |
| 1973 | Budapest | 2nd | 4 | 11 | 0 |

| | | | | |
|---|---|---|---|---|
| | USSR National Teams Match-Tournament | bd. 1 | 2 | 2 | 0 |
| | Leningrad Interzonal | 1-2 | 10 | 7 | 0 |
| | European Team Championship, Bath | bd. 4 | 4 | 2 | 0 |
| | 41st USSR Championship, Moscow | 2-6 | 5 | 11 | 1 |
| | Madrid | 1st | 7 | 8 | 0 |
| 1974 | Nice Olympiad | bd. 1 | 10 | 4 | 0 |
| 1975 | Ljubljana—Portoroz | 1st | 7 | 8 | 0 |
| | 6th USSR Spartakiad, Riga | bd. 1 | 4 | 3 | 0 |
| | Milan | 1st | 4 | 16 | 1 |
| 1976 | Skopje | 1st | 10 | 5 | 0 |
| | USSR Cup | bd. 1 | 2 | 4 | 0 |
| | Amsterdam | 1st | 2 | 4 | 0 |
| | Manila | 2nd | 1 | 4 | 1 |
| | Montilla | 1st | 5 | 4 | 0 |
| | 44th USSR Championship, Moscow | 1st | 8 | 8 | 1 |
| 1977 | Bad Lauterberg | 1st | 9 | 6 | 0 |
| | European Team Championship, Moscow | bd. 1 | 5 | 0 | 0 |
| | Las Palmas | 1st | 12 | 3 | 0 |
| | Leningrad | 4-5 | 5 | 10 | 2 |
| | Tilburg | 1st | 5 | 6 | 0 |
| 1978 | Bugojno | 1-2 | 6 | 8 | 1 |

## MATCHES

| | | | | | |
|---|---|---|---|---|---|
| 1971 | v Korchnoi (training match) Leningrad | drew | 2 | 2 | 2 |
| 1974 | v Polugayevsky (Candidates' ¼ Final) Moscow | won | 3 | 5 | 0 |
| | v Spassky (Candidates' ½ Final) Leningrad | won | 4 | 6 | 1 |
| | v Korchnoi (Candidates' Final) Moscow | won | 3 | 19 | 2 |

Karpov has much less match experience than Korchnoi, but in his brief match career he has been almost uniformly successful. What may prove a handicap to him in Baguio is that he has not yet played a match outside the USSR. Indeed, all of his matches have been in either Moscow or Leningrad.

## 3

# KORCHNOI'S
# PLAYING RECORD

## TOURNAMENTS

|      |                                          | Place      | +  | =  | –  |
|------|------------------------------------------|------------|----|----|----|
| 1946 | USSR Junior Ch., Leningrad               | 11th-12th  | 4  | 2  | 9  |
| 1947 | USSR Junior Ch., Leningrad               | 1st        | 8  | 7  | 0  |
| 1948 | USSR Junior Ch., Tallinn                 | 1st-2nd    | 5  | 0  | 2  |
| 1950 | Leningrad Ch.                            | 2nd        | 8  | 2  | 3  |
|      | ½-final 18th USSR Ch., Tula              | 11th-13th  | 4  | 4  | 7  |
| 1951 | Chigorin Memorial, Leningrad             | 5th-7th    | 6  | 3  | 4  |
|      | ½-final 19th USSR Ch., Leningrad         | 5th-8th    | 6  | 8  | 4  |
| 1952 | ½-final 20th USSR Ch., Minsk             | 2nd-4th    | 7  | 7  | 3  |
|      | 20th USSR Ch., Moscow                    | 6th        | 8  | 6  | 5  |
|      | Leningrad Ch.                            | 4th        | 6  | 3  | 4  |
| 1953 | Leningrad Ch.                            | 2nd        | 8  | 3  | 2  |
|      | ½-final 21st USSR Ch., Vilnius           | 3rd-4th    | 7  | 4  | 3  |
| 1954 | 21st USSR Ch. Kiev                       | 2nd-3rd    | 10 | 6  | 3  |
|      | Bucharest                                | 1st        | 10 | 6  | 1  |
|      | Student Olympiad, Oslo                   | (board 1)  | 3  | 3  | 1  |
|      | ½-final 22nd USSR Ch., Erevan            | 3rd-5th    | 9  | 8  | 3  |
| 1955 | 22nd USSR Ch., Moscow                    | 19th       | 1  | 10 | 8  |
|      | ½-final 23rd USSR Ch., Riga              | 4th-5th    | 8  | 6  | 4  |
|      | Leningrad Ch.                            | 1st        | 16 | 2  | 1  |
|      | Hastings (1955/6)                        | 1st-2nd    | 5  | 4  | 0  |
| 1956 | 23rd USSR Ch., Leningrad                 | 4th        | 6  | 10 | 1  |
|      | Student Olympiad, Uppsala                | (board 1)  | 5  | 2  | 0  |
|      | ½-final 24th USSR Ch., Tbilisi           | 3rd-4th    | 7  | 10 | 2  |
| 1957 | Leningrad Ch.                            | 1st-2nd    | 11 | 4  | 2  |
|      | 24th USSR Ch., Moscow                    | 7th-8th    | 6  | 12 | 3  |
|      | Armenian Ch. (hors concours)             | 1st        |    |    |    |
|      | European Team Ch., Vienna                | (board 8)  | 5  | 1  | 0  |
|      | ½-final 25th USSR Ch., Sverdlovsk        | 1st        | 8  | 11 | 0  |
| 1958 | 25th USSR Ch., Riga                      | 9th-11th   | 4  | 9  | 4  |
|      | RSFSR Ch., Sochi                         | 2nd-4th    | 7  | 10 | 2  |
|      | ½-final 26th USSR Ch., Tashkent          | 2nd-3rd    | 9  | 4  | 2  |
| 1959 | 26th USSR Ch., Tbilisi                   | 9th        | 6  | 8  | 5  |
|      | Krakow                                   | 1st        | 6  | 5  | 0  |
|      | ½-final 27th USSR Ch., Cheliabinsk       | 1st        | 9  | 6  | 0  |

| 1960 | 27th USSR Ch., Leningrad | 1st | 12 | 4 | 3 |
|------|--------------------------|-----|----|----|----|
| | Moscow | 3rd | 6 | 4 | 1 |
| | Buenos Airies | 1st-2nd | 9 | 8 | 2 |
| | Santa Fe | 4th | 3 | 3 | 1 |
| | Corboda | 1st | 5 | 2 | 0 |
| | Leipzig Olympiad | (board 4) | 8 | 5 | 0 |
| | 28th USSR Ch., Moscow | 2nd | 9 | 8 | 2 |
| | European Team Ch., Oberhausen | (board 3) | 8 | 1 | 0 |
| | Budapest | 1st | 9 | 5 | 1 |
| 1962 | Interzonal Stockholm | 4th-5th | 9 | 10 | 3 |
| | Candidates' Tournament, Curacao | 5th | 7 | 13 | 7 |
| | 30th USSR Ch., Erevan | 1st | 8 | 1 | 1 |
| 1963 | Havana | 1st | 14 | 5 | 2 |
| | 31st USSR Ch., Leningrad | 10th | 4 | 12 | 3 |
| 1964 | Leningrad Ch. | 1st | 12 | 4 | 0 |
| | Zonal Tournament, Moscow | 5th-6th | 3 | 5 | 4 |
| | Belgrade | 2nd-3rd | 9 | 5 | 2 |
| | 32nd USSR Ch., Kiev (1964/5) | 1st | 11 | 8 | 0 |
| 1965 | European Team Ch., Hamburg | (board 3) | 4 | 3 | 2 |
| | Gyula | 1st | 14 | 1 | 0 |
| | Erevan | 1st | 6 | 7 | 0 |
| | 33rd USSR Ch., Tallinn | 10th-12th | 6 | 6 | 7 |
| 1966 | Training Tournament, Moscow | 4th-5th | 2 | 4 | 4 |
| | Bucharest | 1st | 11 | 3 | 0 |
| | Sochi | 1st | 10 | 3 | 2 |
| | USSR Team Ch., Moscow | (board 2) | 5 | 5 | 0 |
| | Havana Olympiad | (board 5) | 9 | 3 | 1 |
| | 34th USSR Ch., Tbilisi (1966/7) | 3rd-5th | 4 | 16 | 0 |
| 1967 | Play-off for Interzonal, Tallinn | 1st-3rd | 1 | 2 | 1 |
| | Leningrad | 1st | 10 | 6 | 0 |
| | Interzonal Tournament, Sousse | 2nd-4th | 9 | 10 | 3 |
| 1968 | Wijk aan Zee | 1st | 10 | 4 | 1 |
| | Lugano Olympiad | (board 3) | 9 | 4 | 0 |
| | Palma de Mallorca | 1st | 11 | 6 | 0 |
| 1969 | Sarajevo | 1st | 9 | 6 | 0 |
| | Luhacovice | 1st | 8 | 7 | 0 |
| | Havana | 1st-2nd | 8 | 6 | 1 |
| | Palma de Mallorca | 3rd-4th | 6 | 9 | 2 |
| 1970 | USSR vs Rest of the World, Belgrade | (board 3) | 0 | 3 | 1 |
| | Rovini/Zagreb | 2nd-5th | 7 | 8 | 2 |
| | European Team Ch., Kapfenberg | (board 2) | 2 | 4 | 0 |
| | Siegen Olympiad | (board 3) | 8 | 6 | 1* |
| | 38th USSR Ch., Riga | 1st | 12 | 8 | 1 |
| 1971 | Wijk aan Zee | 1st | 7 | 6 | 2 |
| | Moscow | 11th | 6 | 5 | 6 |
| | Hastings (1971/2) | 1st-2nd | 8 | 6 | 1 |

| 1972 | Amsterdam | 2nd | 7 | 8 | 0 |
| | Skopje Olympiad | (board 2) | 8 | 6 | 1 |
| | Palma de Mallorca | 1st-3rd | 7 | 6 | 2 |
| 1973 | Leningrad Ch. | 8th-9th | 5 | 4 | 5 |
| | Interzonal, Leningrad | 1st-2nd | 11 | 5 | 1 |
| | European Team Ch., Bath | (board 3) | 3 | 2 | 1 |
| | 41st USSR Ch., Moscow | 2nd-6th | 5 | 11 | 1 |
| 1974 | Nice Olympiad | (board 2) | 8 | 7 | 0 |
| 1975 | Moscow | 3rd-5th | 8 | 3 | 4 |
| | Hastings (1975/76) | 4th | 5 | 8 | 2 |
| 1976 | Amsterdam | 1st-2nd | 5 | 9 | 1 |
| 1977 | Montreux | 1st | 4 | 5 | 0 |
| | Dutch Ch., Leeuwarden | 1st | 11 | 2 | 0 |
| 1978 | Wijk aan Zee | 2nd | 5 | 5 | 1 |
| | Beer-Sheva | 1st | 11 | 2 | 0 |

* Korchnoi overslept and lost against Spain by default

## MATCHES

| 1968 | v Reshevsky (Candidates' ¼-final), Amsterdam | won | 3 | 5 | 0 |
| | v Tal (Candidates' ½-final), Moscow | won | 2 | 7 | 1 |
| | v Spassky (Candidates' final), Kiev | lost | 1 | 5 | 4 |
| 1970 | v Bronstein (training match) | lost | 1 | 2 | 3 |
| 1971 | v Karpov (training match), Leningrad | drew | 2 | 2 | 2 |
| | v Geller (Candidates' ¼-final), Moscow | won | 4 | 3 | 1 |
| | v Petrosian (Candidates' ½-final), Moscow | lost | 0 | 9 | 1 |
| 1974 | v Mecking (Candidates' ¼-final), Augusta | won | 3 | 9 | 1 |
| | v Petrosian (Candidates' ½-final), Odessa | won | 3 | 1 | 1 |
| | v Karpov (Candidates Final) | lost | 2 | 19 | 3 |
| 1976 | v Timman, Leeuwarden | won | 4 | 3 | 1 |
| | v Hug, Zurich | won | 2 | 2 | 0 |
| 1977 | v Petrosian (Candidates' ¼-final), Lucca | won | 2 | 9 | 1 |
| | v Polugayevsky (Candidates' ½-final), Evian | won | 5 | 7 | 1 |
| | v Spassky (Candidates' final) Belgrade | won | 7 | 7 | 4 |

# 4

# A HISTORY
# OF THE
# WORLD CHAMPIONSHIP

If you were to ask an ordinary citizen whether he knew more about
Morphy or Smyslov (or whether he had even heard of Smyslov), I am
sure I know which answer would be returned — yet Smyslov was World
Champion for one year, while Morphy was merely a legendary chess
genius, with no official title. The official World Championships began
with the Steinitz-Zukertort match of 1886, yet before that time there
were many talented players who merited the accolade of a World title
which did not yet exist. The most prominent amongst these were the
Frenchmen, Philidor and Labourdonnais, the Englishman, Staunton,
Adolph Anderssen a German, and Morphy himself, from the New World.
But it took a shrewd Austrian Jew, Wilhelm Steinitz, to invent the official
title, and so his name appears first on the official roll of honour.

| | |
|---|---|
| Wilhelm Steinitz (Austria) | 1886-1894 |
| Emmanuel Lasker (Germany) | 1894-1921 |
| Jose Raul Capablanca (Cuba) | 1921-1927 |
| Alexander Alekhine (Russia and France) | 1927-1935 |
| Max Euwe (Holland) | 1935-1937 |
| Alexander Alekhine | 1937-1946 |
| Mikhail Botvinnik (USSR) | 1948-1957 |
| Vassily Smyslov (USSR) | 1957-1958 |
| Mikhail Botvinnik | 1958-1960 |
| Mikhail Tal (USSR) | 1960-1961 |
| Mikhail Botvinnik | 1961-1963 |
| Tigran Petrosian (USSR) | 1963-1969 |
| Boris Spassky (USSR) | 1969-1972 |
| Robert Fischer (USA) | 1972-1975 |
| Anatoly Karpov (USSR) | 1975-?? |

Until the death of Alekhine the destination of the supreme title
depended on free enterprise. There was no way of compelling the reigning
champion to defend his title but the twin incentives of honour and money
ensured that he did so with reasonable frequency. Nobody had an automatic right to challenge the champion but anyone who seemed to have a
reasonable chance of unseating him was liable to be able to find suitable
sponsors.

The free enterprise system did not work too badly but there were justifiable criticisms of it. Some title matches resulted in rather pointless laps of honour for the champion and were held merely because the challenger had suitable financial backing rather than because he had any real chance of winning. Some matches which the chess world would have loved to witness never took place either because the potential challenger was unable to find suitable backing or (some people claimed) because the champion deliberately avoided the encounter by demanding unreasonable terms.

When Alekhine died in harness in 1946 the world chess organisation, FIDE, leapt at the opportunity to assume control of the world championship. They solved the immediate problem of ending the interregnum created by Alekhine's death by organising a tournament (won by Botvinnik) in which the five best players in the world played each other five times. Thereafter FIDE decreed that the champion must defend his title every three years against a challenger selected by a comprehensive system of elimination tournaments. The 'three year rule' should have been sufficient to ensure that the champion did not rest on his laurels and that any defeated champion had an opportunity to regain his title. But FIDE also decreed that a defeated champion should be entitled to a return match within one year. This rule (nicknamed 'the Botvinnik rule' because he twice benefited from it) was manifestly unfair because there was no provision for a 'return return' match and so the champion had two bites at the cherry but the challenger didn't. The Botvinnik rule was dropped in 1963.

Until FIDE took over, the conditions for world championship matches were decided by negotiation between the players and their sponsors. Sometimes the match was the best of a fixed number of games and sometimes it was decided by the first player to win a fixed number of games. Matches varied in length from ten games (Lasker-Schlechter 1910) to thirty-five (Capablanca-Alekhine 1927). FIDE standardised the format by decreeing that every match should be for the best of twenty-four games with the champion retaining is title in the event of a tie.

The FIDE system worked smoothly until the arrival of that strong-willed genius, Fischer on the scene. Negotiations for his match against Spassky 1972 almost broke down and in 1975 negotiations for his match with Karpov actually did break down and Karpov was declared champion by default. Fischer has threatened to go over the heads of FIDE and play an unofficial world championship match. This would seriously undermine the authority of FIDE and result in the unsatisfactory existence of two 'world champions' — one official, the other not. So far this danger has been averted.

The clock was put back in two ways for the 1978 match. The 'Botvinnik' return match rule was reintroduced and the match was to go to the first player to win six games. Both these changes were criticised but at least there was general relief that the best two active players in the world had agreed on a set of rules and a world championship match would take place for the first time in six years.

# 5

# KARPOV'S RECORD AS WORLD CHAMPION

World Champions are not just in competition with their contemporaries, they also have to maintain their historical record against their predecessors and successors in the championship. If we compare Karpov with the eleven former World Champions we see that he has now moved into the lead as regards the number of undivided first prizes in major tournaments obtained throughout their respective tenures. Here is the evidence of each champion, and the number of important firsts he gained in his championship period:

Steinitz 0; Lasker 5; Capablanca 2; Alekhine 5; Euwe 0; Botvinnik 0; Smyslov 0; Tal 0; Petrosian 0; Spassky 1; Fischer 0; Karpov 7.

Karpov's victories were: Ljubljana—Portorozh 1975; Milan 1975; Skopje 1976; USSR Championship 1976; Bad Lauterberg 1977; Las Palmas 1977 and Tilburg 1977.

Tournaments aside, Lasker defended his title successfully in six matches, Steinitz in three, Alekhine and Botvinnik twice, and Petrosian once. All the others shed their title at the first challenge, with the exception of Fischer who let his title go by default. Fischer's reign was, in fact, the most miserable of all, since he played only one game, and this an 'exhibition' draw of no importance against President Marcos of the Philippines. Incredibly, no World Champion won undivided first prize in a major tournament between Alekhine and Spassky. Alekhine's last great victory was Zurich 1934, although I have been generous and allowed him the less impressive Nazi-inspired 'European Championship' at Munich 1942 to build up his total of five.

Karpov's record certainly seems to put most other World Champions to shame, but we have to remember that Karpov started with one big advantage as World Champion: he did not have to play a World Championship match to gain his title! This meant that he had huge reserves of untapped energy to expend on tournament successes — reserves which must have been denied to Euwe, for example, who had to contest 30 tough games with Alekhine, or to Spassky, who had to fight two gruelling matches with Petrosian. On top of this, there is the question of unsatisfied ambition. The majority of World Champions must surely believe that they have proved themselves and need no further self-justification. There must even be a temptation to relax, having achieved the highest title. But

Karpov did not prove himself to be the best player — Fischer merely failed to turn up. So Karpov had to provide the proof himself in tournaments by battering all prospective opposition and critics into silence. After his victories in seven major tournaments, his share of first prize in the super-tournament at Bugojno 1978, and a host of fine performances in lesser events, no one can possibly regard Karpov as a paper tiger, or indeed, as anything less than a worthy and active successor to Fischer's title.

## KARPOV'S SCORE AGAINST THE OTHER WORLD CHAMPIONS

| Karpov's Score | Won | Drawn | Lost |
|---|---|---|---|
| Euwe | 0 | 0 | 0 |
| Botvinnik | 0 | 1 | 0 |
| Smyslov | 1 | 6 | 1 |
| Tal | 0 | 11 | 0 |
| Petrosian | 0 | 10 | 1 |
| Spassky | 6 | 11 | 2 |
| Fischer | 0 | 0 | 0 |
| Total | 7 | 39 | 4 |

Karpov has 26½ points from 50 games (53 per cent) against the other World Champions he has played.

# 6
# KORCHNOI'S PATH TO THE WORLD CHAMPIONSHIP

Towards the end of 1974 Victor Korchnoi succumbed, by the narrowest of margins, to Anatoly Karpov in the Final of the Ninth Candidates' Tournament, which was held in Moscow. The final score of this mammoth struggle was 3 wins to Karpov, 2 wins to Korchnoi and 19 draws. Korchnoi has since claimed that for this contest the Soviet authorities favoured his opponent as the younger man, one who had never met Fischer, or been defeated by him, and who would therefore maintain a more credible image as World Champion if, or when, Fischer failed to show for the title match. Consequently, Korchnoi found it almost impossible to obtain grandmasterly assistance and was constantly subjected to threats and harassment. Anyone who has read the Panovs' account of their life at the Kirov Ballet, after they had applied for exit visas to Israel, will readily comprehend what is meant by this. Korchnoi personally went through the galling experience of seeing an army of the best Soviet chess brains ranged against him.

The Soviet calculation turned out to be correct and Fischer, foundering in a morass of his own 'principles', ceded the World Championship to Karpov without play, early in 1975. But what of Korchnoi? Some unnecessarily sharp remarks he made about Karpov had earned him an even less justifiable banishment from chess tournaments lasting one year. So, while Karpov toured the globe as a conquering hero, Korchnoi had to sit in his home town of Leningrad, twiddling his thumbs and waiting . . . .

Korchnoi is a man of decision. Realising that he could no longer gain his ultimate ambition (the World Championship) in a Soviet context, he resolved to free himself at the earliest opportunity. After a year's 'detention' Korchnoi finally began to receive invitations to foreign tournaments again, and, seizing his chance at the end of the IBM competition at Amsterdam in the summer of 1976, he walked into a police station and requested 'political asylum'. This was less an act of political defiance than a professional gesture. If Korchnoi wished to pursue his goal he had to leave the USSR. A leading professional chess grandmaster cannot risk a sudden and arbitrarily imposed banning at a critical stage of his career if he wants to fight for the World Championship!

By virtue of his second place in the 1974 Candidates' Korchnoi had won the right to compete again in 1977, but the Soviet Federation was quick to strike back, by demanding from FIDE that Korchnoi be expelled from the tournament and thus excluded from participation in the World Championship. To the honour of FIDE, and the President Dr Max Euwe, this request was refused and Korchnoi proceeded to the 10th Candidates' Tournament.

## The 10th Candidates' Cycle, 1977-1978

The knock-out has been in force ever since 1965, when the all-play-all was dropped after Fischer's allegations of 'Commie cheating'.

Quarter-Final matches were for the best of 12 games; Semi-Finals out of 16 and the Final out of 20. There was a provision (actually invoked for Hort-Spassky) for further 2 game mini-matches if deadlock was reached.

| ¼-Final | | ½-Final | | Final | |
|---|---|---|---|---|---|
| **Korchnoi** (Stateless) | 6½ | | | | |
| Petrosian (USSR) | 5½ | **Korchnoi** | 8½ | | |
| **Polugayevsky** (USSR) | 6½ | Polugayevsky | 4½ | | |
| Mecking (Brazil) | 5½ | | | **Korchnoi** | 10½ |
| **Spassky** (USSR) | 8½ | | | Spassky | 7½ |
| Hort (Czechoslovakia) | 7½ | **Spassky** | 8½ | | |
| **Portisch** (Hungary) | 6½ | Portisch | 6½ | | |
| Larsen (Denmark) | 3½ | | | | |

(Final winner: **Korchnoi**)

Details of Korchnoi's matches are given below:

### Quarter Finals
**Il Ciocca 1977**

| Korchnoi | ½ ½ ½ ½ 1 0 ½ 1 ½ ½ ½ ½ | 6½ |
|---|---|---|
| Petrosian | ½ ½ ½ ½ 0 1 ½ 0 ½ ½ ½ ½ | 5½ |

This was Korchnoi's first serious test since his defection, and, ironically, he was drawn against his arch-enemy Petrosian. I will confine comments to Korchnoi's own remarks from *Chess is My Life*.

It was an agonizing experience and in the newspapers they called it the 'match of hate'. We did not speak to each other, did not shake each other's hand, did not allow our gaze to cross. Through the arbiter, Kazic, a draw was offered. It was as well that the chessboard was the only battlefield. My nerves were, however, somewhat stronger. The standard of play was awfully low. In the difficult circumstances mistake just followed mistake.

Hardly an auspicious start for Korchnoi!

### *Semi-Finals*

**Evian 1977**

| | | | | | | | | | | | | | | | |
|---|---|---|---|---|---|---|---|---|---|---|---|---|---|---|---|
| **Korchnoi** | 1 | 1 | 1 | ½ | ½ | 1 | 1 | 0 | ½ | ½ | ½ | ½ | ½ | | 8½ |
| **Polugayevsky** | 0 | 0 | 0 | ½ | ½ | 0 | 0 | 1 | ½ | ½ | ½ | ½ | ½ | | 4½ |

In 1974 I visited Korchnoi in Moscow, during a particularly black patch of his match with Karpov. At that stage he was trailing by 3 points but friendly support (from myself and the Hartstons) helped him to recover, and he even used one of my ideas in the Queen's Indian to win the 21st game. Ever since that time I had the feeling that I could co-operate with him, but the opportunity did not arise until his defection from the USSR. At the Montreux tournament (immediately after his match with Petrosian) Korchnoi invited me to act as his second, an offer which I was delighted to accept. I then recruited Michael Stean to join Korchnoi's squad.

As can be seen, the course of the match was a disaster for the Soviet side — one of the most crushing Candidates' results since Fischer's rampage in 1971. During the match I was pleasantly surprised by the standard of the much-vaunted Soviet adjournment analysis, which became so feeble that we were always confident of getting the right result if a game was adjourned. We knew it wouldn't be so easy against Karpov!

Acting as Korchnoi's second gave me some fascinating insights into the petty political manoeuvres the official Russians were prepared to indulge in to demoralise the opposition. It took me two days of negotiation with V.D. Baturinsky (leader of the Soviet delegation) before they would even agree to let Polugayevsky shake hands at the start of each game, and they were adamant about refusing Korchnoi a flag under which to play. Personally, I believe that Korchnoi is proud of his 'statelessness' and at the preliminary meetings I proposed that Korchnoi play under the 'Skull and Crossbones', but you can guess the answer to that.

### *Final*

**Belgrade 1977/78**

| | | | | | | | | | | | | | | | | | | | | |
|---|---|---|---|---|---|---|---|---|---|---|---|---|---|---|---|---|---|---|---|---|
| **Korchnoi** | ½ | 1 | 1 | ½ | ½ | ½ | 1 | 1 | ½ | 1 | 0 | 0 | 0 | 0 | ½ | ½ | 1 | 1 | | 10½ |
| **Spassky** | ½ | 0 | 0 | ½ | ½ | ½ | 0 | 0 | ½ | 0 | 1 | 1 | 1 | 1 | ½ | ½ | 0 | 0 | | 7½ |

It is clear from the scores of this match that something very unusual occurred after the 10th game, when Korchnoi's winning margin of 5 points was cut to almost nothing, in a dramatic and virtually unprecedented reversal of fortune. There has been too much speculation concerning parapsychology, death rays, black magic and witchcraft surrounding this contest, but in my opinion the strange events can mainly be explained by nervous tension. Spassky spent the second half of the match planning his moves from a closed box off-stage and indulging in other semi-legal behaviour. Korchnoi became infected by this artificially strained atmosphere, but he eventually recovered his poise to secure a substantial and well-deserved victory.

## Facts and Figures

In order to challenge Karpov for the World Championship Korchnoi had to play 43 games in the Candidates' Tournament, of which he won 14, lost 6 and drew 23. This comes to 25½ points or 59.89 per cent. Of his 14 wins 7 were with Black.

Let us compare that with Karpov's performance in the 1974 Candidates', when his defeat of Korchnoi earned him the abortive right to meet Fischer. Karpov also played 43 games, winning 10 losing 3 and drawing 30 (25 points or 58.14 per cent). Karpov only won 2 games with Black, but these 2 included the 17th game of the Final which broke Korchnoi's serve and provided Karpov with his decisive extra point.

The records of the two in their respective Candidates' Tournaments are almost equal, but Karpov had made tremendous progress since he became World Champion, so much so, in fact, that several experts (including Tony Miles in the *New Statesman*) were predicting one year ago that the 1978 World Championship would be a no-contest. The irony of Karpov's position in 1975 was that he was universally regarded as second best to Fischer, an assessment which he could not disprove, in spite of his own willingness to play against the American Grandmaster. In compensation, Karpov ran up a truly amazing series of tournament successes, but Korchnoi has also performed with terrible force since his near-fiasco against Petrosian, and we can now look forward to that rare phenomenon — a World Championship with both players in peak form.

# 7
# KARPOV'S STYLE

One senses sacrilege in the air when speaking of Karpov and style in the same breath, since Karpov is a near-perfect player who almost rises above stylistic considerations. Nevertheless, Karpov still exhibits certain subtle preferences, there are still certain operations which he carries out with greater or lesser degrees of dexterity, and he has certain characteristics which any prospective opponent would examine in detail.

The hallmark of Karpov's games is fluency and ease. He is the Mozart of the chessboard and in chess terms he enjoys Capablanca's speed of play, the invincibility of Petrosian in his best days and the killer instinct of Fischer. This killer instinct is not expressed by any overt show of tempestuous aggression but by a machine-like insistence which gradually wears down the most stubborn of opponents.

The strengths (and possible weakness) of Karpov's style can be more easily defined under four headings:-

## Speed of Play

If one examines the 24 games played between Karpov and Korchnoi in their 1974 match it becomes obvious that Karpov was by far the more rapid player. Only Capablanca in his prime played so consistently fast in important matches. Very rarely Karpov's speed leads to superficial decisions, but in the practical struggle it usually turns out to be a devastating weapon which leaves the opponent floundering in time-trouble. Against Olafsson at Bad Lauterberg 1977 Karpov had used 2¼ hours after 2 sessions of play, while the Icelandic Grandmaster had consumed 5¼ hours. In the *New Statesman* Tony Miles asked whether the time difference at the end of that game was a record for modern chess.

To illustrate Karpov's speed of play here is his rapid demolition of Lajos Portisch, rated at that time at 2625.

Portisch — Karpov, King's Indian Attack, Europa Cup, Moscow 1977

| 1 N-KN3 | N-KB3 |
| 2 P-KN3 | P-QN3 |
| 3 B-N2 | B-N2 |
| 4 0-0 | P-K3 |
| 5 P-Q3 | |

It is a matter of taste, but I think 5 P-B4 is more active.

| 5 . . . | P-Q4 |
| 6 QN-Q2 | QN-Q2 |

21

### 7 R-K1      B-B4

Fluid development is typical of Karpov's style but one cannot deny the originality of developing the KB at QB4 in a Flank Opening.

### 8 P-B4

This shows that Portisch had been driven into a passive frame of mind by the prospect of facing the World Champion. The consistent course now is 8 P-K3 (to blunt the operation of Black's KB) followed by the fianchetto of White's QB.

| 8 . . . | 0-0 |
| 9 PxP | PxP |
| 10 N-N3 | B-N5 |
| 11 B-Q2 | P-QR4 |

More ambitious than 11 . . . BxB 12 QxB P-QB4 which would have been good enough for equality.

| 12 QN-Q4 | R-K1 |
| 13 QR-B1 | P-B4 |
| 14 N-B5 | N-B1 |
| 15 P-Q4? | |

Provoking a sharp struggle at the wrong moment.

| 15 . . . | N-K5 |
| 16 PxP? | |

White's position is already bad but this is a blunder losing material.

| 16 . . . | NxB |

### 17 NxN      Q-N4!

Forking White's knights. If now 18 N-K3 RxN 19 PxR QxP+ wins.

| 18 N-Q6 | BxN |
| 19 NxB | BxR(K8) |
| 20 QxB | RxP |
| 21 QxR | QxR+ |
| 22 Q-B1 | Q-Q7 |
| 23 PxP | R-QB1 |

**White Resigns.**

I was playing on top board for England in this event and during my game with Smejkal our deliberations were rudely interrupted by an explosion of cheering and shouting in the tournament hall. It transpired that Karpov had crushed Portisch and the crowd was registering its appreciation. I wandered over to their board and looked at the clock times: Portisch had taken 2 hours and 10 minutes. If his position had not been bad enough to resign then he would soon have found himself in time-trouble. I then looked at Karpov's clock. He had taken just 1 hour to annihilate a semifinalist from the Candidates' tournament!

### Precision of Calculation

At nearly all times Karpov sees his way very clearly. He holds the structure of future events in his mind, rather like Michelangelo, who claimed he could see the future shape of his sculpture in the rough block of stone. Many people regard Karpov as an icy calculating machine without nerves, and he exerts an impressive personal power precisely because he is so calm and controlled.

As an example of this I want to cite his game against Miles from Tilburg 1977. The English Grandmaster caught Karpov in a sharp prepared variation, which involved a rook sacrifice to trap the White king in the centre of the board — now read on . . .

**Karpov — Miles, English Opening, Tilburg 1977**

1 P-QB4 P-QB4 2 N-KB3 N-KB3 3 N-B3 N-B3  4 P-Q4 PxP  5 NxP P-K3 6 P-KN3 Q-N3 7 N-N3 N-K4 8 P-K4 B-N5 9 Q-K2 P-QR4 10 B-K3 Q-B3  11 P-B3 0-0  12 N-Q4 Q-R3 13 N-N5 P-Q4

Miles had had this position once before in 1977. Then he was White against Nunn in a game from the 2nd T.V. Master Game Tournament and the game had continued: 14 BPxP PxP 15 B-Q4 PxP 16 Bx N PxP 17 Q-B4 P-B7+ 18 K-Q1 R-Q1+ 19 K-B1 B-K3 with obscure complications which ended in a draw. Watch how Karpov wields his intellectual machete to cut his way through the tangled jungle of variations.

**14 N-B7!**          **Q-Q3**

The alternative is 14 . . . Q-B3 when Karpov gives the following plausible main line: 15 NxR Nx

QBP 16 B-Q4 P-K4 17 PxP NxQP 18 QxN PxB  19 QxQ PxQ  20 P-QR3 PxN 21 PxB BPxP 22 R-QN1 PxP  23 RxP B-B4 24 N-N6! NxN 25 RxP and White has the superior ending.

| 15 NxR | PxKP |
|--------|------|

More complicated is 15 . . . Nx QBP. After the text Black's attack fizzles out.

| 16 PxP | NxKP |
|--------|------|
| 17 R-Q1 | Q-B3 |
| 18 B-N2 | NxBP |
| 19 B-Q4 | BxN+ |
| 20 PxB | P-B4 |
| 21 0—0 | N/B5-Q3 |
| 22 N-N6 | P-K4 |
| 23 NxB | RxN |
| 24 RxKP | Q-B4+ |
| 25 B-Q4 | |

**Black Resigns.**

## Virtuoso in Space

Ever since the days of Dr Tarrasch any strong player knows how to cramp the opposing position with pawns, if given the opportunity. Karpov, however, has mastered the difficult art of maintaining, and consistently exploiting, a space advantage in fluid, open positions *by piece control alone*. This is a particularly striking facet of his style which I will illustrate with a thematic game against the Soviet Grandmaster Mark Taimanov.

**Karpov — Taimanov, Sicilian Defence, USSR Team Championship, Moscow 1972.**

1 P-K4 P-QB4  2 N-KB3 P-K3  3 P-Q4 PxP 4 NxP P-QR3 5 B-Q3 B-B4

6 N-N3 B-N3  7 0-0 N-K2  8 Q-K2
QN-B3   9 B-K3 N-K4   10 P-QB4
BxB  11  QxB  Q-B2  12 P-B5!

The first step in a strategy designed to dominate the dark squares.

12 ...            NxB
13 QxN            P-QN3

Black immediately takes measures to challenge the advanced pawn, but even after it has disappeared it leaves a strong square for White in its wake.

14 PxP            QxNP
15 N/1-Q2         P-Q4
16 P-K5!

Although this gives Black a passed pawn it increases White's network of dark square domination.

16 ...            B-Q2
17 KR—B1          0-0
18 Q-Q4

Methodically driving Black back. After 18 . . . QxQ 19 NxQ KR-B1 20 N/2-N3 N-B3 21 NxN BxN 22 N-Q4 White enjoys a favourable ending.

18 ...            Q-N1
19 N-B3           N-B3
20 Q-K3           R-B1
21 R-B5           P-QR4
22 R/1-QB1        P-R5
23 N/N3-Q4        N-R4

Black does everything he can to achieve Q-side counterplay. His threat of . . . N-B5 forces White to isolate his QNP.

24 RxR+           BxR
25 P-QN3          B-Q2
26 P-R4           P-R3
27 P-KN4!

The manoeuvre inaugurated by the text goes beyond a mere technical exploitation of a spatial plus. Karpov not only uses his central grip to defend his potentially shaky Q-side, but also to launch a sudden raid against the Black king. White's QR, innocently controlling a Q-side file is, in fact, destined to join in an attack on the other side of the board.

27 ...            Q-N2
28 P-R5           N-B3
29 P-N5           NxN
30 NxN            KRPxP
31 QxP

Threatening P-R6.

31 ...            K-R2
32 R-B3           Q-N5
33 R-N3           R-KN1
34 N-B3           PxP
35 PxP            QxP

DIAGRAM

The culmination of Black's Q-side

initiative — he wins the isolated pawn. Unfortunately, White has been given sufficient time to build up a mating attack.

| 36 Q-B1 | Q-R7 |
| 37 N-N5+ | K-R1 |
| 38 NxP+ | K-R2 |
| 39 Q-N5 | Q-N8+ |
| 40 K-R2 | Resigns. |

There is no defence to Q-N6+.

## Karpov's Weakness

If Karpov has a weakness it is a slight hesitancy when faced by unusual openings, often of the old-fashioned, classical variety. I exploited this in my game against Karpov from Bad Lauterberg 1977 by playing the virtually unexplored Philidor Defence against him.

Karpov scored 7½/8 with White in that tournament, and my game was the half. As further evidence here is a rather unconvincing Karpov draw with this kind of opening against an opponent Karpov would normally expect to beat.

**Haase — Karpov, Centre Game, Skopje Olympiad 1972**

1 P-K4 P-K4  2 P-Q4 PxP  3 QxP N-QB3  4 Q-K3 P-Q3  5 N-QB3 N-B3  6 B-Q2 B-K2  7 0-0-0 0-0  8 Q-N3 P-QR3  9 P-B4 P-QN4  10 P-K5 N-Q2  11 N-B3 R-N1  12 N-Q5 N-B4  13 B-K3 N-K5  14 Q-K1 P-B4  15 P-KR3 B-K3  16 R-N1 K-R1  17 P-KN4 PxKP  18 NxB QxN  19 Nx P NxN  20 PxN R/N1-Q1  21 B-Q3 B-Q4 **Drawn**

# 8
# KORCHNOI'S STYLE

Most of what has been written about Korchnoi's style (including some remarks of my own which appeared at the time of the 1974 match) is now hopelessly out of date. Usually one reads about the heroic defender in hectic time-trouble, the veins on his brow bursting with his immense will to win, always ready to snatch material and weather the attack etc. . . Probably this was the stereotyped impression Spassky had of him before their match in Belgrade last year.

The keynotes are still striving and determination, but Korchnoi's style has rounded and developed in remarkable fashion since he came to the West. He has successfully eliminated that drop of poison which vitiated his earlier achievements. He now avoids time-trouble if possible, instead of revelling in it, as he seemed to do in former times, and he no longer overestimates material in relation to the initiative. Indeed, he has developed a very fine feeling for the initiative and is particularly dangerous with Black, when he sees the chance to offer a pawn sacrifice early in the game to disorganise his opponent's position. In this respect he bears comparison with Alekhine, as well as with his own hero, the Apostle of the Struggle, Emanuel Lasker.

I will illustrate these points with two of his games from the 1977 Candidates' cycle.

**Polugayevsky — Korchnoi, English Defence, Evian 1977 (Game 6)**

| 1 P-Q4 | P-K3 |
| 2 P-QB4 | P-QN3 |
| 3 P-K4 | |

Played with an air of disbelief by Polugayevsky who obviously regarded Black's formation as a bad joke.

| 3 . . . | B-N2 |
| 4 Q-B2 | |

Polugayevsky's idea is to defend his KP without playing N-QB3 which would risk doubled pawns after . . . B-N5.

| 4 . . . | Q-R5! |

26

An unpleasant surprise for Polugayevsky and one which appears to break a number of sound, elementary rules. However, it is surprisingly difficult to drive away the annoying Black queen.

**5 N-Q2**

Nineteen minutes spent over this, so Black's strange opening was already justified in a practical sense.

| 5 . . . | B-N5 |
| 6 B-Q3 | P-KB4 |
| 7 N-B3 | BxN+ |
| 8 K-B1? | |

Feeble. To be consistent White must sacrifice two pawns with 8 BxB Q-N5 9 N-K5! QxNP 10 0-0-0 PxP 11 B-K2 when vast complications ensue. After the text White gains a pawn but he loses the right to castle and also allows his pawn structure to be ruined.

| 8 . . . | Q-R4 |
| 9 BxB | N-KB3 |
| 10 PxP | BxN |
| 11 PxB | N-B3 |
| 12 B-B3 | 0-0 |
| 13 R-K1 | Q-R6+ |

Significantly preferring pursuit of the attack to re-establishment of material equality with 13 . . . QxBP.

| 14 K-K2 | QR-K1 |
| 15 K-Q1 | P-K4! |

.     **DIAGRAM**

Spurning pawns, Korchnoi introduces an imaginative combination which exploits the shaky position of White's king in the middle of the board. I must say, the position at the moment looks like a reversed King's Gambit, where everything has gone wrong for White.

| 16 PxP | NxP |
| 17 B-K2 | |

Or  17 BxN RxB  18 RxR QxP+ and . . . QxR.

| 17 . . . | NxKBP! |

The point of Black's play.

| 18 Q-Q3 | RxB |
| 19 RxR | |

If 19 KxR Q-R4 and Black wins.

| 19 . . . | Q-N7 |
| 20 KR-K1 | NxR |
| 21 KxN | QxRP? |

Jeopardising victory. By interposing 21 . . . Q-N8+ 22 K-Q2 and only then . . . QxRP Korchnoi could have prevented the invasion of his position which now occurs.

| 22 R-K7 | Q-N8+ |
| 23 K-K2 | Q-N5+ |
| 24 K-K1 | P-KR4 |
| 25 Q-N3! | |

A difficult decision to make, but it is the right one. Exchange of queens eases the task of defence. From now until the adjournment Polugayevsky plays excellently and brings about a drawish ending.

25 . . . QxQ 26 PxQ R-B2 27 BxN PxB 28 R-K8+ K-N2 29 K-B2 K-R3 30 P-QN4 K-N4 31 R-QR8 KxP 32 RxP P-Q3 33 P-R4 K-K3 34 P-R5 PxP 35 RxRP P-KB4 36 P-B5

R-R2   37 PxP PxP   38 P-N5 P-R5
39 PxP RxP   40 R-R8 R-QN5 41
R-QN8 K-Q4

The adjourned position. Polugayevsky seemed to be anxious to set up some kind of time record for sealed moves since he now consumed 51 minutes, leaving himself just over 8 minutes for 14 moves nex day.

Our adjournment analysis was not particularly fruitful. Of course, we did not know Polugayevsky's sealed move and we could find nothing very convincing against 42 R-N6!; 42 K-B3 also seemed impossible to crack by orthodox methods.

42 K-B3          R-N6+!?

A psychological blow. It looks nonsensical to free White's king, but Korchnoi was relying on the fact that Polugayevsky would probably have analysed more 'dangerous' tries. With only 8 minutes until move 56 there was plenty of scope for error, even against 'nonsense'.

43 K-B4          K-B4
44 R-QB8+?

The losing check. The immediate KxP should draw. Korchnoi now played his remaining moves in-

stantly, so that Polugayevsky had no time to think at all.

44 ... KxP 45 KxP R-K6 46 K-B4 R-K8   47 R-Q8 K-B4   48 R-QB8+ K-Q5 49 K-B3 P-Q4 50 K-B2 R-K4 51 R-QR8 K-B6 52 R-R3+ K-N5 53 R-R1 P-Q5 54 R-QB1 P-Q6 55 R-B8 P-Q7 56 R-QN8+ K-B6 57 R-QB8+ K-Q6 58 R-Q8+ K-B7 59 R-QB8+ K-Q8 White Resigned.

It is apparent from this game that Korchnoi is also a great master of the endgame. In fact, from my own experience of his endgame analysis, I would say that he is fully the equal of all the practitioners in this branch of the art of chess, both from the past and in the present day. His psychological approach to the question of the adjourned position is also worthy of deep study.

Spassky — Korchnoi, French Defence, Belgrade 1977, Game 2
1 P-K4 P-K3 2 P-Q4 P-Q4 3 N-QB3 B-N5 4 P-K5 P-QB4 5 P-QR3 BxN+ 6 PxN N-K2  7 Q-N4 PxP 8 QxNP R-N1 9 QxRP Q-B2 10 N-K2 QN-B3  11 P-KB4 B-Q2  12 Q-Q3 PxP 13 B-K3 P-Q5!

Korchnoi had specially prepared this sharp line as a psychological weapon. Black seizes the initiative at the cost of one or two pawns — extremely uncongenial for Spassky who prefers attack to defence.

| 14 B-B2 | 0-0-0 |
| 15 NxQP | NxN |
| 16 QxN | P-N3 |
| 17 B-R4 | B-N4 |
| 18 Q-K4 | BxB |
| 19 RxB? | |

Spassky could have drawn with 19 Q-R8+ K-Q2 (19 . . . Q-N1 is too risky) 20 0-0-0+ N-Q4 21 Rx N+ PxR 22 QxQ—+ K-B1 23 Q-R8+ etc.

| 19 . . . | R-Q4 |
| 20 BxN | QxB |
| 21 R-B3 | K-N1 |
| 22 K-B1 | |

If 22 RxP Q-R5+ 23 K-B1 R-Q7 is unpleasant. A significant improvement is 22 P-N3! e.g. 22 . . . R-Q7 23 R-P RxRP 24 0-0-0, as pointed out by Najdorf.

| 22 . . . | R-Q7 |
| 23 R-B2 | R(1)-Q1 |
| 24 Q-B3 | RxR+ |
| 25 KxR | R-Q7+ |
| 26 K-N3 | |

Or 26 K-B1 Q-B4 with advantage to Black.

| 26 . . . | Q-Q1 |

Although White is a pawn ahead his defence is hampered by the insecure position of his king. Note that 26 . . . RxBP 27 Q-Q3 gives Black nothing but now he threatens to capture on QB7.

| 27 Q-K4 | Q-N1+ |
| 28 K-R3 | Q-R1+ |
| 29 K-N3 | Q-N2+ |

| 30 K-R3 | R-Q1 |

Threatening mate. Now Black's queen and rook develop amazing versatility and hammer White from all directions.

| 31 P-N4 | R-R1+ |
| 32 K-N3 | Q-R3 |
| 33 Q-N2 | Q-R5+ |
| 34 K-B3 | R-Q1 |
| 35 Q-N3 | Q-K2 |
| 36 P-N5? | |

In time-trouble Spassky lets slip his last chance, 36 R-K1.

| 36 . . . | R-Q7 |
| 37 K-N4 | Q-N2 |
| 38 QxP | R-N7+ |
| 39 K-R3 | R-B7 |
| 40 K-N4 | Q-K5 |

**White Resigns.**

To encapsulate the contrast in style between Karpov and Korchnoi I would say it was a matter of Fluency v Dynamism. We know that Karpov has always admired Capablanca, while Korchnoi looks to Lasker for inspiration and I have compared his recent games to those of Alekhine. So, the question is — will Baguio 1978 be a repetition of Capablanca v Lasker 1921, or Capablanca v Alekhine 1927?

## 9

# CLOSE ENCOUNTERS: PREVIOUS GAMES BETWEEN KORCHNOI AND KARPOV

Karpov and Korchnoi have played 35 serious games against each other, and also one game in a simultaneous display, given by Korchnoi when Karpov was 11 years old. Their full results are given below in tabular form:

| Year | Event | Karpov | Korchnoi |
|------|-------|--------|----------|
| 1962 | Simultaneous Display | ½ | ½ |
| 1970 | 38th USSR Championship | 0 | 1 |
| 1971 | Training Match | +2=2-2 | +2=2-2 |
| 1971 | Alekhine Memorial | 1 | 0 |
| 1971/2 | Hastings | 0 | 1 |
| 1973 | Interzonal | ½ | ½ |
| 1973 | 41st USSR Championship | 1 | 0 |
| 1974 | Candidates' Final | +3=19-2 | +2=19-3 |

The complete tally is: Karpov 7 wins, Korchnoi 6 wins, and 23 draws.

The little-known training match in 1971 was unusual in that Korchnoi took Black in 5 out of the six games *and forewarned Karpov what opening he was proposing to play.*

Most of the games played since Karpov won his spurs are well known, but the following fairy-tale beginning to the Korchnoi-Karpov relationship is worth reproducing.

**Simultaneous Display, Cheliabinsk 1962, Korchnoi — Karpov, Four Knights**

1 P-K4 P-K4 2 N-KB3 N-QB3 3 P-Q4 PxP 4 NxP N-B3 5 N-QB3 P-Q3 6 B-QN5 B-Q2 7 0-0 B-K2 8 R-K1 0-0 9 B-B1 R-K1 10 P-KR3 NxN 11 QxN B-B3 12 B-K3 Q-Q2 13 QR-Q1 B-B1 14 B-KN5 B-K2 15 B-B1 P-QR3 16 P-KN4 P-R3 17 P-B4 QR-Q1 18 B-N2 Q-B1 19 Q-Q3 P-QN4 20 P-R3 Q-N2 21 Q-B3 B-B1 22 P-KR4 P-QR4 23 P-N5 PxP 24 RPxP N-R2 25 B-R3 P-Q4 26 PxP RxR+ 27 RxR BxQP 28 NxB QxN 29 QxQ RxQ 30 P-N6 B-B4+ Drawn.

# Part II

# THE RUN-UP TO THE MATCH

Garlands greeted Viktor Korchnoi and the rest of his party (Petra Leeuwerik, Michael Stean, Yasha Murei and myself) when we arrived in Manila, for the purpose of acclimatisation, two weeks before the start of the match. The whole atmosphere was reminiscent of Disneyland and our spirits were only slightly dampened when the monsoons set in a few days after our arrival.

From Manila we moved in state to Baguio City where Karpov and his entourage had already arrived a few days earlier. Baguio (which means gold in the local language Tagolog) is on North Luxon, an island 150 miles north of Manila, and, being cooler than the main capital, is the summer capital of the Philippines. The City itself is a fortress set in a valley between 5000 ft. mountains and appropriately the organisers had placed the Korchnoi and Karpov parties in separate hotels on mountains on either side of the city so that they could gaze across at each other like the two towers of Minas Ethil and Minas Morgul in Tolkien's *Lord of the Rings*.

Despite reluctance from the Russians to meet the dissident leper Korchnoi more than was necessary, President Marcos insisted on receiving the two players together at the Presidential Palace Malacanung. At the reception he made a statement saying "This match will focus attention on the Philippines especially after the distorted reporting of the Western Press on this country." Curiously he singled out Leonard Barden for criticism on the grounds that he had claimed that the Philippines lacked funds to stage the match. In fact a number of reports in England had expressed doubts based mainly on the fact that no US network was interested in the TV rights which had been expected to raise £1,000,000.

From my own experience I can testify that no expense or effort was spared in the interest of the complete comfort of the players and their delegations. One small example was that, when I ordered soup at the Philippina Plaza, it arrived in a bowl encased in a moulded block of ice into which flowers had been frozen. An even smaller example was the miniature bed which the diminutive world champion had specially made for him by a local carpenter.

I have already introduced the players themselves in the Introduction and I must now introduce their respective heads of delegation who were to play such an important role in the various squabbles which arose both before and during the match.

The Russian leader was one V.D. Baturinsky, a retired colonel — not however the sort of retired colonel who writes to the *London Daily Telegraph*, since his commission was in the KGB. There was no love lost between him and the Korchnoi camp since he was one of the soviet chess bureaucrats who had contributed to Korchnoi's decision to leave the USSR. Korchnoi had clashed with him since, when he led the USSR delegations in the Candidate's matches. At his press conference Korchnoi said Baturinsky should be hung, drawn and quartered for his role as a political prosecutor during the Stalin era.

Baturinsky was confronted by Ms. Petra Leeuwerik. She had previously had little interest in chess when she met Korchnoi in Holland a few months after his defection. But they soon found that the coincidence of their views on communists was more than enough to forge a bond between them and she has been a loyal champion of Korchnoi ever since. Her own reasons for remaining cheerless in the company of Russians are substantial enough. When she was nineteen she was kidnapped from the Russian zone of Vienna on the pretext of being a spy and spent ten years in the notorious Vorkuta concentration camp. She is a stimulating and entertaining person and in view of her history it is hard to blame her for her fierce hatred of the Russians. But even before the match I was worried that she would prove *plus royaliste que le roi* and fan Korchnoi's already fiery disposition. As the match progressed my worries were unfortunately proved to be justified.

After settling in, the two contestants were confronted by the press. Karpov, dressed in a barong with the championship logo topped by a crown embroidered on it, was serene but rather dull and he avoided political questions. In particular he declined to comment on Korchnoi's request that his family be allowed out of the USSR on the grounds that this issue was nothing to do with chess. Asked by Petra Leeuwerik to comment on the fact that his chess autobiography *'Chess is My Life'* bore the same title as Korchnoi's, published a few months earlier, he replied that the title was his publishers' choice. He was, however, provoked into commenting on Korchnoi: "He is a fighter in the full meaning of the word. His play and method are good. He is a very strong chess player but as to his character, I do not appreciate it highly." On the issue of the result of the match, after being told of Korchnoi's confidence in winning he replied, "Maybe Karpov is as sure of victory as he was three years ago. Then I was sure I'd win as I am now." However he declined to make any predictions on the length of the match. "It is very difficult," he said.

Not surprisingly, Korchnoi was more forthcoming. He objected to the size of the Soviet delegation of 16 which included not only strong chess players such as the ex-world champion Tal (officially designated a journalist) and grandmaster Balashov but also, he alleged, "a medician, a PT expert, a psychologist or psychiatrist, a chemistry expert (!), an expert to conduct physical tests during the match and two members of the KGB secret police."

Korchnoi used the quaint word "medician" to mean simply a doctor. But one journalist missheard him and reported that he had said "magician". The report spread rapidly and it is an interesting reflection on the atmosphere surrounding the match that nobody seemed to regard the suggestion of black magic as implausible!

The issue of the size of Karpov's delegation simmered on after the press conference. Petra Leeuwerik, as head of the Korchnoi delegation, demanded that the names and functions of all 16 be disclosed. "It is impossible," she argued, "for them to come here without specific functions since the category of tourist does not exist for Soviet travellers." Baturinsky declined to supply the information on the grounds that the rules of the match did not compel him to do so and his contention was upheld by the Philippino organiser of the match, Campomanes.

Returning to the press conference, Korchnoi said that his life would be in danger from Soviet agents if he damaged Soviet prestige by beating the champion. It was generally considered that this fear was rather far fetched but I was still relieved that I was not invited to act as Korchnoi's food taster!

The centrepiece of Korchnoi's conference was his announcement that he had written an open letter to Chairman Brezhnev demanding that his wife and son should be allowed out of the USSR, thus emulating Martina Navratilova in using his position in the limelight to publicise a private grievance. He denied that Karpov could disclaim responsibility for the acts of a government he supports and called him "one of the jailers of my family". The letter concluded:

"I appeal to you to demonstrate the goodwill necessary for the fulfillment of the conditions of the Helsinki International Agreement, which prescribes the reunification of divided families.

"I invoke your mercy, Mr. Chairman; I beg you to show compassion for two citizens af the USSR, whose life, by decree of fate, is no longer bound to the life of Soviet society. Permit them to leave the Soviet Union."

A copy of this letter was sent to the Russian ambassador to the Philippines. Forewarned of its contents, he returned it unopened.

Korchnoi was only persuaded to speak briefly about the match itself. He said the chances were 50-50 and predicted the contest would be over in 20 games. He castigated the new rule that Karpov should be entitled to a re-match if he lost and left the audience in doubt whether he would abide by this rule if the case arose.

No report of a chess match seems complete these days without a paragraph on death rays, so here goes . . . Petra Leeuwerik prophylactically announced that Korchnoi had brought an anti-ray device with him. Baturinsky retaliated by demanding that Korchnoi's special chair, an olive-green stoll giroflex type costing £700, should be x-rayed but all that was found by an incredulous radiographer was foam rubber.

But the main pre-match dispute concerned which flag Korchnoi should play under. He wanted the Swiss flag on the grounds that he has now resided in Wohlen, Switzerland, for almost a year and proposes to make Switzerland his home and play for the Swiss in the Olympics. He had applied for Swiss nationality and had a letter from the Swiss government consenting to the use of their flag. But all this was not good enough for the Soviets who wanted him to play under a plain white flag with the word *'stateless'* on it. They rejected his counter-proposal that he would play under the hammer and sickle provided that the words 'I've escaped' appeared on it. The dispute dragged on perilously close to the scheduled start of the match and was not resolved until two days before the match was due to start. In the end, after two critical meetings at one of which Baturinsky stormed out bellowing threats to cancel the match unless he got his own way, what Korchnoi called "the diplomacy of the fist", triumphed. Despite the last-minute arrival of an independent legal opinion from Professor Karl Doehring of Heidelberg University, which supported Korchnoi, the jury voted against the Swiss flag. Eventually on the proposal of Colonel Edmondson (USA) a compromise was reached. The Soviet flag would be displayed on the stage but neither player would have a flag on the chess table.

The match now being on again preparations were made for the opening ceremony on 17th July. It was arranged that the Soviet national anthem would be played for Karpov while Korchnoi chose part of the last movement of Beethoven's Ninth symphony, which features the 'Ode to Joy' which Schiller had originally entitled *'Freiheit'* (Liberty) until the censors intervened. This was a case of pseudo-military kitsch in competition with great classical music. Korchnoi had intended to sit down ostentatiously during the Russian national anthem but this gesture proved unnecessary because the orchestra got their music mixed up and played instead the Internationale, which Stalin had dropped as the Soviet National Anthem in 1943. This produced scowls from the Soviets and guffaws from the Korchnoi camp.

The whole chess world was now anxiously waiting for the start of the match.

# GAME ONE

## 18th July

After all the preliminary alarms and excursions the stage now seemed set for the first game — but there was one final hiccup. Although both players had previously settled and approved the chess pieces to be used in the match, they both decided at the last minute (finally agreeing on something) that they were too light-weight. Thus a match which had been planned months in advance was in danger of failing to start on time because no suitable chess set was available. Happily, as in 1972, the situation was saved by a *deus ex machina*, cunningly disguised as a human millionaire. But, whereas Jim Slater had to fork out £50,000 to save the Fischer-Spassky match, all that was required of our new hero, Manila magnate Manuel Zamora (may his tribe increase!) was one heavy chess set. This was rushed 150 miles from Manila over tortuous mountain roads and arrived with 15 minutes to spare — 14 minutes too early for full dramatic effect.

The first game itself was an anti-climax. President (Prexy in the local language, Tagolog) Marcos was watching but this did not spur the players to great efforts and after minor inaccuracies on each side the game burnt out to an early draw.

**White: Korchnoi**
**Black: Karpov**

### Queen's Gambit Declined

| | |
|---|---|
| 1 P-QB4 | N-KB3 |
| 2 N-QB3 | P-K3 |
| 3 N-B3 | P-Q4 |
| 4 P-Q4 | B-K2 |
| 5 B-N5 | P-KR3 |
| 6 B-R4 | 0-0 |
| 7 P-K3 | P-QN3 |
| 8 R-B1 | B-N2 |
| 9 B-Q3 | PxP(?) |

9...P-B4 is correct.

| | |
|---|---|
| 10 BxP | QN-Q2 |
| 11 0-0 | P-B4 |

**12 PxP(?)**

12 Q-K2 is a better attempt to retain White's opening advantage, e.g. 12...N-K5 13 NxN BxB 14 N-B3 B-KB3 15 KR-Q1 Q-K2 16 B-R6 QR-N1 17 BxB RxB 18 N-K4 with a plus (Alekhine - Bogoljubow, Mannheim 1937). Alekhine recommended 12...P-R3 13 KR-Q1 P-QN4 as an improvement but White can retain a slight advantage by playing 13 P-R4.

| | |
|---|---|
| 12 ... | NxP |
| 13 Q-K2 | P-R3 |
| 14 KR-Q1 | Q-K1 |
| 15 P-QR3 | KN-K5 |

35

| 16 NxN | NxN |
| 17 BxB | QxB |
| 18 N-Q4 | KR-B1 |

### DIAGRAM

**Draw** **agreed** on Karpov's proposal. The position is lifeless. (Times: 0.52 — 0.52)

# GAME TWO

## 20th July

Although countless chess fans all over the world would have been delighted to watch the match, draws and all, if only they could have afforded the fare to the Philippines, in Baguio itself interest temporarily plummetted after the boring first game. The price of tickets was reduced but still the playing hall was almost empty and it proved necessary to enlist a troop of local military cadets to swell the audience.

The second game, although also drawn, was considerably more interesting than the first and featured some splendid theoretical preparation by Korchnoi which extended up to move 24! Korchnoi surprised everyone by shelving the French in favour of the Open Ruy Lopez. Karpov reached an ending with the nominal advantage of bishop for knight but he could make nothing of it and the game was drawn in 29 moves. At the close of the game Korchnoi said "Karpov heard somewhere that bishop was better than knight − in Leonid Stein's hands maybe, but not in his!"

The game was encouraging for the Korchnoi camp, partly because we maintain Karpov plays less well in open positions and partly because Karpov was always behind on the clock - at one point he had used 50 minutes against Korchnoi's 4 minutes.

**White: Karpov**
**Black: Korchnoi**

### Ruy Lopez

| | |
|---|---|
| 1 P-K4 | P-K4 |
| 2 N-KB3 | N-QB3 |
| 3 B-N5 | P-QR3 |
| 4 B-R4 | N-B3 |
| 5 0-0 | NxP |
| 6 P-Q4 | P-QN4 |
| 7 B-N3 | P-Q4 |
| 8 PxP | B-K3 |
| 9 P-B3 | B-QB4 |
| 10 QN-Q2 | 0-0 |
| 11 B-B2 | B-B4 |
| 12 N-N3 | B-KN5 |

| | |
|---|---|
| 13 NxB | NxN |
| 14 R-K1 | |

This position is well known to Karpov — see for example his

37

games against Smyslov at Leningrad 1977 and Tilburg 1977 and against Belyavsky at Leningrad 1977. But now Korchnoi produced a new move which clearly caught Karpov unawares.

| | |
|---|---|
| 14 ... | P-Q5 |
| 15 P-KR3 | B-R4 |
| 16 PxP | BxN |
| 17 QxB | NxQP |
| 18 Q-B3 | Q-Q4 |
| 19 B-K3 | NxB |
| 20 QxN(B2) | N-Q6 |
| 21 KR-Q1 | KR-Q1 |
| 22 QxP | |

22 QR-B1 may be a little better.

| | |
|---|---|
| 22 ... | QxKP |
| 23 QxQ | NxQ |
| 24 P-QN3 | P-B3 |

| | |
|---|---|
| 25 B-N6 | RxR+ |
| 26 RxR | R-QB1 |
| 27 R-Q2 | P-KR4 |
| 28 B-K3 | K-B2 |
| 29 P-B4 | |

Draw agreed
(Times: 1.55 — 1.35)

# GAME THREE

## 22nd July

During the second game a yoghurt was delivered to Karpov and nobody appeared to take any notice but when the same thing happened in game 3 the audience burst out laughing – for by now the Great Yoghurt Controversy, for which the match may be remembered long after the chess has been forgotten, was in full swing.

After the second game the Korchnoi camp, in an attempt to ease the tension and parody some of the earlier protests, issued a formal protest claiming that the delivery of a yoghurt could convey a kind of coded message. "Thus a yoghurt after move 20 could signify 'we instruct you to offer a draw'; or a sliced mango could mean 'we order you to decline a draw'. A dish of marinated quails eggs could mean 'play N-N5 at once' and so on. The possibilities are limitless."

Predictably only Baturinsky and Ms. Leeuwerik appeared to take the protest seriously but their intransigence was sufficient to blow the dispute up out of all proportion. After a long meeting of the jury had failed to solve the problem, Lothar Schmid finally saved the day by decreeing that Karpov could have his yoghurt provided that he had only the violet coloured variety served at a fixed time by a designated waiter.

The Great Yoghurt Controversy gave the press a field day and Ian Ward must have enjoyed himself when commenting in *The London Daily Telegraph* on the compromise: "But will the yoghurt crisis now really subside? Herr Schmid is the first to admit the tenuousness of the situation. He fully realises that yoghurt can come in many colours – green, blue, pink, yellow, to name but a few. Under the Schmid ruling a change in the colour of the yoghurt passed to Karpov throws the whole compromise into confusion: for then the Russians must seek official permission once again. 'If it is a violet yoghurt again no mention need be made in advance to me or to the deputy arbiters. In case Mr. Karpov wishes to change beverages, please let an arbiter know in advance of the game by describing the new beverage in a short note.' And in this rarified atmosphere that only chess grandmasters appear to comprehend fully, it appears that there might be serious complications if Herr Schmid is asked to distinguish between, say, mauve and violet yoghurt. The implications remain frightening."

The third game was by far the sharpest of those to date. Korchnoi allowed the Nimzo-Indian Defence for the very first time in all his games

39

against Karpov and achieved an opening advantage using a line he had analysed with Furman in 1967! Furman, ironically, later became Karpov's trainer, and his death earlier this year deprived Karpov of a valuable friend and supporter.

Korchnoi rapidly built up a dominating position, and for most of the game the assembled experts (Najdorf, Byrne, Tal, Euwe etc.) believed he would win with a crushing king-side assault. Korchnoi also held a time advantage of half an hour until the latter stages of the game. However, Korchnoi faltered on move 24 and Karpov was allowed to wriggle out with a draw. White has nothing better at the end.

**White: Korchnoi**
**Black: Karpov**

### Nimzo-Indian Defence

| 1 | P-QB4 | N-KB3 |
| 2 | P-Q4 | P-K3 |
| 3 | N-QB3 | B-N5 |
| 4 | P-K3 | P-B4 |
| 5 | N-K2 | |

Rubinstein's move, which avoids doubled pawns. It is the best antidote to the popular Hubner variation (5 B-Q3 N-B3 6 N-B3 BxN+ 7 PxB —Q3) which Black is trying to introduce with his fourth move.

| 5 . . . | | PxP |
| 6 | PxP | P-Q4 |
| 7 | P-B5 | N-K5 |
| 8 | B-Q2 | NxB |
| 9 | QxN | P-QR4 |

I believe this is a new move for published theory, although Korchnoi had analysed it privately with Furman. Karpov played 9... P-QR4 very quickly, but he soon slowed down.

Previous tries by Black in this position have been:
(A) 9...P-QN3 10 P-QR3 BxN+ 11 NxB PxP 12 PxP P-QR4 13 B-N5 B-Q2 14 R-B1 P-R5 with approximate equality in Averbakh

-Panno, Portoroz Interzonal 1958.
(B) 9...N-B3 10 P-QR3 B-R4 11 P-QN4 B-B2 12 P-N3 P-QN3 13 B-N2 PxP 14 QPxP R-QN1 15 R-QN1 0-0 16 0-0 (16 P-B4!?) 16...B-K4 17 KR-Q1 with a small plus in Korchnoi-Spassky, USSR Championship 1973.

| 10 | P-QR3 | BxN |
| 11 | NxB | B-Q2 |
| 12 | B-Q3 | P-R5 |

Here is the point of Black's ninth move. He lames White's queenside pawns, but at the cost of development tempi which White invests to inaugurate a kingside attack.

| 13 | 0-0 | 0-0 |
| 14 | P-B4 | |

According to Korchnoi White could also maintain a small plus by operating on the queenside, e.g. 14 QR-B1 P-QN3 15 N-N5 etc. The text is more violent and more creative.

| 14 . . . | | P-KN3 |
| 15 | K-R1 | N-B3 |
| 16 | B-B2 | N-K2 |

Black rushes one reserve to the defence of his threatened kingside.

| 17 | QR-K1 | P-N3 |
| 18 | R-B3 | |

White's whole game plan revolves around pushing through the

advance P-KB5, but if Black prevents this with the blockade move ...P-KB4 he will suffer from a weak king pawn and a restricted queen bishop hemmed in by its own pawns.

18 ...                    R-K1?

Black should have played 18... PxP 19 PxP P-B3! setting up a barrier around his king.

19 R(3)-K3!

A very fine and deep attacking conception, the point of which should be to force through P-KB5.

19 ...                    B-B3
20 PxP                    QxP

21 P-KN4

White could strike at once with the combinational blow 21 P-B5 with the following variations:

A) 21...NxP 22 BxN KPxB 23 NxQP! Q-Q1 24 RxR+ BxR 25 RxB+ QxR 26 N-B6+ and wins.
B) 21...NPxP 22 R-N3+ N-N3 23 P-R4 Q-Q1 24 P-R5 Q-R5+ 25 R-R3 Q-B5 26 R(1)-K3 winning.
C) 21... NPxP 22 R-N3+ N-N3 23 P-R4 Q-B2 24 N-K2! B-N4 25 N-B4 K-R1 (If 25...Q-Q1 26 N-R5 QxP+ 27 R-R3 Q-K2 28 Q-R6 P-B3 29 RxP! wins) 26 N-R5 Q-Q1 (Or 26...Q-R4 27 Q-N5! QxR+ 28 K-R2 when the threat of Q-B6+ wins for White, or 26...

R-KN1 27 Q-N5 Q-Q1 28 N-B6 with the lethal P-R5 coming.) 27 Q-R6 QxP+ 28 R-R3 QxR(K8)+ 29 K-R2 R-KN1 30 N-B6 R-N2 31 QxPch RxQ 32 RxR mate. The geometry of the two variations with the rook sacrifice on K1 is striking (Q-R4xR+ or Q-KR5x R+). However, Black has a big improvement after 26...P-B3! 27 RxN PxR 28 Q-R6+ Q-R2 29 QxQ+ KxQ 30 NxP+ K-N2 31 NxR+ RxN 32 R-K3 when White has only a slightly better ending.

21 ...                    Q-B2
22 P-B5

If 22 R-R3 Black can hold on by 22...Q-Q3! 23 P-B5 KPxP 24 Q-R6 Q-B3! but not, however, 22...K-N2 23 P-B5 N-N1 24 P-B6+ NxP 25 Q-R6+ K-N1 26 R-KB1 Q-K2 27 P-N5 N-R4 28 RxN PxR 29 QxP+ K-R1 30 Q-R8 mate.

22 ...                    KPxP
23 PxP                    Q-Q3
24 R-R3?

Optically impressive but it allows a draw. White can maintain the pressure with 24 R-K5! Q-B3 25 Q-R6 when he still has a strong attack. Another promising idea is 24 R-N3 with slow build up of pressure on the Black king.

24 ...                    NxP
25 BxN                    PxB
26 R-N1+                  K-R1
27 R-R6                   R-K3
28 RxR                    QxR!

Not 28...PxR 29 Q-N5 Q-B1 30 N-K2 followed by N-B4 with advantage to White in spite of his pawn minus, e.g. 30...P-K4 31 N-N3 PxP 32 NxP P-Q6 33 N-Q4! 

29 Q-N5                   Q-N3
30 Q-R4                   Q-K3

41

**Draw agreed**

White has nothing better than repetition of the position.

(Times: 2.33 − 2.17)

# GAME FOUR

## 25th July

While the Great Yoghurt Controversy was rumbling on, Karpov created a minor diversion by complaining that his chair was too low. A cushion was supplied but Karpov complained this made the chair too high and so a duplicate of the original chair, brought over from Manila, was specially modified to make it four centimetres higher. But Karpov rejected this too and finally plumped for the original chair with a smaller cushion. The Little Russian Bear was now satisfied.

In the fourth game Korchnoi varied from game 2 on move 14 and Karpov, although sitting comfortably, could gain absolutely no advantage, conceding a draw by repetition on move 19. Such a game is caviar to the general and some non-chess playing journalists were going berserk with frustration, dubbing Baguio "a land based ship of fools". There were fears that if it carried on raining we would not be land based much longer. Nevertheless, game 4 was of great theoretical importance, fitting in with Korchnoi's overall match strategy of nullifying Karpov's White openings, comparable to neutralising the serve in tennis.

White: Karpov
Black: Korchnoi

### Ruy Lopez

| | | | |
|---|---|---|---|
| 1 P-K4 | P-K4 |
| 2 N-KB3 | N-QB3 |
| 3 B-N5 | P-QR3 |
| 4 B-R4 | N-B3 |
| 5 0-0 | NxP |
| 6 P-Q4 | P-QN4 |
| 7 B-N3 | P-Q4 |
| 8 PxP | B-K3 |
| 9 P-B3 | B-QB4 |
| 10 QN-Q2 | 0-0 |
| 11 B-B2 | B-B4 |
| 12 N-N3 | B-KN5 |
| 13 NxB | NxN |
| 14 R-K1 | |

All so far as in the second game where Black played 14...P-Q5.

**14 . . .        B-R4**

A surprise as Korchnoi himself in Volume C of the *Encyclopedia of Chess Openings* published in 1974 claims this move to be a blunder losing to 15 B-N5 BxN (or 15... Q-Q2 16 B-K3 N-K3 17 BxP+!) 16 QxB QxB 17 QxQP (Bronstein-Flohr, USSR 1944). However, since then he had discovered that Black can equalise by 17...QR-K1! Karpov now thought for 40 minutes but was unable to find any way of obtaining the advantage.

**15 P-KR3        R-K1**

43

| 16 B-B4 | N-K3 |
|---------|------|
| 17 B-Q2 | N-B4 |
| 18 B-B4 | N-K3 |
| 19 B-Q2 | |

DIAGRAM

**Draw agreed**
(Times: 0.50 – 0.41)

# GAME FIVE

### 27th, 28th and 30th July

After the uneventful fourth game the audience were desperate for some real action and they were not disappointed. The fifth game proved to be one of the most dramatic ever played in a world championship match.

After Karpov had rashly tried to exploit his time trouble by playing a very loosening move, Korchnoi adjourned in an apparently won position. The following morning there was a small breakfast party to celebrate the second anniversary of Korchnoi's defection. The centrepiece was a birthday cake, supplied by the Pines Hotel, decorated with a knight, two candles and the words "Happy Birthday Viktor Korchnoi — Good Luck". Asked if he wanted any special present, Korchnoi answered "It's not difficult to guess".

But after the ball was over Korchnoi arrived at the battlefield to find that Karpov had sealed an unexpected cavalry manoeuvre. However, he kept his head while Karpov did his best to lose his. But alas, just when Napoleon should have met his Waterloo, the Duke of Wellington fell off his horse and the battle was again evenly poised. Further inaccuracies allowed Korchnoi to adjourn a second time in a favourable position, but this time no win could be found. Korchnoi nonetheless resumed the game and made Karpov demonstrate that he knew how to draw. Eventually Korchnoi was satisfied and delivered stalemate on move 124.

The game set two records. It was the longest ever world championship game, breaking the record previously held by the fourteenth game of the 1961 Tal-Botvinnik match, and the first ever to end in stalemate.

**White: Korchnoi**
**Black: Karpov**

### Nimzo-Indian Defence

| | |
|---|---|
| 1 P-QB4 | N-KB3 |
| 2 P-Q4 | P-K3 |
| 3 N-QB3 | B-N5 |
| 4 P-K3 | P-B4 |
| 5 N-K2 | P-Q4 |

Varying from 5...PxP with which he failed to equalise in the third game.

| | |
|---|---|
| 6 P-QR3 | BxN+ |
| 7 NxB | BPxP |
| 8 KPxP | PxP |
| 9 BxP | N-B3 |
| 10 B-K3 | 0-0 |
| 11 0-0 | P-QN3 |
| 12 Q-Q3 | |

More pointed is 12 Q-B3 B-N2 13 B-Q3 according to our analysis after the game. The text follows ancient precedent, but against Karpov's accurate defence it promises very little.

| | |
|---|---|
| 12 . . . | B-N2 |
| 13 QR-Q1 | P-KR3 |

Improving on Botvinnik-Tolush, USSR 1965, where Black played 13 . . . N-K2 which allowed 14 B-KN5.

**14 P-B3!**

A new move which prepares a highly original kingside pawn storm. The move was unexpected and, according to Korchnoi, Karpov now began to dislike the position although objectively Black stands quite well. Further points of 14 P-B3 are to blunt the power of Black's QB and to prepare a new avenue for White's own QB.

| | |
|---|---|
| 14 . . . | N-K2 |
| 15 B-B2 | N(B3)-Q4 |
| 16 B-R2 | N-B5 |
| 17 Q-Q2 | N(B5)-N3 |

The point of this artificial manoeuvre was to deprive White's QB of his KR4 square but White achieves this anyway by a thrust of his KRP.

| | |
|---|---|
| 18 B-N1 | Q-Q2 |
| 19 P-KR4 | KR-Q1 |
| 20 P-R5 | N-KB1 |
| 21 B-R4 | P-B3 |

Intended to limit the scope of White's bishop but now the weakness of Black's KP becomes significant.

| | |
|---|---|
| 22 N-K4 | N-Q4 |

DIAGRAM

**23 P-KN4**

Not everyone would have the courage to play such a move. There is an ever-present danger that White may become severely

overextended. Opinions were divided as to who stood better. Najdorf favoured White, Stean preferred Black, and l had no idea at all. A typically difficult 'Korchnoi position' has in fact now arisen. The press rooms were in the cellars beneath the auditorium, and much excitement was generated at the Byrne-Najdorf 'Experts Table'.

| | |
|---|---|
| 23 . . . | QR-B1 |
| 24 B-N3 | B-R3 |
| 25 KR-K1 | R-B3 |
| 26 R-QB1 | N-K2 |
| 27 RxR | QxR |

This looks careless. After 27... NxR 28 N-Q6 I believe the position is still in equilibrium. The move played loses tempi.

| | |
|---|---|
| 28 B-QR2 | Q-Q2 |
| 29 N-Q6 | B-N2 |

Now White gains the permanent advantage of the two bishops, but if Black challenges the knight by 29...N-B1? 30 RxP! NxR 31 Q-K3 is a winning sacrifice.

| | |
|---|---|
| 30 NxB | QxN |
| 31 Q-K3 | K-R1 |
| 32 R-QB1 | N-Q4 |
| 33 Q-K4 | Q-Q2 |
| 34 B-N1 | Q-N4 |
| 35 P-N4 | Q-Q2 |

A retreat, but if Black plays

incautiously 35...P-R4 36 B-Q6!
RxB 37 R-B8 K-N1 Q-R7+
etc. wins.

| 36 Q-Q3 | Q-K2 |
| 37 K-B2 | P-B4? |

Typical Karpov. With Korchnoi
in time trouble he plays 'va-
banque' instead of going for the
objectively best defence. It is of
course extra risky to break the
position open when White has the
two bishops.

| 38 PxP | PxP |
| 39 R-K1 | Q-B3 |
| 40 B-K5 | Q-R5+ |
| 41 B-N3 | Q-B3 |
| 42 R-R1 | |

We all thought this ingenious
move would win. Karpov now
spent nineteen minutes sealing.

| 42 ... | N-R2! |

A brilliant move which gives
Black tremendous counterchances,
in spite of the loss of a pawn.
Curiously, the whole defensive
concept behind Black's move was
entirely overlooked by grandmasters Byrne and Najdorf and, I
hate to admit, by Korchnoi's
whole group (including Korchnoi
himself) despite one whole night
of analysis. A case of mass hypno-
tism??? This was in fact the first
game where Zukhar was noticed

in the audience trying to stare
Korchnoi down.

| 43 B-K5 | Q-N4 |
| 44 QxP | Q-Q7+ |
| 45 K-N3 | N(2)-B3 |

The intention becomes clear.
The knights support each other,
and White faces extreme danger
from the devastation which
surrounds his own king. Korchnoi
played the next few moves superbly (without the aid of adjournment analysis) but he got into
raging time trouble finding them.

| 46 R-N1 | R-K1 |
| 47 B-K4! | |

It seems that this stroke escaped
the Soviet analysts, since Karpov
now spent fifty minutes on his
reply. White cannot play the
apparently logical 47 K-R3 in
view of 47...RxB followed by
...N-B5+ and White is crushed.

| 47 ... | N-K2 |
| 48 Q-R3 | R-QB1 |
| 49 K-R4 | |

A unique method of clearing the
KN-file, but Korchnoi, now on
top again, only had a couple of
minutes for seven moves. Faced
with this predicament Karpov
tried to solve his problems by
blitzing Korchnoi, but during the
blitz he himself played some
extremely weak moves.

| 49 ... | R-B8 |
| 50 Q-N3 | |

50 Q-N2, forcing exchanges, is
more clearcut.

| 50 ... | RxR |

If 50...Q-N4+ 51 QxQ PxQ+ 52
RxP R-R8+ 53 K-N3 R-N8+ 54
K-B4 N(3)-Q4+ 55 BxN NxB+
56 K-B5 N-K2+ 57 K-K6 RxR 58
KxN RxP 59 P-B4 followed by
P-Q5, P-Q6 etc. winning.

| 51 QxR | K-N1 |
|--------|------|

Beginning an insane king march.

| 52 Q-N3 | K-B2? |
|---------|-------|
| 53 B-N6+ | K-K3? |

The foolhardy king continues his march to the scaffold, but fortunately the hangman is asleep.

| 54 Q-R3+ | K-Q4 |
|----------|------|

**55 B-K4+??**

With only two moves to go to the time control Korchnoi throws his whole advantage away by one of the worst blunders in world championship history, ranking with Tchigorin's horrendous oversight in the last game of his second match with Steinitz. Of course, 55 B-B7+ followed by 56 Q-K6+ wins easily.

| 55 ... | NxB |
|--------|-----|
| 56 PxN+ | KxP |
| 57 Q-N4+ | K-Q6 |
| 58 Q-B3+ | |

The calm has descended after the storm. Korchnoi thought forty minutes over this move in a desperate attempt to find winning chances but to no real avail. He has a slight advantage due to the weakness of Black's pawn on KN2 but it is virtually certain that the 'wrong-coloured rook's pawn' will eventually play a decisive role.

| 58 ... | Q-K6 |
|--------|------|

| 59 K-N4 | QxQ+ |
|---------|------|
| 60 KxQ | P-N3? |

This makes Black's defensive task more difficult and gives Korchnoi new hope. 60..K-N4 draws easily. Perhaps Karpov couldn't believe he was still on the board and found it hard to concentrate.

| 61 B-Q6 | N-B4 |
|---------|------|
| 62 K-B4 | |

Karpov had apparently overlooked this move. If now 62... NxB 63 PxP N-K1 64 K-K5 followed by 65 P-Q5 and Black cannot prevent one of the two White passed pawns queening. Now he has to sacrifice his knight but the position is still just tenable.

| 62 ... | N-R5 |
|--------|------|
| 63 K-N4 | PxP+ |
| 64 KxN | KxP |
| 65 B-N8 | P-R4 |
| 66 B-Q6 | K-B5 |
| 67 KxP | P-R5 |
| 68 KxP | K-N6 |
| 69 P-N5 | K-B5 |
| 70 K-N5 | KxP |

As White's bishop does not control his RP's queening square his only chances of winning lie in either capturing both Black pawns while the Black king is too far away from the queening square or stalemating the black king temporarily and so forcing Black to play ...P-N5 when White's rook's pawn is converted to a winning knight's pawn. But Karpov defends perfectly and neither eventually occurrs.

| 71 K-B5 | K-R3 |
|---------|------|
| 72 K-K6 | K-R2 |
| 73 K-Q7 | K-N2 |
| 74 B-K7 | K-R2 |

| 75 | K-B7 | K-R1 |
|----|------|------|
| 76 | B-Q6 | K-R2 |
| 77 | K-B8 | K-R3 |
| 78 | K-N8 | P-N4 |
| 79 | B-N4 | K-N3 |
| 80 | K-B8 | K-B3 |
| 81 | K-Q8 | K-Q4 |
| 82 | K-K7 | K-K4 |
| 83 | K-B7 | K-Q4 |
| 84 | K-B6 | K-Q5 |
| 85 | K-K6 | K-K5 |
| 86 | B-B8 | K-Q5 |
| 87 | K-Q6 | K-K5 |
| 88 | B-N7 | K-B5 |
| 89 | K-K6 | K-B6 |
| 90 | K-K5 | K-N5 |
| 91 | B-B6 | K-R4 |

Here the game was adjourned a second time. Korchnoi has made no progress in the last twenty moves but now had a chance to consult reference books and analyse the position thoroughly. I telexed Bob Wade to consult his Library in London but no win was to be found. Our own ending books had been lost with Murei's luggage in Tel Aviv, but miraculously they arrived on the morning the game was to be resumed. Alas they merely confirmed the position was a draw.

| 92 | K-B5 | K-R3 |

| 93 | B-Q4 | K-R2 |
|----|------|------|
| 94 | K-B6 | K-R3 |
| 95 | B-K3+ | K-R4 |
| 96 | K-B5 | K-R5 |
| 97 | B-Q2 | K-N6 |
| 98 | B-N5 | K-B6 |
| 99 | B-B4 | K-N7 |

The only move! One typical way to lose is 99...K-B7 100 K-K4 K-K7 101 B-N8 K-B7 102 K-Q5 K-B6 103 K-B5 K-K5 104 KxP K-Q4 105 B-R2 K-K3 106 KxP K-Q2 107 K-N5 K-B1 108 K-B6 and Black's king is cut off. The existence of such pitfalls for Black show that Korchnoi's playing on so long in a theoretically drawn position was not just bloody-mindedness.

| 100 | B-Q6 | K-B6 |
|-----|------|------|
| 101 | B-R2 | K-N7 |
| 102 | B-B7 | K-B6 |
| 103 | B-Q6 | K-K6 |
| 104 | K-K5 | K-B6 |
| 105 | K-Q5 | K-N5 |
| 106 | K-B5 | K-B4 |
| 107 | KxP | K-K3 |
| 108 | K-B6 | K-B3 |
| 109 | K-Q7 | K-B2 |
| 110 | B-K7 | K-N1 |
| 111 | K-K6 | K-N2 |
| 112 | B-B5 | K-N1 |
| 113 | K-B6 | K-R2 |
| 114 | K-B7 | K-R1 |
| 115 | B-Q4+ | K-R2 |
| 116 | B-N2 | K-R3 |
| 117 | K-N8 | K-N3 |
| 118 | B-N7 | K-B4 |
| 119 | K-B7 | K-N4 |
| 120 | B-N2 | K-R3 |
| 121 | B-B1+ | K-R2 |
| 122 | B-Q2 | K-R1 |
| 123 | B-B3+ | K-R2 |
| 124 | B-N7 stalemate | |

(Times: 6-02 — 6.01 — a moral victory for Karpov?)

# GAME SIX

29th July

The sixth game was played in the interval between the second and third sessions of the fifth game. Many people were surprised that neither player exercised his right to postpone the game after their traumatic experiences in the previous encounter. No doubt each player would have been delighted if the other had chosen to postpone but neither wished to waste one of his ration of three postponements.

As it was the game cannot have taken much out of the players, as it was drawn in 23 moves. Korchnoi stood slightly better in the final position and in normal circumstances would probably have played on.

Karpov switched from 1 P-K4 to the English Opening, but again obtained no advantage with White. It was suggested that Karpov was deliberately soft pedalling with White in order to discover Korchnoi's main line defences and thus prepare more deeply for them at a later stage. If this policy was deliberate it certainly exposed him to a rough time with Black and at this stage in the match he was observed to be looking tired and haggard.

**White: Karpov**
**Black: Korchnoi**

### English Opening

| | |
|---|---|
| 1 P-QB4 | P-K4 |
| 2 N-QB3 | N-KB3 |
| 3 N-B3 | N-B3 |
| 4 P-KN3 | B-N5 |
| 5 B-N2 | 0-0 |
| 6 0-0 | P-K5 |
| 7 N-K1 | BxN |
| 8 QPxB | P-KR3 |
| 9 N-B2 | R-K1 |

So far we have been following the ninth game of the 1974 match. In that game Karpov was Black and play continued 9...P-QN3 10 B-K3 B-N2 11 N-Q5 N-K4. In the present game Korchnoi varies by developing his QB on KB4 and overprotecting his KP à la Nimzowitsch.

| | |
|---|---|
| 10 N-K3 | P-Q3 |
| 11 Q-B2 | P-QR4 |
| 12 P-QR4 | Q-K2 |
| 13 N-Q5 | |

If 13 P-B4 PxP e.p. 14 PxP Q-K4 15 B-Q2 Q-QB4 16 QR-K1 B-K3 17 P-N3 P-Q4 Black has some initiative as the White knight on K3 hinders the co-ordination of his pieces.

| | |
|---|---|
| 13 ... | NxN |
| 14 PxN | N-N1 |
| 15 B-K3 | B-B4 |
| 16 P-R3 | N-Q2 |

50

| 17 P-QB4 | P-QN3 |
| 18 Q-B3 | N-B4 |
| 19 P-N3 | Q-Q2 |
| 20 K-R2 | R-K2 |
| 21 B-Q4 | P-KB3 |
| 22 QR-B1 | Q-K1 |
| 23 Q-K3 | |

### DIAGRAM

**Draw agreed**

Black stands better and should have declined the draw, e.g. 23...
Q-R4 24 R-B3 B-N5 25 R-K1 QR-K1 with the threat of 26... N-Q6 27 PxN PxP 28 QxR RxQ 29 RxR P-Q7 winning. (Times: 1.25 − 1.05)

# GAME SEVEN

## 1st and 2nd August

The seventh game provided high drama, but still no result. Korchnoi played the first half of the game superbly. He produced an opening innovation as early as move six and Karpov was soon forced to sacrifice the exchange for inadequate compensation. But the position remained very complex and gradually Korchnoi ran short of time. His position steadily deteriorated and when the game was adjourned he was faced by two connected passed pawns on the sixth rank which seemed certain to decide the game after a few spite checks. Nobody at that stage doubted that Karpov was about to register the first win and Baturinsky triumphantly heralded the victory on Philippino television that evening.

We started analysing the adjourned position in a state of deep depression but it gradually became clear that Korchnoi could fight on. The key defensive resource was found by Murei, appropriately enough on his thirty-eighth birthday. When we finally abandoned analysis at 7 a.m. we had still not solved the position. We had found neither a clear win for Karpov nor a clear draw for Korchnoi. To our astonishment Karpov came to the board next day and offered a draw, which was of course accepted. As the players were seen signing the score sheets most of the spectators assumed Korchnoi had resigned and pandemonium broke loose when it was announced that the game was drawn. "They'll never believe me in Argentina" lamented Najdorf.

Asian Junior Champion, Murray Chandler, articulated the question in everyone's mind for New Zealand radio:

"Why was Karpov so sure that Korchnoi had found the crucial saving continuation? Why did he not even probe to find out just how much Korchnoi knew? Personally I think Karpov was just plain gutless. He could have played on and forced Korchnoi to prove he had found a saving variation. Karpov would not have risked anything."

Is it too devious to suggest that, having decided the position was drawn and that Korchnoi would almost certainly find the correct defence, Karpov was trying to mock Korchnoi's action in playing on so long in the drawn ending in the fifth game?

The seventh game incidentally set a new record for the number of draws at the start of a world championship match, depriving the 1966 Petrosian vs. Spassky encounter of that dubious honour. Wags were predicting that the match would last till Christmas — 1979. More seriously there was speculation that the World Team Championship, scheduled to begin in mid-October, would be postponed.

**White: Korchnoi**
**Black: Karpov**

**Nimzo-Indian Defence**

| 1 P-Q4 | N-KB3 |
|---|---|
| 2 P-QB4 | P-K3 |
| 3 N-QB3 | B-N5 |
| 4 P-K3 | 0-0 |

Karpov varies from 4...P-B4 with which he got into hot water in the third and fifth games, but Korchnoi still has something up his sleeve.

| 5 B-Q3 | P-B4 |
|---|---|
| 6 P-Q5 | |

An entirely new move suggested by Murei. The idea is either to reach a Benoni-like structure after 6...PxP 7 PxP P-Q3 or else after 6...P-QN4, which Karpov actually plays, to achieve the sort of position in which Karpov does not feel at home. If Black tries 6...PxP 7 PxP NxP 8 BxP+ KxB 9 QxN White has some advantage, due to his central grip and the exposed Black king, for which the bishop pair offers insufficient compensation.

| 6 ... | P-QN4 |
|---|---|

After twenty minutes thought Karpov accepts the challenge and plays the most active move. This must have been a difficult decision as he never feels particularly comfortable when he has to offer a gambit.

| 7 PxKP | BPxP |
|---|---|
| 8 PxP | B-N2 |
| 9 N-B3 | P-Q4 |
| 10 0-0 | QN-Q2 |
| 11 N-K2 | Q-K1 |

Black certainly has counterplay for his pawn in the shape of a powerful centre, but this move looks too artificial and supports the view that Karpov is not a gambit master.

| 12 N-N3 | P-K4 |
|---|---|
| 13 B-B5 | P-N3 |
| 14 B-R3 | P-QR3 |

If Black tries to prevent White's next move by 14...P-KR3, 15 P-K4 smashes the position open to White's advantage.

**15 N-N5!**

A very good move which wins the exchange. Although the position is tense, and indeed one of the most original ever to occur in the opening of a World Championship game, there was a general feeling in the press room that White was now on top. Another idea for White is 15 PxP BxP 16 BxN QxB 17 NxP but it looks too risky.

| 15 ... | PxP |
|---|---|
| 16 N-K6 | P-B5 |
| 17 B-Q2 | B-B4 |

| | |
|---|---|
| 18 N-B7 | Q-K2 |
| 19 NxR | RxN |
| 20 P-R3 | N-N3 |
| 21 Q-B2 | B-B1 |
| 22 BxB | RxB |
| 23 B-R5 | |

Also good is the pawn sacrifice 23 B-N4 BxB 24 PxB QxP 25 R-R7 opening lines for the rooks. Korchnoi is one of the greatest exponents in exploiting the advantage of the exchange, but from now on he begins to contradict this image.

| | |
|---|---|
| 23 . . . | QN-Q2 |
| 24 Q-Q2 | B-Q3 |
| 25 B-N4 | N-B4 |
| 26 BxN | BxB |
| 27 K-R1 | Q-Q3 |
| 28 QR-Q1 | |

I prefer 28 P-B4 trying to blast open lines at once.

| | |
|---|---|
| 28 . . . | K-R1 |

**29 Q-B2**

Korchnoi was now losing the thread of the game and drifting into time trouble and so Black begins to get superb compensation. Correct was 29 P-K4 P-Q5 30 Q-N5 N-Q2 31 P-B4 PxP 32 N-K2 followed by NxBP. and N-Q5 when White should win.

| | |
|---|---|
| 29 . . . | Q-K3 |
| 30 N-K2 | Q-B3 |

| | |
|---|---|
| 31 P-R3 | R-K1 |
| 32 P-QN4?? | |

Every schoolboy knows you can't play moves like that. Now Black obtains two lusty passed pawns.

| | |
|---|---|
| 32 . . . | B-N3 |
| 33 Q-N2 | K-N1 |
| 34 KR-K1 | K-B2 |
| 35 Q-B2? | |

Another lemon which eases the advance of Black's passed pawns.

| | |
|---|---|
| 35 ... | P-Q5 |
| 36 N-N3 | R-Q1 |
| 37 PxP | PxP |
| 38 Q-Q2 | P-Q6 |

38...R-Q2 looks safer but the text is good enough.

**39 Q-R6**

A desperate attempt to obtain counterplay which is remarkably successful.

| | |
|---|---|
| 39 . . . | P-B6 |
| 40 N-K4 | NxN? |

Karpov was now also in time trouble and throws away the win with the last move before the time control. 40...K-N1 leaves White with no counter to the expansion of the passed pawns.

| | |
|---|---|
| 41 QxRP+ | K-B1 |

The famous adjourned position.

**42 Q-R8+**

The sealed move after which a

draw was **agreed**. Here now is a summary of the analysis which led us to the unexpected conclusion that Black has no clear win:

A) 42 Q-R8+ K-B2 43 Q-R7+ K-B3 44 Q-R4+ K-N2 (or 44... N-N4 45 P-B4 followed by PxN+) 45 RxN R-K1 46 RxR QxR 47 RxP Q-K8+ (or 47...P-B7 48 Q-KB4 Q-K8+ 49 K-R2 P-B8=Q 50 R-Q7+) 48 K-R2 B-B2+ 49 P-N3 QxP+ with a draw since White has the threat of R-Q7+ and if Black takes the rook there is perpetual check.

B) 42 Q-R8+ K-B2 43 Q-R7+ K-K1 44 Q-N8+ K-Q2 45 RxP+ K-B1 46 RxR+ BxR 47 K-N1! This is Murei's miracle ingredient. Black now has trouble co-ordinating his pieces and the position can become double edged, which is probably what frightened Karpov off, e.g.:

B1) 47...K-Q2 48 P-QR4 PxP 49 P-N5 QxP 50 QxP (Not 50 RxN? Q-N8+) 50...N-Q3 51 Q-N7+ and QxP.

B2) 47...P-N4 48 P-QR4 N-B3 (48...PxP? 49 P-N5) 49 PxP NxQ (49...QxKNP+ only liberates White's king) 50 PxQ N-K2 51 R-R5 N-N3 52 R-K2. White then puts his rook on QB2 and leaves it there, even allowing ...NxR KxN with a draw.

B3) 47...N-Q7 (If 47...P-B7 48 R-QB1 plus Q-N3 or Q-R2) 48 R-QB1 Q-B5 (Or 48...P-N4 49 P-KR4 PxP 50 Q-N4+ K-N1 51 Q-N8 etc.) 49 QxP N-K5 (or 49... N-N6 50 Q-B5+ and another check will win the pawn on Black's QB6.) 50 R-B2 Q-Q6 51 RxPch QxR 52 QxN and Black's extra piece cannot win. But if Black wishes to play for a win he can try 50...Q-Q4 when the position remains obscure, but Black cannot stand worse.

(Times: 2.32 − 2.40)

# GAME EIGHT

### 3rd August

It is well known that Korchnoi plays less well when he is angry and before the eighth game the Soviets pulled off a master stroke which made him see red. Without warning Karpov coyly refused the customary handshake at the beginning of the game and Korchnoi was left with his hand suspended pointlessly in mid-air.

Simultaneously, in the press centre beneath the playing hall, the Soviet press chief Roshal issued a rather vague statement justifying Karpov's action: "Recent events have shown that the challenger has not given up his line of intensification of the tension of the situation .... Under such circumstances Mr. Karpov does not wish to shake hands with Mr. Korchnoi."

This immoral, but astute, action by the Russians appeared to throw Korchnoi off balance. Mistaking, according to one commentator, the playing hall for a casino, he played an absurdly risky innovation which formed no part of our prepared analysis. Karpov refuted this with crisp efficiency and finished off with some nice fireworks. After seven indecisive games the business of winning suddenly looked so easy!

After the game Korchnoi relieved his feelings a little by refusing to sign the scoresheet but the following morning he relented and signed.

I stumbled into a hornet's nest by remarking that Karpov's refusal to shake hands would at least save Korchnoi having to go and wash his hands. This provoked the sharp rebuke from Baturinsky that, by associating with the likes of Korchnoi and Ms. Leeuwerik, I had lost "the traits characterising an English gentleman" (whatever they may be). Suitably contrite I withdrew my offending comment and sent Baturinsky a cigar of peace but this was returned (unsmoked!) together with a cake of soap autographed by the great man himself. I haven't had the heart to use it, and it now forms one of my favourite souvenirs of this soap opera.

After the game Karpov celebrated his victory with the laconic comment "At last!". The following day the Terraces Plaza Hotel threw a party for him and, not to be outdone by Korchnoi's earlier 'birthday party' at the Pines Hotel, they provided a cake with one candle on it. I was not invited and unfortunately missed the sight of a beaming Baturinsky dancing in traditional Ifugao garb.

Karpov now led 1-0 with 7 draws.

**White: Karpov**
**Black: Korchnoi**

### Ruy Lopez

| | |
|---|---|
| 1 P-K4 | P-K4 |
| 2 N-KB3 | N-QB3 |
| 3 B-N5 | P-QR3 |
| 4 B-R4 | N-B3 |
| 5 0-0 | NxP |
| 6 P-Q4 | P-QN4 |
| 7 B-N3 | P-Q4 |
| 8 PxP | B-K3 |
| 9 QN-Q2 | |

Varying from 9 P-B3 which was played in the second and fourth games.

| | |
|---|---|
| 9 . . . | N-B4 |
| 10 P-B3 | P-N3 |

A new provocative and weak move. This unwise innovation was improvised by Korchnoi at the board and formed no part of our preparation. The move is partly motivated by our theory that Karpov does not like to gambit pawns, but the gambit which the text allows is more murderous than speculative.

Despite the weakness of Black's move, Karpov must have been disappointed to be denied the chance to play his innovation 11 N-N5! after the standard move 10...P-Q5. But he was to get his opportunity in his next game with White.

| | |
|---|---|
| 11 Q-K2 | B-N2 |
| 12 N-Q4 | |

#### DIAGRAM

| | |
|---|---|
| 12 . . . | NxP? |

Consistent but suicidal. Black duly wins a pawn but at the cost of allowing his kingside to be smashed and losing the right to castle — far too high a price.

| | |
|---|---|
| 13 P-B4 | N-B5 |

13...N(K4)-Q6 is a small improvement but it is also not very promising, e.g. 14 P-B5 NxB 15 QRxN PxP 16 NxBP 0-0 17 B-B2 with a fierce attack in prospect.

| | |
|---|---|
| 14 P-B5 | PxP |
| 15 NxP | R-KN1 |

Making the best of a bad job. In some lines Black sneaks some counterplay on the KN file.

**16 NxN**

A simple solution, quite in Karpov's style, but 16 B-B2 is probably more deadly.

| | |
|---|---|
| 16 . . . | QPxN |

Korchnoi thought for thirty-five minutes over this move, which showed that something had gone wrong. 16...NPxN was also bad, e.g. 17 B-B2 K-Q2 18 NxB RxN 19 Q-K5 Q-KN1 20 R-B2 P-B3 21 QxKBP R-B2 22 Q-Q4 RxR 23 QxN R-KB1 24 QxN B-R6 25 B-K4 PxB 26 B-N5 and wins. This is only a sample variation but it illustrates the unhappy plight of Black's exposed king.

If instead 16...NxB 17 RPxN PxN 18 PxP PxP 19 B-R6 and Black will be mown down in the centre.

**17 B-B2**

Best. If 17 NxB+ RxN 18 Q-K5, forking two pieces, 18...RxP+ 19 KxR Q-Q4+ 20 QxQ BxQ+ followed by ...PxB gives Black counterplay.

**17 . . .          N-Q6?**

By now it is just a question of choosing the lesser evil, which would have been 17...Q-Q4 18 B-R6 BxB 19 NxB R-KB1.

**18 B-R6!**

Korchnoi freely admitted he had overlooked this move.

**18 . . .          B-B1?**

Two better chances were 18...B-R1 or 18...BxB 19 NxB R-N3 20 NxP Q-K2, though both are fairly forlorn.

| **19 QR-Q1** | **Q-Q4** |
| **20 BxN** | **PxB** |
| **21 RxP** | **Q-B3** |

The original idea was 21...B-B4+ 22 K-R1 RxP 23 QxR QxR

24 QxR+ K-Q2 and Black wins. But now Korchnoi saw that instead 23 RxQ RxQ 24 RxB wins for White.

**22 BxB          Q-N3+**

If 22...KxB 23 N-Q4 wins a piece.

| **23 K-R1** | **KxB** |
| **24 Q-B3** | |

The position now looks like a Muzio King's Gambit where White has not had to sacrifice a piece.

| **24 . . .** | **R-K1** |
| **25 N-R6** | **R-N2** |
| **26 R-Q7!** | |

Simple but pleasing. 26...BxR allows 27 QxP+ RxQ 28 RxR mate. The threat is now 27 RxP+ and there is no satisfactory defence.

| **26 . . .** | **R-QN1** |
| **27 NxP** | **BxR** |
| **28 N-Q8+** | **Black resigned** |

(Times 1.58 — 2.25)

# GAME NINE

## 5th August

The spotlight now falls on Dr. Vladimir Zukhar, a noted hypnotist (parapsychologist, necromancer or what you will) who was suspected by Korchnoi of trying to hypnotise him by sitting at the front of the audience and rivetting his gaze onto Korchnoi throughout the games.

He was first recognised by Ms. Leeuwerik during the fifth game. Ever resourceful, she frightened him away by sitting down beside him and offering him a copy of the *Gulag Archipelago*, but he later reappeared on a more distant tuffet and the dispute which was to take over the headlines from the Great Yoghurt Controversy was under way.

As Korchnoi was clearly being disturbed by Zukhar I wrote to Campomanes before the eighth game setting out our objections and asking that Zukhar be seated with the rest of the Soviet delegation at the back of the playing hall. The matter was considered by the jury which resolved that if the Chief Arbiter Schmid considered that Korchnoi was being disturbed he should exercise his powers under match regulation 4.56 which states: "The arbiter shall not permit the players to be unnecessarily disturbed." The dispute lay dormant during the eighth game, when it was overshadowed by the handshaking issue, but at the beginning of the ninth game Ms. Leeuwerik asked Schmid to exercise his powers to have Zukhar removed. Schmid asked Zukhar to join the rest of the Soviet delegation at the back of the hall, but in the end he merely moved from the fifth to the seventh row.

After this coup Ms. Leeuwerik announced proudly "Viktor does not know anything about this because he did not notice him." Later, on her own initiative, she tried to get play moved to a closed room, but Korchnoi was not at that time disturbed by Zukhar and he did not want to move. Ms. Leeuwerik commented angrily and illogically, "Viktor has gone crazy. He doesn't know he is being disturbed." She was obviously unaware of the undertones of self-satire in her remarks.

The ninth game itself followed the pattern which had become all too familiar. Korchnoi obtained the better position as White and converted this to a winning advantage but ran short of time and allowed Karpov to escape with a draw.

So far Korchnoi had obtained won positions in four games, the third (probably), fifth, seventh and ninth, whereas Karpov had only obtained two won positions, in the seventh and eighth games. Yet it was Karpov who was leading the match by one game. On the basis of this contradictory evidence opinions were divided as to who was favourite to win the match. Karpov supporters claimed that Korchnoi was likely to run out of steam and that if Korchnoi was already one down before Karpov had played himself into form there could be little hope for him when Karpov really got going. Korchnoi supporters retorted that Karpov was in fact playing to his normal standard and Korchnoi's dynamism was exposing his weaknesses more efficiently than his other recent opponents have been able to achieve. If Korchnoi continued to obtain won positions with such ease he was bound to start winning them eventually. Events in the next few games were to lend suppport to both these views.

Karpov now led 1-0 with 8 draws.

**White: Korchnoi**
**Black: Karpov**

### Queen's Gambit Declined

| | |
|---|---|
| 1 P-QB4 | N-KB3 |
| 2 N-QB3 | P-K3 |
| 3 N-B3 | P-Q4 |
| 4 P-Q4 | B-K2 |
| 5 B-B4 | 0-0 |
| 6 P-K3 | P-B4 |
| 7 QPxP | BxP |
| 8 Q-B2 | N-B3 |
| 9 R-Q1 | Q-R4 |
| 10 P-QR3 | B-K2 |
| 11 N-Q2 | P-K4 |
| 12 B-N5 | P-Q5 |
| 13 N-N3 | Q-Q1 |
| 14 B-K2 | |

14 . . .        P-KR3?
Better was 14...N-KN5 as played

in Portisch-Spassky, Havanna 1966.

| | |
|---|---|
| 15 BxN | BxB |
| 16 0-0 | B-K3 |
| 17 N-B5 | Q-K2 |
| 18 NxB | QxN |
| 19 N-Q5 | QR-Q1 |
| 20 B-Q3? | |

This allows Black to equalise. Correct was 20 P-K4 N-K2 21 B-B3 NxN 22 KPxN followed by P-B5 with a clear advantage since White's passed pawns are the more dangerous. If Black does not swap knights White's mobile pawns (P-QN4/P-B5/B-B4 etc.) are worth more than Black's blockaded passed pawn.

| | |
|---|---|
| 20 . . . | N-K2 |
| 21 NxB+ | QxN |
| 22 PxP | PxP |
| 23 KR-K1 | R-Q2? |

A mistake which allows White to secure the only open file. 23... N-N3!, planning to exchange this knight for White's bishop, would have maintained equality.

| | |
|---|---|
| 24 R-K4 | N-B3 |
| 25 Q-K2 | P-KN3 |
| 26 R-K1 | K-N2 |
| 27 P-QN4 | P-N3 |
| 28 Q-N4! | |

Korchnoi cleverly translates his central grip into a kingside attack. But now he only had twenty-five minutes for his next twelve moves.

| 28 ... | KR-Q1 |
| 29 P-KR4 | P-KR4 |
| 30 Q-N3 | |

30 Q-N5 keeps Black sewn up positionally but the text is more aggressive.

| 30 ... | Q-Q3 |
| 31 P-B4 | |

Threatening a devastating sacrifice with R-K6!

| 31 ... | R-K2 |
| 32 RxR | NxR |
| 33 R-K5 | P-R4! |

A good practical decision. When in extreme danger Karpov usually manages to complicate matters and exploit Korchnoi's time-trouble.

**34 RxKRP**

After the game Korchnoi claimed that 34 PxP PxP 35 RxQRP would win, but the text is also excellent.

| 34 ... | PxP |
| 35 PxP | QxNP |

### DIAGRAM

**36 R-QN5**

A time-trouble reaction, after which Karpov crawls out unscathed. Logical is 36 R-K5!

which recentralises the rook, creates threats of P-B5 and P-R5 and defends White's own hinterland. I believe this wins, e.g. 36 R-K5 N-B3 37 R-K2 Q-B6 38 P-B5 N-N5 39 Q-K5+ K-N1 40 PxP QxB 41 PxP+.

| 96 ... | Q-Q7 |
| 37 K-R2 | Q-K6 |
| 38 RxP | R-QR1 |
| 39 QxQ | |

39 P-B5 retained some winning chances.

| 39 ... | PxQ |
| 40 R-N2 | R-R6 |
| 41 B-K4 | R-B6 |

The sealed move. The game was **agreed drawn** without resumption. At first Korchnoi feigned horror at Karpov's temerity in offering a draw a pawn down but he was soon persuaded to accept the inevitable.

(Times: 2.37 — 2.26)

# GAME TEN

## 8th August

While the game of musical chairs was still in progress during the ninth game, the Russians distributed their formal reply to my letter on Zukhar in which they denied the hypnosis charges. The day after the ninth game they went on to the offensive and issued a formal protest against Schmid's action regarding Zukhar during the ninth game. The protest was signed by Karpov himself and contained the significant words "It is with regret that I must note that these as well as some other actions on the part of the Chief Arbiter generate doubts as to his objectiveness and impartiality." So the jury met again and after a six (sic!) hour meeting decided that, although he had acted in good faith, Schmid had misinterpreted his powers and that he was not authorised to adjudicate on subjective or mental disturbances — merely on objective or physical ones. This legal nicety would no doubt have delighted A.P. Herbert but it must have seemed to Schmid like a straight reversal of the earlier decision. The official minute of the meeting carefully omits to say what should be done about Zukhar in future! Rumour has it that a gentleman's agreement was reached that Zukhar should not be required to join the rest of the Soviet delegation, but should move back from the fifth to the seventh row. But nobody seems quite sure about this and, not being a gentleman myself, I must confess myself unable to throw light on the matter!

After the meeting Ms. Leeuwerik continued to win over more friends by issuing a statement on behalf of Korchnoi accusing the jury, organisers and president of being pro-Soviet. An extract from this interesting example of international diplomacy will give an indication of its general tone: "Viktor Korchnoi has requested me to say that from now on, until the end of the match, he will be animated by a special feeling when playing the games — he will hear, resounding in the pockets of his adversary, the clank of the chains that fetter his family in the prison camp that is the Soviet Union."

She finished off a busy day by submitting a protest withdrawing her consent to sit in pre-arranged places in the auditorium, demanding that the Russians be searched on entry and insisting that all further draws be offered through the arbiter.

Fortunately the tenth game was sufficiently interesting to divert some attention from the disputes front. It was a close shave for Korchnoi thanks to a startling innovation which apparently emanated from Tal. Korchnoi described Karpov's eleventh move as the kind you find once in a century, and even Golombek was bold enough to declare "It is not a move you see readily. It can easily be overlooked." But Karpov then committed the classic error of attempting to blitz his opponent. Korchnoi gradually outplayed Karpov from a worse ending and gained the upper hand himself. However, Karpov snatched a draw at the end of the session as Korchnoi's time was running out. It was basically an unimpressive game by Karpov who wrongly sacrificed accuracy and artistry for purely practical considerations such as playing quickly.

Karpov now led 1-0 with 9 draws.

**White: Karpov**
**Black: Korchnoi**

### Ruy Lopez

| | |
|---|---|
| 1 P-K4 | P-K4 |
| 2 N-KB3 | N-QB3 |
| 3 B-N5 | P QR3 |
| 4 B-R4 | N-B3 |
| 5 0-0 | NxP |
| 6 P-Q4 | P-QN4 |
| 7 B-N3 | P-Q4 |
| 8 PxP | B-K3 |
| 9 QN-Q2 | N-B4 |
| 10 P-B3 | P-Q5 |

Consigning 10...P-N3, played in the eighth game, to the scrap heap where it so deservedly belongs. Korchnoi's excuse for that insane move was that he feared Karpov had a theoretical bombshell prepared and in this game it exploded.

**11 N-N5!**

As soon as this was played the Soviet delegation exchanged knowing winks and made a move for the bar. Korchnoi was left on the burning deck to work out whether the move was brilliance or bluff. Understandably, after 13 minutes thought, he decided to decline the Russian gift. It remains a open question whether the sacrifice is objectively correct since, perhaps significantly, Karpov did not repeat this variation later in the match.

Here is a selection from the myriad of variations to which the sacrifice could give rise:

A) 11...QxN 12 Q-B3 B-Q2 13 BxPch K-K2! 14 B-Q5 NxKP 15 R-K1 K-Q1 16 RxN QxR 17 BxR B-Q3 18 N-B1 PxP 19 PxP R-B1 with some advantage to Black. But White can improve by 15 Q-K2 with horrible threats, e.g. 15...B-N5 16 N-B3 or 15...P-Q6 16 Q-K1.

B) 11...QxN 12 Q-B3 K-Q2? 13 B-Q5.

C) 11...NxB 12 NxB PxN 13 PxN is rather uncomfortable for Black as he has trouble completing his development.

D) 11...B-Q4 12 NxBP KxN 13

Q-B3ch K-K3 14 Q-N4ch K-K2
(If 14...K-B2 15 Q-B5ch and
P-K6) 15 N-B3 N-K3 16 B-N5
NxB 17 NxN BxB 18 PxB Q-Q4
19 P-QB4 PxP 20 PxP QxBP 21
QR-B1 Q-Q4 22 R-B5 NxP 23
R-K1 QxR 24 Q-K6ch K-Q1 25
N-B7ch NxN 26 Q-K8 mate. A
beautiful variation.

**11 . . .**         **PxP**

Safety first, but Black now has a
difficult defensive task ahead.

**12 NxB**         **KBPxN**
**13 PxP**         **Q-Q6**

Korchnoi tries to exchange
queens as he does not fear Karpov
in the ending.

**14 N-B3?**

This eases Black's problem
slightly. 14 P-QB4 was best.

**14 . . .**         **QxQ**
**15 BxQ**

Of course Karpov wants to keep
the two bishops, but 15 RxQ NxB
16 PxN is more painful for Black
who cannot connect his rooks.
From now on Karpov is steadily
outplayed.

**15 . . .**         **B-K2**

Black does not castle since he
wants to keep his king near the
weakened KP which is in need of
constant protection.

**16 B-K3**

Better is 16 P-QR4 P-N5 17
B-K3 PxP 18 R-B1 in order to
break up the position for his
bishops.

**16 . . .**         **N-Q6**

Korchnoi now counter-attacks by
exploiting the weakness of White's
KP.

| 17 B-N3 | K-B2 |
| 18 QR-Q1 | N(6)xKP |
| 19 NxN | NxN |
| 20 B-KB4 | N-B5 |

**21 BxN?**

Now White's advantage vanishes.
21 R-Q7 was the last chance.

**21 . . .**         **PxB**
**22 R-Q4**         **B-Q3**
**23 B-K3**

K3 was an unlucky square for
Karpov in this game. The text
hands over the initiative to Black
whereas 23 BxB would have
drawn comfortably.

| 23 . . . | KR-QN1 |
| 24 RxP | R-N7 |
| 25 P-QR4 | R-R7 |
| 26 P-N3 | R-QN1 |
| 27 R-Q1 | R(1)-N7 |
| 28 R(1)-Q4 | R-N8+ |
| 29 K-N2 | R(8)-R8 |
| 30 R-R4 | P-R3 |
| 31 B-B5 | P-K4 |
| 32 B-R7 | K-K3 |
| 33 R(B4)-KN4? | |

White's rooks are placed more
clumsily than Black's in any case,
but this crude attempt to blitz
Korchnoi gets Karpov into hot
water. His rook is driven to the
pathetically stupid square KR5.

**33 . . .**         **B-K2!**

Did Karpov overlook this?

**34 R-R5**         **B-B3**

34...B-N4 35 P-R4 P-N3 is too
dangerous. So too is 34...N-N4 35
P-R4 K-B4 36 PxB KxR 37 PxP!
PxP 38 RxKP with too much
compensation for the exchange.

**35 R-QB4**

DIAGRAM

**35 . . .**         **K-Q2?**

35...RxP 36 RxP R-QB8 gives
Black winning chances. In
desperate time trouble Korchnoi
heads for a draw.

| 36 B-N8 | P-B3 |
| 37 R-K4 | RxRP |
| 38 P-QB4 | R-R4 |

| | |
|---|---|
| 39 BxP | BxB |
| 40 R(R5)xB | RxR |
| 41 RxR | R-R5 |
| 42 R-K4 | R-R4 |
| 43 P-R4 | P-R4 |
| 44 R-B4 | |

**Draw agreed**

(Times: 1.39 − 2.51)

# GAME ELEVEN

## 10th August

The number of protests was now increasing exponentially and rival press conferences were littering all the public buildings.

The Russians issued a reply to Ms. Leeuwerik's inflammatory statement of 8th August. It was entitled "Chess Match in The Philippines Is Not A Training Ground For The Cold War" and contained attacks on Korchnoi, myself and especially Ms. Leeuwerik:

"This woman, who never had anything to do with chess and the international chess movement, who openly declares of her spiteful hatred to the USSR, is trying to convert the distinguished sporting competition, that the World Chess Championship Match is, into the training ground of the Cold War and impede the consolidation of friendship and cultural co-operation, to which admittedly serve chess, between countries."

Even the Chairman of the Jury, Professor Lim Kok Ann joined in the fun, defending himself against Ms. Leeuwerik's accusations of bias and concluding with the words "The Lady doth protest too much, methinks."

Murray Chandler and I diverted ourselves by composing a do-it-yourself protest kit which we were proposing to patent under the brand name 'Gens Una Sumus' the motto of FIDE. In our advertising literature we claimed: "Tests with dummy heads of delegations have proved scientifically that up to 600 protests every 24 hours can be served indiscriminately on match organisers, jury chairmen and chief arbiters."

There was one note of genuine reconciliation. Karpov's accusation of bias against Schmid had not been retracted despite the jury's exoneration of the Chief Arbiter. Schmid was offended and during the tenth game he had a diplomatic illness and his deputy Filip took over. But before the eleventh game he had discussions with Karpov and they issued a joint statement reporting that Karpov now recognised Schmid's impartiality.

In the eleventh game Korchnoi's psychological decision to employ a non-classical opening led to brilliant success. Karpov moved very quickly throughout the whole game, as Golombek put it "... so that he would have plenty of time to regret his errors." The World Champion's middle-game play was extraordinarily pusillanimous and he seemed unable to form a plan. On move 26 he blundered and the rest of the game was a formality. In a way it was a pity that Korchnoi's win should come from this rather easy game instead of one of his more heavyweight creative achievements in earlier games with White.

After the game Korchnoi's group plus Colonel Ed Edmondson and Murray Chandler celebrated at the Pines Hotel with caviar and champagne. Houdini had at last been trapped.

The score was now 1-1 with 9 draws.

**White: Korchnoi**
**Black: Karpov**

### Sicilian Defence

| | |
|---|---|
| 1 P-KN3 | P-QB4 |
| 2 B-N2 | N-QB3 |
| 3 P-K4 | P-KN3 |
| 4 P-Q3 | B-N2 |
| 5 P-B4 | |

We have now reached by transposition a Closed Sicilian Defence, a very unusual opening for a world championship match reminiscent of some Spassky games from 1965 and 1966 in matches against Geller, Larsen and Petrosian.

| | |
|---|---|
| 5 ... | P-Q3 |
| 6 N-KB3 | N-B3 |
| 7 0-0 | 0-0 |
| 8 P-B3 | R-N1 |
| 9 Q-K2 | |

A new plan simply intending to grasp the centre with his pawns. 9 P-KR3 or 9 K-R1 would have been more conventional.

| | |
|---|---|
| 9 ... | N-K1 |

Korchnoi favoured 9...P-QN4 10 P-K5 N-Q4 and he even thought Black might then be slightly better.

| | |
|---|---|
| 10 B-K3 | N-B2 |
| 11 P-Q4 | PxP |
| 12 PxP | B-N5 |
| 13 R-Q1 | P-Q4 |

Black now becomes cramped and his KB is imprisoned, but if 13...N-K3 14 Q-KB2 Q-N3 15 P-Q5 QxP 16 QN-Q2 wins.

| | |
|---|---|
| 14 P-K5 | Q-Q2 |

| | |
|---|---|
| 15 N-B3 | KR-QB1 |

Better was 15...B-R6 16 B-R1 when Korchnoi planned KR-QB1 followed by N-Q1-B2 to embarrass the far-flung prelate. But after the text Korchnoi seizes the bishop pair, and makes better use of it than Karpov in the previous game.

| | |
|---|---|
| 16 Q-B1 | |

A fine move to break the pin.

| | |
|---|---|
| 16 ... | P-QN4 |
| 17 P-KR3 | BxN |

**18 BxB**

A matter of taste. It was possible to attack on the kingside with 18 QxB P-K3 19 P-KN4 plus N-K2-N3 etc., but Korchnoi observes a subtle possibility to counterattack on the queenside, which appears to be Black's domain.

Although his pieces appear to be eccentrically placed, they soon start to exhibit a kind of mystical co-operation.

| | |
|---|---|
| 18 ... | P-N5? |

Black should have played 18...P-K3 with equal chances. Karpov

67

probably overlooked the zwischenzug 19 B-N4 which avoids the
variation 18...P-N5 19 N-R4
NxQP 20 N-B5 NxB with check.
Thus White gains the square QB5
for a knight.

| 19 B-N4 | P-K3 |
| 20 N-R4 | N-R4? |

He had to play 20...B-B1
preparing to surrender the bishop
for White's knight on QB5 which
could have produced a situation
similar to the fifteenth game of
the 1974 match.

| 21 N-B5 | Q-K1 |
| 22 B-K2 | N-N2? |

Feeble. The best chance was the
pawn sacrifice ...N-B5 to obtain
light square control.

| 23 NxN | RxN |
| 24 R(Q1)-B1 | Q-Q2 |
| 25 R-B2 | P-N6 |
| 26 PxP | RxP?? |

Losing by force. After 26...
R(1)-N1 27 P-QN4 White has an
extra pawn but Black is not
devoid of counterplay.

**27 Q-B1!**

This neat move not only defends
the bishop on K3 but also
threatens 28 B-R6 to which Black
has no satisfactory answer.
Karpov is therefore forced to
surrender the exchange without
compensation and in a normal
match he would probably have
resigned in a few moves instead of
prolonging the agony.

| 27 ... | R-N2 |
| 28 B-R6 | R(1)-N1 |
| 29 BxR | RxB |
| 30 R-R3 | P-KR3 |
| 31 R(R3)-B3 | N-N4 |
| 32 R-B8+ | K-R2 |
| 33 R(B2)-B6 | P-B3 |
| 34 K-N2 | Q-KB2 |
| 35 Q-B2 | P-QR4 |
| 36 P-KN4 | PxP |
| 37 BPxP | P-R5 |
| 38 R-QR8 | N-R2 |
| 39 R-R6 | Q-K2 |
| 40 RxRP | R-B2 |
| 41 Q-N3 | N-B3 |
| 42 R-R1 | N-N5 |
| 43 R-QB1 | R-B5 |
| 44 R-QN8 | |

44 RxR PxR 45 QxP Q-N2+ was
best avoided.

| 44 ... | RxR |
| 45 BxR | Q-QB2 |
| 46 RxN | QxB |
| 47 Q-Q3 | P-R4 |
| 48 R-N6 | B-R3 |
| 49 PxP | Q-N4+ |
| 50 Q-N3 | Q-Q7+ |
| 51 Q-B2 | Black resigns |

(Times: 3.16 — 1.41)

# GAME TWELVE

15th August

After his loss in game eleven Karpov postponed the twelfth game. In this match each player was entitled to three automatic 'time outs' before game 24. The players had agreed to drop the hypocritical custom which had applied in previous world championship matches, whereby a doctor's certificate was required for a time out but was in fact always granted. What a fruitful source of disputes this could have produced. One can envisage each player demanding that his own doctor examine his opponent and prescriptions of bloodletting etc. being rife.

Philippinos have the endearing habit of calling storms by girls' names and during the lull in hostilities we were visited by tropical storm 'Heling' which forced everyone to stay indoors. AIPE (the International Chess Journalists Association) organised a blitz tournament to keep everyone happy. This was won by Karpov's press secretary Roshal (playing with rather more vigour than the World Champion himself had so far displayed!) ahead of such worthies as Edmondson, Baturinsky, Radoicic and Lothar Schmid's son.

Karpov's rest did not infuse him with much new life and he failed to exploit some over-ambitious play by Korchnoi. Shortly before the adjournment Karpov offered a draw directly to Korchnoi but was merely answered by mute gesticulations. During the adjournment Korchnoi complained to Schmid that Karpov's offer had disturbed him and was contrary to Korchnoi's new policy, announced by Ms. Leeuwerik after the handshake row, that draws must be offered through the arbiter. Schmid misunderstood and thought Korchnoi was offering a draw. He communicated this bogus offer to the Russians and it was accepted. Not wishing to embarrass Schmid, and as the position was drawn anyway, Korchnoi acquiesced in this premature result. It must be the first time that a draw has been offered not through but by the arbiter!

The score was now 1-1 with 10 draws.

| White: Karpov | | 2 N-KB3 | N-QB3 |
| Black: Korchnoi | | 3 B-N5 | P-QR3 |
| | | 4 B-R4 | N-B3 |
| Ruy Lopez | | 5 0-0 | NxP |
| 1 P-K4 | P-K4 | 6 P-Q4 | P-QN4 |

| | |
|---|---|
| 7 B-N3 | P-Q4 |
| 8 PxP | B-K3 |
| 9 Q-K2 | |

Varying from 9 QN-Q2 and 9 P-B3 played in earlier games. The fact that Karpov does not try to repeat the opening of game ten makes one wonder whether the spectacular 11 N-N5 was bluff after all.

| | |
|---|---|
| 9 ... | B-K2 |
| 10 R-Q1 | 0-0 |
| 11 P-B4 | NPxP |
| 12 BxP | B-QB4 |
| 13 B-K3 | BxB |
| 14 QxB | Q-N1 |

I believe this manoeuvre is Korchnoi's own invention.

| | |
|---|---|
| 15 B-N3 | N-R4 |
| 16 N-K1 | |

| | |
|---|---|
| 16 ... | Q-N3! |

Improving on Hubner-Demarre, Dresden 1969, in which White obtained the advantage after 16... NxB 17 PxN Q-N3 18 QxQ PxQ 19 P-QN4! threatening 20 P-B3. The point of Korchnoi's move order is to avoid the knight being stranded on K5. White has not achieved much from the opening.

| | |
|---|---|
| 17 QxQ | PxQ |
| 18 P-B3 | NxB |
| 19 RPxN | N-B4 |
| 20 P-QN4 | N-Q2 |

Not 20...N-N6 21 R-R3 P-Q5 22 N-Q2 ultimately winning a pawn.

| | |
|---|---|
| 21 N-Q3 | P-KN4? |

An incredibly risky move. The point is to cut off lines of communication for White's KP, but it seriously loosens Black's kingside and he eventually loses a pawn.

Korchnoi rejected the plausible 21...P-QR4 because of 22 N-B3 PxP 23 RxR RxR 24 NxNP NxP 25 N(4)xP BxN 26 NxB and White wins a pawn by force. Best was 21...KR-B1 after which the position is about level.

| | |
|---|---|
| 22 N-B3 | KR-B1 |
| 23 N-B2 | P-Q5 |

A volatile measure designed to avoid White obtaining a good knight on Q4 against Black's bad bishop on K3.

| | |
|---|---|
| 24 N-K2 | P-Q6 |

The only chance to disco-ordinate White's cavalry. If 24...NxP 25 NxP followed by N-K4 and White's centralised knights breathe fire.

| | |
|---|---|
| 25 NxP | B-B5 |

More accurate is 25...B-N6 26 R-Q2 R-B7 or 25...B-N6 26 R-K1 B-B5 27 N(2)-B1 R-K1 planning ...QR-Q1 followed by ...N-N1-B3-Q5 with full compensation. After the text Black has to struggle a bit.

DIAGRAM

**26 N-N3**

This looks suspect. Karpov overlooked Black's 28th move.

If 26 N-B3 P-R3 followed by recapture of the pawn, but 26 P-B4 clinging to the extra material poses more problems, although Korchnoi considered the weakness of White's KP gave good drawing chances.

| 26 ... | BxN |
|---|---|
| 27 RxB | NxP |
| 28 R-Q5 | N-N3 |

Before this move Golombek, Panno and I were worried about Black's prospects, but we suddenly realised now that everything was OK.

If 28...P-B3 29 N-K4 K-N2 30 NxP wins.

| 29 RxP | R-B7 |

Black's active pieces (rook on the seventh and possibility of ...N-B5 etc.) guarantee Black near equality. Anyway, as I have stressed before, Korchnoi does not fear Karpov in the ending.

| 30 P-N3 | R-N7 |
| 31 N-B5 | |

31 P-R4 transposes, but 31 P-B4 is somewhat more dangerous.

Now Black liquidates to a total draw.

| 31 ... | RxQNP |
|---|---|
| 32 P-R4 | K-B1 |
| 33 P-R5 | N-K2 |
| 34 NxN | KxN |
| 35 R-K1+ | K-B1 |
| 36 R-K4 | P-R4 |
| 37 R(4)-N4 | K-K2 |
| 38 PxP | RxRP |
| 39 P-R6 | RxR |
| 40 RxR | P-N4 |
| 41 R-N7 | R-N8+ |
| 42 K-R2 | R-Q8 |
| 43 RxRP | R-Q1 |
| 44 R-N7 | |

| 44 ... | R-KR1 |

The sealed move. The game was **agreed drawn** without resumption. (Times: 2-31 — 2-34)

# GAME THIRTEEN

**17th and 20th August**

Back to the infamous Dr. Zukhar. He was by now again sitting in the fifth row despite the alleged gentleman's agreement that he should sit in the seventh. Whether or not this man really does possess hypnotical or psychological powers or is merely an eccentric-looking quack who enjoys staring at Korchnoi for five hours on end is basically irrelevant. The point is that the Soviets were clearly trying to present a facade of disturbance which the organisers were powerless to prevent since the idiot jury refused to recognise the existence of mental disturbance. Although earlier it had appeared that Petra Leeuwerik was more worried by the staring zombie than Korchnoi, it was now clear that Korchnoi himself had become petrified. His fears were not assuaged by the receipt of an unsolicited academic opinion from Cambridge that hypnosis from a distance is at least possible.

Korchnoi recruited an anti-missile-missile in the person of Israeli psychologist Dr. Vladimir Bergina. Whether he had less powers than Zukhar or whether Karpov is less vulnerable to mental disturbance, Karpov was not in the least put off by Bergina. For some reason Ms. Leeuwerik objected to Bergina's presence. Although he appeared to me be having a beneficial effect on Korchnoi, Ms. Leeuwerik persuaded Korchnoi to send him home after only a few days.

We had by now also obtained the services of Oscar Panno, thinly disguised as a reporter for *Clarion*, the biggest paper in Buenos Aires. And so our secret delegation was beginning to match the Soviet one.

The thirteenth game resumed the unhappy pattern of Korchnoi's encounters with White which had at last been broken in the eleventh game. Korchnoi built up a dominating position, let it slide into equality and then actually lost by a tragic blunder.

He adjourned in what appeared to be a very favourable position. But he wasted a full forty minutes sealing a rather obvious move which only left him 20 minutes for his next 15 moves. I sat glued to my seat for this period going crazy with worry while minutes ticked away. Korchnoi was clearly incredibly nervous and when he had finally decided on the sealed move he put it in the envelope and took it out again several times to make absolutely sure he had written down the move he wanted to play. It was quite obvious to me that he was undergoing acute mental disturbance while trying to seal the move.

After a night of analysis we decided, in view of Korchnoi's time shortage, that it was necessary to take time out for the adjournment session in order to avoid any surprises which might throw him off balance after the adjournment. In retrospect this was the wrong decision. In the extended period of analysis we discovered the position was not a win. It contained good chances but against accurate defence there was very little to be done. This demoralised Korchnoi somewhat. Moreover, before resumption of the thirteenth game, Korchnoi adjourned the fourteenth in a hopeless position and this led him to try desperate and unjustified winning attempts in game thirteen, leading ultimately to his blunder on move 56 in what was by then a totally drawn position.

The thirteenth game reinforced our fear that the Soviet analysts were slightly superior to us. Our analysis was very thorough but theirs had a spark of genius which I suspect was infused by the presence of the brilliant ex-world champion Tal.

Karpov now led 2-1 with 10 draws.

| White: Korchnoi | | 14 N-K1 | KR-K1 |
| Black: Karpov | | 15 N-Q3 | |

Queen's Gambit Declined

| 1 P-QB4 | N-KB3 |
| 2 N-QB3 | P-K3 |
| 3 N-B3 | P-Q4 |
| 4 P-Q4 | B-K2 |
| 5 B-N5 | P-KR3 |
| 6 B-R4 | 0-0 |
| 7 R-B1 | P-QN3 |
| 8 BxN | BxB |
| 9 PxP | PxP |
| 10 P-KN3 | |

A new departure. I had analysed this idea in 1968 and Panno played it against Esposito in 1963 in an Argentine club match. But it was Stean who revived the idea and persuaded Korchnoi to use it. At least it avoids the super-solid main lines.

| 10 ... | P-B3 |
| 11 B-N2 | B-B4 |
| 12 0-0 | Q-Q3 |
| 13 P-K3 | N-Q2 |

Korchnoi based his strategy in this game on the eighth game of his 1977 match with Petrosian. The plan is to exchange off Black's QB and then slowly advance on the queenside to enhance the power of White's fianchettoed KB.

| 15 ... | P-N3 |

I don't like this move much as it cuts off the retreat of the QB. I believe 15...P-QR4 to restrict

White's queenside expansion must be better.

| | |
|---|---|
| 16 N-B4 | B-N2 |
| 17 P-KN4 | |

A bold move, the point of which I did not immediately grasp. Now Black's QB, which defends the light square pawn chain, is exposed to a swap, although White has to pay a small price in the weakening of his king protection.

| | |
|---|---|
| 17 . . . | B-K3 |
| 18 P-KR3 | N-B1 |
| 19 NxB | NxN |
| 20 Q-Q3 | QR-Q1 |
| 21 R-B2 | N-B2 |

Korchnoi criticised this retreat and recommended ...Q-K2 plus ...Q-R5 and ...N-N4 with more tangible counterplay. I have noticed, however, that Karpov, with Black, tends to play possum in the earlier stages, waiting for the fifth hour and Korchnoi's time trouble before he really comes out and starts a fight.

| | |
|---|---|
| 22 N-R4 | Q-Q2 |
| 23 P-N3 | |

An interesting speculative piece sacrifice is 23 P-N4 P-QB4 24 NPxP QxN 25 PxP N-K3 26 P-N7. It could also be tried next move when Black's knight can no longer go to K3.

| | |
|---|---|
| 23 . . . | R-K3 |
| 24 N-B3 | R-Q3 |
| 25 P-N4 | B-B1 |
| 26 N-K2 | P-QN4 |

Trying to get his knight to QB5. But Korchnoi has enough time to undermine Black's queenside structure first.

| | |
|---|---|
| 27 Q-N3 | N-R1 |
| 28 P-QR4 | PxP |

If 28...P-R3 29 P-R5 and the knight is incarcerated.

| | |
|---|---|
| 29 QxRP | N-N3 |
| 30 Q-N3 | R-N1 |
| 31 N-B4 | N-B5 |
| 32 Q-R4 | P-KB4 |

Typical Karpov — a move in the same league as his 33...P-R4 in game nine. He chooses just the right moment psychologically and practically to randomise the position. Objectively I feel Black is now hovering near the brink of defeat, but it takes a great effort to push him over, and meanwhile Korchnoi was getting tired and the clock was ticking away precious minutes.

| | |
|---|---|
| 33 PxP | QxP |
| 34 QxRP | RxP |
| 35 R-R2 | Q-B1 |
| 36 R-B1 | R-N2 |
| 37 Q-R4? | |

This I do not understand. Why not 37 Q-R6 putting the queen in a more active position and pinning Black's rook? If queens are exchanged White will drive off Black's well placed knight with B-B1, with potentially overwhelming pressure against Black's queenside pawns.

| | |
|---|---|
| 37 . . . | R-KB2 |

Black has successfully consolidated his scattered forces and

White's advantage is now in question. In fact his best chance is the following exchange sacrifice.

| 38 RxN | PxR |
| 39 QxP(4) | Q-B4 |
| 40 N-Q3 | B-N2 |

**41 R-R7**

The sealed move over which Korchnoi thought for so long.

41 ... R(3)-B3

Probably best, although Black has a huge number of playable alternatives which are very hard to crack, such as 41...P-R4 or even the retraction 41...B-B1, now that White's KB2 is no longer protected. This complicated our task of analysis. It also transpired that White could never win if the queens and one rook each were exchanged.

**42 RxR**

42 N-K5 allows 43...QxP+ drawing.

42 ... RxR
43 P-Q5

It seemed more aggressive to push the pawn to QB6 but this allows a black square blockade and so simply 43 BxP was better.

43 ... B-K4

A fine resource which prevents White's king reaching safety at KR2. Now Korchnoi should have given up trying to win.

| 44 PxP | K-N2 |
| 45 B-K4 | Q-N4+ |
| 46 K-B1 | B-Q3 |
| 47 B-Q5 | R-K2 |
| 48 B-B3 | P-R4 |
| 49 B-Q1 | Q-KB4 |
| 50 K-K2 | R-K5 |
| 51 Q-B3+ | Q-B3 |
| 52 Q-N3 | Q-B4 |
| 53 Q-N7+ | |

Rashly rejecting repetition by 53 Q-B3+.

| 53 ... | R-K2 |
| 54 Q-N2+ | K-R2 |
| 55 Q-Q4 | B-B2 |

**56 Q-KR4??**

With only one move to go to the time control, White throws the game away.

56 ... R-K5
57 P-B4

The only way to save the trapped queen, but now White's position collapses.

| 57 ... | B-N3 |
| 58 B-B2 | RxP+ |
| 59 K-Q2 | Q-R4+ |
| 60 K-Q1 | Q-R8+ |
| 61 K-Q2 | R-K5 |

**White resigned.**
(Times: 3-58 — 3-56)

# GAME FOURTEEN

The fourteenth game, started in the interval between the first and second sessions of the thirteenth, witnessed yet another Open Variation of the Ruy Lopez. Earlier in the match this had served Korchnoi well and he had the advantage that he had access to Kevin O'Connell's new book on this opening while Karpov was relying on Korchnoi's contribution to *The Encyclopedia of Chess Openings* published in 1974 and now becoming out of date. Korchnoi had likened Karpov's conduct of the opening to a pupil learning his lesson and then being confronted by his teacher for the examination. But latterly the pupil had been going outside the syllabus and embarrassed his teacher with awkward questions in games 8, 10 and 12.

Once again Karpov got the better position from the opening but Korchnoi had a defensible position when he overlooked a simple exchange sacrifice. Initially Karpov only obtained one pawn for his investment but, following another mistake by Korchnoi, further dividends were declared. In the second session, played immediately after Korchnoi's debacle in the thirteenth game Karpov rapidly registered his second win of the day. The game illustrated Karpov's skill at exploiting small advantages in an unspectular but effective manner.

Karpov now led 3-1 with 10 draws.

White: Karpov
Black: Korchnoi

### Ruy Lopez

| | | | |
|---|---|---|---|
| 1 P-K4 | P-K4 | 11 B-B2 | B-B4 |
| 2 N-KB3 | N-QB3 | 12 N-N3 | B-KN5 |
| 3 B-N5 | P-QR3 | 13 P-KR3 | |
| 4 B-R4 | N-B3 | | |
| 5 0-0 | NxP | | |
| 6 P-Q4 | P-QN4 | | |
| 7 B-N3 | P-Q4 | | |
| 8 PxP | B-K3 | | |
| 9 P-B3 | B-QB4 | | |
| 10 QN-Q2 | 0-0 | | |

A new departure which is actually the most straightforward attempt to refute Black's opening. Black could have tried a pseudo-Dilworth sacrifice with 13...BxN 14 PxB NxKBP 15 RxN BxR+ 16 KxB NxP but after my suggestion 17 Q-N1! White is still on top, e.g. 17...R-K1 18 B-N5 Q-Q3 19 Q-N3 N-N5+ 20 BPxN R-K7+ 21 K-B3 QxQ+ 22 KxQ

76

RxB  23 N-Q4  RxNP  24  B-B1
winning.

| 13 ... | B-R4 |
| 14 P-N4 | B-KN3 |

Korchnoi assesses this position as
unclear in ECO but it soon
becomes evident that White will
exert a permanent dark square
grip.

| 15 BxN | PxB |
| 16 NxB | PxN |
| 17 B-B4 | QxQ |

If 17...Q-K2 18 Q-Q5 N-R4 19
P-N4 Black's front KBP is ultimately doomed and this, combined with White's control of
space, would give White a distinct
advantage.

| 18 QRxQ | N-Q1 |
| 19 R-Q7 | N-K3 |
| 20 NxN | PxN |
| 21 B-K3 | QR-B1 |
| 22 KR-Q1 | |

Also excellent is 22 B-B5 KR-K1
23 R-K1 playing to exclude
Black's bishop from the game.
Karpov had been moving very
rapidly and I feared, justifiably,
that he had prepared the variation
far into the ending. Since Black
does not have a wide choice in his
cramped quarters, this would not
have been too difficult a task for
him.

| 22 ... | B-K5 |
| 23 B-B5 | KR-K1 |
| 24 R(7)-Q4 | B-Q4 |
| 25 P-N3 | P-QR4 |
| 26 K-R2 | R-R1 |
| 27 K-N3 | R-R3? |

Commencing a faulty manoeuvre
which overlooks entirely that
Black can sacrifice the exchange.
The best chance was 27...B-B3
followed by ...P-R5 though it
would still not be easy for Black.

| 28 P-KR4 | R-B3 |

**29 RxB!**
Of course. For some inexplicable
reason Korchnoi had not even
considered this.

| 29 ... | PxR |
| 30 RxP | R(3)-K3 |
| 31 B-Q4 | P-B3 |
| 32 R-B5 | R-KB1? |

Usually I watched the games
from the press centre, but today I
was invited to give a speech at the
closing ceremony of the Philippino
championship, which was also
held in Baguio. During the speech
I was handed a note with this
position from the game on it. I
saw at once that Black had to play
32...R-Q1 33 KxP R-Q4 and if 34
K-K4 R(K3)xKP+. White's only
chance to play for a win would be
34 RxR PxR, although with one

rook exchanged and Black's K5 in his control Black should hold the position.

After the text Black goes irrevocably downhill.

| | |
|---|---|
| 33 P-R4 | PxP |
| 34 PxP | P-N3 |
| 35 RxRP | R(3)-K1 |
| 36 R-R7 | R-B2 |
| 37 R-R6 | R-B2 |
| 38 B-B5 | R(2)-B1 |
| 39 B-Q6 | R-R1 |
| 40 RxP | RxRP |
| 41 KxP | P-R4 |

### DIAGRAM

The adjourned position which is easily won for White.

| | |
|---|---|
| 42 PxP | PxP |
| 43 P-B4 | R-R7 |
| 44 R-N6 | K-B2 |
| 45 P-B5 | R-R5 |
| 46 P-B6 | K-K3 |
| 47 P-B7 | K-Q2 |

| | |
|---|---|
| 48 R-N8 | R-QB1 |
| 49 K-K3 | |

Not at once 49 P-K6+ KxP 50 RxP KxB.

49 . . .       RxRP

In view of the threat of P-B4, P-B5 etc. Black has nothing better.

**50 P-K6+**     **Black resigns**

50...KxP now fails to the *zwischenzug* 51 B-N3.

(Times: 2-48 — 2-54)

# GAME FIFTEEN

**22nd August**

When the thirteenth game was adjourned Korchnoi had appeared to have good chances of going 2-1 up but now he was suddenly 3-1 down. The gods could not let such a dramatic reversal go unnoticed so they chose to mark the occasion by means of an earthquake of force six on the Richter Scale (I am not sure what the equivalent Elo rating is). Lightning even penetrated Harry Golombek's bedroom. Why the gods chose to pick on this innocent bystander I don't know, but fortunately he was unharmed.

Although shaken by his recent experiences Korchnoi decided not to postpone the fifteenth game. However, the game was a limp affair and the first time since the first game that Korchnoi failed to make any impression with White. He played the Catalan for the first time in the match and was confronted by a sharp pawn sacrifice which Karpov had obviously prepared beforehand. Naturally wishing to steady his nerves after Sunday's disaster, Korchnoi did not try to refute the sacrifice by hanging on to the pawn and the game rapidly petered out into a draw.

The only excitement was provided by an altercation on stage when Karpov started rocking his chair, which drew forth sharp words from Korchnoi. A jury meeting the following morning decided that such disturbances would henceforth be forbidden.

Karpov now led 3-1 with 11 draws.

**White: Korchnoi**
**Black: Karpov**

### Catalan Opening

| | |
|---|---|
| 1 P-QB4 | N-KB3 |
| 2 N-QB3 | P-K3 |
| 3 N-B3 | P-Q4 |
| 4 P-Q4 | B-K2 |
| 5 P-KN3 | 0-0 |
| 6 B-N2 | PxP |
| 7 N-K5 | N-B3 |

An odd looking move which saddles Black with tripled pawns.

The point is that White has to waste time capturing these and Black is happy to sacrifice a pawn for a lead in development.

| | |
|---|---|
| 8 BxN | PxB |
| 9 NxP(B6) | Q-K1 |
| 10 NxB+ | QxN |
| 11 Q-R4 | P-B4 |
| 12 QxBP | PxP |
| 13 QxQP | P-K4 |
| 14 Q-KR4 | R-N1 |
| 15 B-N5 | |

An unambitious move. White

could have put Black's opening sacrifice to the test by trying to hold on to the pawn with 15 P-QR3 or 15 0-0 R-N5 16 Q-N5 etc.

15 ...       RxP

16 0-0

White could have settled for a draw at once with 16 N-Q5 Q-N2 17 NxN+ PxN 18 0-0 PxB 19 QxNP+. He might as well have done so as the text also leads to a clearly drawn position.

| 16 ... | Q-K3 |
|--------|------|
| 17 BxN | QxB |
| 18 QxQ | PxQ |
| 19 QR-N1 | RxR |
| 20 RxR | B-K3 |
| 21 P-B3 | R-B1 |
| 22 R-QB1 | R-N1 |
| 23 R-B2 | R-QB1 |
| 24 K-B2 | BxP |
| 25 RxB | |

Draw agreed
(Times: 1-28 — 0-52)

# GAME SIXTEEN

## 24th August

The weather continued to cast a damper on the proceedings. It rained twenty-four hours a day and even the fish were drowning. Two people were actually killed by a landslide at the back of the playing hall. Rain streamed through the hotel roof and Stean aquired a private lake in his bedroom. Not being able to swim he chose to evacuate.

There were fears that the generator in the playing hall might collapse and the sixteenth game have to be postponed but Campomanes gave the green light. After the game the generator at the Pines Hotel did indeed explode and we were plunged into darkness for hours. I was interested to learn that the Philippinos picturesquely describe such events as brownouts.

After much pleading from his seconds Korchnoi finally dropped the Open Ruy Lopez for the sixteenth game. To be honest his choice of the French was as much a surprise to his seconds as it must have been to Karpov. We were planning a different half-open defence but at the last minute Korchnoi discovered a flaw in our analysis and so resorted to the French Defence without much prior analysis, relying on his great experience with this opening to pull him through.

Korchnoi's choice of opening was a success. Karpov was obviously not expecting the line Korchnoi played and missed the best continuation on move 12. He retained a slight advantage but Korchnoi defended adequately and the game was adjourned in a drawn position which was not resumed.

The Tarrasch Variation which Karpov plays against the French gives Black very few chances of winning and it may be for this reason that Korchnoi had not allowed it before. However, it simplifies the position to such an extent that Black should be able to draw by suitably patient defence and so it is not ideal for a match such as this where a draw can always be regarded as a satisfactory result for Black. Perhaps, therefore, Korchnoi should have adopted the French Defence earlier, but the spectators can be grateful he did not in view of the seven tedious draws the opening led to in the 1974 match.

Karpov now led 3-1 with 12 draws.

White: Karpov
Black: Korchnoi

### French Defence

| 1 P-K4 | P-K3 |
| 2 P-Q4 | P-Q4 |
| 3 N-Q2 | P-QB4 |
| 4 KPxP | KPxP |
| 5 B-N5+ | |

In the 1974 match Karpov had invariably played 5 KN-B3 and the games continued 5...N-QB3 6 B-N5.

| 5 ... | B-Q2 |

Karpov seemed surprised by this move. Was he expecting 5...N-B3 6 KN-B3 transposing back into the lines played in the 1974 match? If so, why did he play 5 B-N5ch rather than 5 KN-B3?

| 6 Q-K2+ | Q-K2 |

In the twenty-second game Korchnoi played the more complicated alternative 6 . . . B-K2 but also failed to equalise.

| 7 BxB+ | NxB |
| 8 PxP | NxP |
| 9 N-N3 | QxQ+ |
| 10 NxQ | NxN |
| 11 RPxN | B-B4 |

**12 B-Q2**

Better is 12 N-B3 which leads to a plus for White after either 12 . . .

N-B3 13 N-R4 or 12 . . . 0-0-0 13 R-R5 (Hort-Ivkov, Wijk aan Zee 1970).

| 12 ... | N-K2 |
| 13 N-B4 | 0-0 |
| 14 0-0 | KR-Q1 |
| 15 N-Q3 | B-N3 |
| 16 P-B3 | P-B3 |
| 17 KR-Q1 | K-B2 |
| 18 K-B1 | N-B4? |

Black immediately has to retract this careless move which withdraws support from the vulnerable QP. 18...N-B3 would have been quite satisfactory, especially as it prevents 19 N-N4.

| 19 B-K1 | N-K2 |
| 20 N-N4 | R-Q2 |
| 21 R-Q3 | QR-Q1 |
| 22 QR-Q1 | K-K3 |
| 23 B-Q2 | N-B3 |

At this stage I thought Black had comfortable equality, but my optimism was dispelled by Karpov's next few moves. By impressively accurate play he maintained his grip and lured Black's rook to the horribly passive square QN3.

| 24 NxN | PxN |
| 25 P-QN4 | K-B2 |
| 26 B-K3 | BxB |
| 27 RxB | R-QN1 |
| 28 R-K2 | R-N4 |
| 29 R-R1 | R(Q2)-N2 |
| 30 R-Q2 | K-K3 |
| 31 R-R6 | R(N4)-N3 |
| 32 R-R2 | K-Q3 |
| 33 K-K2 | R-K2+ |
| 34 K-Q3 | P-QR3 |

DIAGRAM

**35 R-Q1?**

Karpov succumbs to his besetting sin of trying to blitz Korchnoi and throws away most of his advantage

opportunities for manoeuvring.

| 36 . . . | K-Q1 |
|----------|------|
| 37 P-B3 | R-K4 |
| 38 K-Q4 | K-B2 |
| 39 R-K1 | K-Q3 |
| 40 P-KB4 | RxR |
| 41 RxR | P-QR4 |
| 42 PxP | RxP |

The sealed move. The game was agreed drawn during the adjournment.

by a hasty move. Better alternatives would have been 35 P-KN3 or 35 R-K2 swapping Black's active rook and leaving him with the miserable beast on QN3.

**35 . . .　　　K-B2**
**36 R(R2)-R1**

36 R(Q1)-R1 followed by R-R4, P-QN3 and eventually P-B4 would still have left White with some

A plausible continuation at the end would have been 43 R-QR1 P-B4+ 44 K-Q3 R-N2 45 P-R6 R-R2 46 P-B4 P-Q5 47 R-R5 K-B3 48 P-N3 and if 48...K-N3 49 R-N5+ etc. White can also draw by leaving his rook on QR1 meeting ...K-N3 with R-N1+ KxP R-N5 R-B2 creating a totally drawn position a pawn down.

(Times: 2-12 — 2-32)

# GAME SEVENTEEN

## 26th August

The Zukhar dispute had been quietly simmering during the last few games. The main development was Ms. Leeuwerik's new habit of trying to distract him by kicking his shins and jabbing the small of his back with a pen. This approach was less successful than the more subtle *Gulag Archipelago* Gambit she had adopted earlier, and Ms. Leeuwerik's only success was to make an exhibition of herself.

Now the dispute really boiled over again. At the beginning of the game Korchnoi objected violently to Zukhar's presence and threatened to evict him by physical violence if necessary. Eventually Campomanes agreed to move him back but warned that this would be the last time.

The seventeenth game was yet another tragedy for Korchnoi. Following the familiar pattern he built up a won position with White after improving on his play in game seven. His position in the early middle game was so good that he retained winning chances even after a number of inaccuracies in the later middle game. But he no longer had winning chances when disaster struck: Korchnoi allowed an elegant but obvious mate in three. His resignation was greeted by singing and screaming from thirty tourists who had fortuitously arrived from Russia that day. This must have taken Korchnoi's mind back to the partisan crowds who watched his 1974 match against Karpov in Moscow.

Korchnoi had wasted thirteen precious minutes on his clock by his fulminations against Zukhar at the start of the game. Perhaps forgetting this he commented after the game: "I don't know where my time went. I thought I was moving quickly." Would the extra thirteen minutes have been enough time to allow Korchnoi to have won his overwhelming position? Thirteen seconds should have sufficed to at least avoid the loss at the end.

After each win Karpov had a party and this time the Terraces Plaza Hotel presented him with a cake showing the final position of the seventeenth game. The first thing he did was eat White's king!

Karpov now led 4-1 with 12 draws.

| White: Korchnoi | | |
|---|---|---|
| Black: Karpov | 1 P-QB4 | N-KB3 |
| | 2 N-QB3 | P-K3 |
| Nimzo-Indian Defence | 3 P-Q4 | B-N5 |

| 4 P-K3 | O-O |
|--------|-----|
| 5 B-Q3 | P-B4 |
| 6 P-Q5 | P-QN4 |

Repeating the sharp method adopted in the seventh game. This may not in fact be the best move. The paradoxical 6...P-KR3, which bypasses the possibility of BxRP+ and leaves White with some anxiety about his centre, e.g. 7 P-K4 PxP 8 KPxP BxN+ 9 PxB R-K1+ 10 N-K2 P-Q3 and the position is about equal.

| 7 PxKP | BPxP |
|--------|------|
| 8 PxP | P-QR3 |

Varying from 8...B-N2 played in the seventh game.

9 N-K2

Improving his strategy in the seventh game when he developed this knight on KB3.

| 9 ... | P-Q4 |
|-------|------|
| 10 O-O | P-K4 |
| 11 P-QR3 | PxP |
| 12 BxNP | BxN |
| 13 PxB | B-R3 |
| 14 R-N1 | Q-Q3 |
| 15 P-QB4 | P-Q5 |
| 16 N-N3 | |

By now it was clear that Karpov's handling of the opening had been inauspicious to say the least. I felt that Black was already lost. Not only was he a pawn down,

but his own centre pawns were not mobile and there were a number of weak squares in his camp, such as KB4.

| 16 ... | N-B3 |
|--------|------|
| 17 P-QR4 | N-QR4 |
| 18 Q-Q3 | Q-K3 |
| 19 PxP | BPxP |
| 20 P-B5 | KR-B1 |
| 21 P-B4 | |

21 B-N5 is a good alternative, but the text, ripping open lines against Black's insecure kingside, is quite sufficient to win.

| 21 ... | RxP |
|--------|-----|
| 22 BxB | QxB |
| 23 QxQ | |

Better was 23 R-N8+ K-B2 24 R-N5 displacing Black's king, keeping queens on the board and introducing unpleasant threats such as PxP and Q-B5. Incredibly Korchnoi did not even consider this obvious manoeuvre and from now on we witness his decline.

| 23 ... | RxQ |
|--------|-----|
| 24 B-R3 | R-Q4 |
| 25 N-B5 | K-B2 |
| 26 PxP | RxP |
| 27 R-N5? | |

This is a blunder which allows Black to complicate things in White's time pressure. Again the simple course would have been 27

85

NxQP and White still has good chances to win.

Down in the press room I was beginning to become pessimistic.

| 27 ... | N-B5 |
|---|---|

A typical example of Karpov's eel-like defensive skill after earlier unimpressive play. If now 28 N-Q6+ RxN 29 RxR R-Q2 and the Black knight on QB5 is forking two pieces.

| 28 R-N7+ | K-K3 |
|---|---|
| 29 NxQP+ | K-Q4 |
| 30 N-B3? | |

Better was 30 B-B8 KxN 31 BxP R(K)-K3 32 R-B7 K-K4 33 P-N4 P-R3 34 R-B5+ or 33...N-K6 34 R(B1)xN RxR 35 P-N5 and wins. In view of this Black would have to play 31...N-K5. White can then get rook plus pawns for two knights in much more favourable circumstances than the game. All this was proposed by Murei.

Perhaps the simplest, however, was the line proposed by Panno: 30 N-B2 NxB 31 N-N4+ or 30 N-B2 RxP 31 B-B8 and Black is still in deep water.

| 30 ... | NxB |
|---|---|
| 31 NxR | KxN |
| 32 R-K7+ | K-Q5 |
| 33 RxP | N-B5 |
| 34 R-B4+ | |

Better was 34 R-B7.

| 34 ... | N-K5 |
|---|---|
| 35 R-Q7+ | K-K6 |
| 36 R-B3+ | K-K7 |
| 37 RxP | N(B)-Q7 |
| 38 R-QR3 | R-QB3 |
| 39 R-R1?? | |

Now the 'kremlins' get at White's position. 39 P-R4 also lost to 39... R-B8+ 40 K-R2 N-B8+ 41 K-R3 N-B7 mate. But simply 39 P-N4 should draw since after 39... N-B6+ 40 RxN KxR 41 P-R4 the ending is still drawn even if Black wins all White's pawns.

| 39 ... | N-B6+! |
|---|---|

Very pretty. It is mate after 40 K-R1 N-B7 or 40 PxN R-N2+ 41 K-R1 N-B7.

**White** therefore **resigned.**
(Times: 2-28 — 2-92)

# GAME EIGHTEEN

## 2nd and 3rd September

Korchnoi was now trailing 1-4 and his position appeared desperate. Nobody since Steinitz in 1886 had yet won a world championship after being three games down, though as recently as 1954 Smyslov managed at least to draw his match against Botvinnik after starting with one draw and three losses. Korchnoi's main consolation was that, as the match was of unlimited duration, Karpov needed to win two more games and so could not canter home with draws as he had done in the 1974 match. Nonetheless Korchnoi's task of winning five games while conceding only one loss was a daunting one.

Many people were predicting that Korchnoi would now find a pretext for defaulting the match rather than suffer the indignity of defending a hopeless cause. I never gave much credence to this fear for two reasons. Firstly Korchnoi disapproves in principle of not fighting out to the bitter end, as witnessed by his expressions of contempt for Spassky's action in threatening to walk out of the Candidates' final. Secondly the loser's prize offered 100,000 good reasons for completing the match! The joker in the pack was Ms. Leeuwerik. She clearly had considerable influence over Korchnoi and I was afraid that, if she thought that Korchnoi could no longer win the match, she might regard a political bust-up as a more satisfactory end to the match than a clear-cut chess victory for Karpov. Despite our disagreement on policy Ms. Leeuwerik and I remained on good terms personally. We both wanted what we thought was best for Korchnoi but we happened to disagree radically on how this should be achieved.

The day after the seventeenth game we were sidetracked by rather a trivial issue. Despite our defeat over the flag issue Ms. Leeuwerik was still insisting that our delegation be referred to as the Swiss delegation rather than the Korchnoi delegation. Lim Kok Ann sent a telegram to the Swiss Chess Federation asking two questions — 1. Did Ms. Leeuwerik represent Korchnoi only or the Swiss Chess Federation itself? 2. If she did represent the Swiss Chess Federation did they accept responsibility for her "violent political statements" and "damaging allegations"? The Swiss Chess Federation merely answered the second question, denying responsibility, and left the first question unanswered. There was a meeting to discuss the matter which I attended in the Gilbertian dual capacity of translator and chief second. Inside the jury room I was translator but I had to leave the chamber occasionally and revert to my role as chief second to sign certain documents. At one time a fog from rain outside penetrated our deliberations which added to the unreal nature of the proceedings. In the end I managed to have the whole silly matter suppressed without a vote.

Korchnoi now decided to take two 'time-outs' before the eighteenth game. This was a gamble. It meant that he would not be entitled to any more postponements unless the match lasted for more than 24 games. But it also gave Korchnoi a chance to recharge his batteries (and Karpov his Batuniskys?) and make a fresh start.

Korchnoi chose to take his rest in Manila rather than Baguio and he flew off there with Ms. Leeuwerik. In her absence I was appointed acting head of the Korchnoi delegation and I was determined to make the most of this opportunity. By now I was convinced that Ms. Leeuwerik had not been acting in Korchnoi's best interests. She seemed more intent on using the match as a political platform for attacking the Russians rather than squashing side-issues which might distract Korchnoi and so enabling him to give of his best in the match.

In my new role as head of the Korchnoi delegation I attended a meeting to reconsider the Zukhar question. I decided to follow R.A. Butler's maxim that politics is the art of the possible and approached the meeting in a concilatory mood. I started the meeting by ordering a round of drinks and Baturinsky mellowed considerably. He very soon agreed that Zukhar should sit at the back of the Playing Hall with the rest of the Soviet delegation, which was all we had ever wanted from our negotiations. The only concession we had to make in exchange was that Korchnoi should stop wearing the special proplylactic reflective glasses which he had been wearing even before the Zukhar controversy arose. Why Karpov should find his own reflection disturbing I don't know, but the glasses had been giving Korchnoi headaches anyway and so this point was readily agreed. The joint communiqué issued by Baturinsky and myself concluded: "The participants' representatives have expressed their hope that all this will contribute to the further course of the match in the interest of chess and in the spirit of FIDE principles".

I was happy to have settled in one meeting the problem which had defied solution for five weeks. I was flattered when Panno wrote comparing me to Disraeli, assuming that the more seedy machinations of that student of Machiavelli have not found their way into the Argentinian history books. But I was brought down from the clouds by the news that Korchnoi had just given a press conference in Manila threatening to walk out of the match unless the organisers installed a one-way mirror in the Playing Hall which would allow the audience to see the players, but not the players the audience. I hastily despatched a delegation consisting of Stean Murei and Edmondson to Manila to inform Korchnoi that the war was over and prevent him from continuing hostilities in ignorance of this conclusion, like Japanese cut off in the jungle after World War II. Fortunately their counsels prevailed. Korchnoi withdrew his new demands and my original compromise was reinstated. Although Edmondson was not an official member of our delegation he proved himself a tower of strength, no doubt drawing on his experience in persuading that other turbulent genius, Fischer, to play in 1972, and so I continued in charge of negotiations. Michael Stean commented on this takeover: 'It was a bloodless coup. Petra's exuberance has lost us much goodwill'.

Twenty minutes before the start of the eighteenth game I summoned an informal meeting of the jury and, toasting peace, expressed the hope that our future meetings would be over drinks and not over protests. I also presented olive branches in the form of carved wooden horses to all.

The audience for the eighteenth game was swelled by the august presence of the USSR ambassador. He originally sat in the second row but after a brief discussion with Camponanes I had him moved to join the rest of the Soviet delegation before the start of play. After all the problems in shifting Zukhar I was very pleased to be able to shift the USSR ambassador in two minutes.

In the eighteenth game Korchnoi played the Pirc Defence for the first time in the match. This was in accordance with our policy of chopping and changing his defences with Black in order to sidetrack Karpov's preparation. Unfortunately Karpov got in with a novelty first. Korchnoi slipped into a slightly dubious middle game and only succeeded in saving himself after adjournment by some fine endgame play. None-the-less, this was a reasonable achievement considering he had spent the preceding week in Manila issuing ultimatums rather than preparing for the game. Afterwards Tal praised Korchnoi's defensive skill in a difficult situation.

Karpov now led 4-1, with 13 draws.

**White: Karpov**
**Black: Korchnoi**

### Pirc Defence

| 1 P-K4 | P-Q3 |
|--------|------|
| 2 P-Q4 | N-KB3 |
| 3 N-QB3 | P-KN3 |
| 4 N-B3 | |

Recently Karpov has invariably played the Two Knights variation against the Pirc Defence rather than one of the more aggressive systems beginning with 4 P-B4

Korchnoi's own high point with this opening was his win against Fischer in the Candidates' tournament in 1962.

| 4 ... | B-N2 |
|-------|------|
| 5 B-K2 | 0-0 |
| 6 0-0 | B-N5 |
| 7 B-K3 | N-B3 |
| 8 Q-Q3 | |

Karpov has made a specialty of 8 Q-Q2 in this position — see for example his games against

Timman at Tilburg 1977 and against Adorjan at Las Palmas 1977. The idea of this new move is to have the square Q2 available for the king's knight. Korchnoi pondered for fifteen minutes over his reply.

| 8 . . . | P-K4 |
| 9 P-Q5 | N-N5 |

Korchnoi spent a further twenty minutes on this move. The alternative is 9 . . . N-K2 10 N-Q2 B-Q2 11 N-B4 N-K1 12 P-B4 when white has the advantage as black cannot manoeuvre a knight towards K4.

| 10 Q-Q2 | P-QR4 |
| 11 P-KR3 | |

Korchnoi was more afraid of 11 N-K1. The exchange of the light square bishops whould then help White in view of the fixed central pawn chain. But if Black's QB retreats then 12 P-QR3 followed by 13 N-Q3 shuts Black's QN out of the game for a long time.

Karpov used sixteen minutes here so he was obviously out of his prepared line.

| 11 . . . | B-Q2 |
| 12 B-KN5 | |

More unpleasant for Black is 12 P-R3 N-R3 13 QR-N1 intending P-QN4 when Black's knight on QR3 is a liability. If then 13. . . N-B4 14 BxN PxB 15 NxP is good for White.

| 12 . . . | Q-K1 |
| 13 N-R2 | |

13 N-K1 was a better method of preparing for . . . P-KB4 than this decentralisation.

| 13 . . . | K-R1 |
| 14 P-R3 | N-R3 |
| 15 B-R6 | BxB |

| 16 QxB | N-KN1? |

This prepares an incorrect plan. Korchnoi overestimates the virtues of . . . P-KB4 which turns out merely to create weaknesses. Black could have equalised by 16 . . . N-B4 17 Q-K3 P-B3 e.g. 18 P-QN4 PxP 19 PxN P-Q5 20 Q-Q3 PxN 21 PxP B-B3 and Black will easily surround the White pawn on Q3.

| 17 Q-K3 | P-KB4 |
| 18 PxP | BxP |
| 19 QR-B1 | N-B3 |
| 20 P-KN4! | |

An excellent move over which Karpov spent twenty-five minutes. The fact that he can continue to dominate Black's QN and QB outweighs any slight weaknesses in his own camp. This move is typical of Karpov's skill in positions where he has a space advantage.

| 20 . . . | B-Q2 |
| 21 P-B4 | PxP |
| 22 QxP | N-B4 |
| 23 QR-K1 | |

We were more worried by 23 Q-Q4 Q-K4 (not 23 . . . QN-K5 24 RxN! RxR 25 P-N5) 24 QxQ PxQ 25 N-B3

| 23 . . . | KN-K5 |
| 24 Q-K3 | Q-K4 |

| 25 NxN | NxN |
|--------|-----|
| 26 B-B3 | N-N4 |

The only chance is to simplify.
26 . . . Q-N6+? would lead Black
to an impasse.

| 27 QxQ | PxQ |
|--------|-----|

Now Black's weak KP guarantees
White a small but lasting advantage.

| 28 B-N2 | RxR+ |
|---------|------|
| 29 NxR | R-K1 |
| 30 N-Q2 | P-R5 |
| 31 R-K3 | |

Karpov decides not to rush
matters by 31 P-B4 or 31 N-K4 and
instead plays for the adjournment — rather a surprising decision
as Korchnoi only had thirteen
minutes for his next ten moves.

| 31 ... | K-N2 |
|--------|------|
| 32 K-B2 | R-K2 |
| 33 P-B4 | P-N3 |
| 34 R-QB3 | P-R4 |

By exchanging a pair of pawns
on the kingside, Black prevents
White from later expanding there
by P-R4 and P-N5.

| 35 K-N3 | PxP |
|---------|-----|
| 36 PxP | B-K1 |
| 37 P-B5 | PxP |
| 38 N-K4 | NxN |
| 39 BxN | K-B3 |
| 40 RxP | K-N4 |

The adjourned positions. White

clearly has a pull as Black's pieces
are passive and there are a number
of vulnerable pawns in his camp,
but I thought at first it would not
be too difficult to hold. Korchnoi
even opined that this was the best
positon he had had for the whole
game. However we gradually became more and more pessimistic
as the active plans for Black (such
as playing for . . . R-KB5) all
seemed too dangerous. Korchnoi
does not like to defend passively
but eventually the decision was
taken to do as little as possible.
Over the next eight moves White
plays non-committally hoping that
Black will become active but
Korchnoi did not oblige.

| 41 B-Q3 | R-B2 |
|---------|------|
| 42 B-K2 | R-R2 |
| 43 B-B3 | R-B2 |
| 44 R-B4 | R-K2 |
| 45 R-N4 | R-K2 |
| 46 K-B2 | B-Q2 |
| 47 K-N3 | B-K1 |
| 48 K-B2 | B-Q2 |
| 49 K-K3 | |

White gets moving at last but
Black is ready.

| 49 ... | P-K5 |
|--------|------|

The correct moment to obtain a
passed KNP.

| 50 BxP | KxP |
|--------|-----|
| 51 K-B2 | K-N4 |
| 52 B-B2 | R-K4 |
| 53 BxRP | BxB |
| 54 RxB | RxP |
| 55 K-K3 | R-N4 |
| 56 P-N4 | R-K4+ |
| 57 K-Q4 | K-B5 |
| 58 R-R8 | P-N4 |
| 59 R-QB8 | R-K5+ |
| 60 K-Q5 | R-K4+ |
| 61 K-B6 | P-N5 |

| 62 RxP | P-N6 |
| 63 K-N6 | P-N7 |
| 64 R-B1 | K-B6 |

### DIAGRAM

**Draw agreed.** A possible conclusion would have been 65 P-R4 K-B7 66 P-R5 R-K8 67 R-B2+ R-K7 68 R-B1 R-K8 69 R-B2+ with a draw by repetition. If Black forces White to give up his rook in this variation by 67 . . . K-B8 the position is still drawn after e.g. 68 RxP KxR 69 P-R6 R-QR8 70 P-R7 K-B6 71 K-N7 K-K5 72 P-R8=Q

RxQ 73 KxR K-Q4 and Black wins White's last pawn.

(Times: 4.02 — 4.07)

# GAME NINETEEN

## 7th September

After the eighteenth game the new spirit of détente was marked by a party given for both delegations by the wife of President Marcos. She had recently been nominated for the Nobel Peace prize and on the evidence of this occasion she certainly deserved it. It was a pity that adverse weather conditions prevented her from attending the party herself.

The party started a little frostily but as the evening wore on the two delegations began to intermingle. Everyone obviously enjoyed themselves and by the end of the evening even the sinister Dr. Zukhar was to be observed in a tired and parapsychological condition happily dancing to the strains of Mozart and Liszt.

When dawn broke there were obviously those who wished it hadn't, and the Russians decided to postpone the nineteenth game. This may seem rather surprising as the game was not due to start till 5 p.m., but Karpov had two postponements in reserve before game 24 and so he could easily afford to use one of them.

For the nineteenth game Ms. Leeuwerik flooded the audience with parapsychologists and gurus, thus brilliantly solving the problem of the sparse audience for the match.

One group consisted of girl parapsychology students of Father Jaime Bulatao the Jesuit priest from Ateneo de Manila University. They were an ornamental addition to the audience and Korchnoi had reason to be grateful that he had not pressed his demand for a one-way mirror. This nubile bunch was busy conjuring up good vibrations for Korchnoi, though it later transpired that none of them could play chess. It was charming to watch them thinking positively and willing Korchnoi to victory in positions where a draw was all he could reasonably hope for.

The other group, who appeared to be rivals of the first, was composed of two members of the fanatical religious sect Ananda Marga, called Stephen Dwyer and Victoria Shepherd. Resplendent in saffron robes and turbans they adopted the lotus position in the immediate vicinity of the Soviet delegation. This colourful couple were on bail pending appeal against conviction for the attempted murder, by stabbing, of a diplomat, for which they had each received a seventeen year sentence. It was there-fore readily understandable that the Russians swiftly evacuated their benches and trooped *en masse* into the restaurant in the bowels of the Convention Centre. The picturesque pair were later persuaded to move a few seats away from the Soviet enclosure so that the Russians could return. As soon as they complied they were encircled by security agents who kept them under nervous surveillance for the rest of the game.

Before the match Korchnoi had predicted that it would be over in twenty games. When the nineteenth game started, Karpov needed only two more wins to retain his title. Did Korchnoi remember his earlier prediction?

The course of the nineteenth game suggests that Korchnoi was still trying to consolidate his nerves after earlier traumatic experiences. He adopted the Catalan Opening with which he had obtained no advantage in the fifteenth game. Again Karpov equalised comfortably and it seemed to me, from the amount of time Korchnoi took over the early phase of the game, that Korchnoi was not entirely at ease. The game fluctuated slightly but it was always objectively drawn and Korchnoi's only real danger came from his old enemy the clock. But he managed to find some good moves fast and shortly before the adjournment the game was agreed drawn by means of a mutual shrug of the shoulders.

Karpov now led 4-1, with 14 draws.

**White: Korchnoi**
**Black: Karpov**

### Catalan Opening

| | |
|---|---|
| 1 P-QB4 | N-KB3 |
| 2 P-KN3 | P-K3 |
| 3 B-N2 | P-Q4 |
| 4 N-KB3 | B-K2 |
| 5 P-Q4 | O-O |
| 6 QN-Q2 | P-QN3 |
| 7 O-O | B-N2 |
| 8 PxP | |

Varying from 8 P-N3 which Korchnoi played against Petrosian in their eleventh Candidates' game last year.

| | |
|---|---|
| 8 . . . | PxP |
| 9 N-K5 | QN-Q2 |
| 10 QN-B3 | P-B4 |
| 11 P-N3 | P-QR4 |

Korchnoi felt this was not good but I disagree. The weakening of Black's QN4 square never turns out to be important, while the threat of . . . P-QR5 hanging over White's head is very annoying.

| | |
|---|---|
| 12 B-N2 | N-K5 |

**13 R-B1**

Korchnoi even considered 13 R-N1 here, which shows that he was perturbed by the possibility of . . . P-QR5.

| | |
|---|---|
| 13 . . . | R-K1 |
| 14 NxN? | |

This prematurely reduces the tension. White should have kept things on the boil with 14 P-K3 though I doubt if he could then boast of any objective advantage.

| | |
|---|---|
| 14 . . . | QxN |
| 15 N-K5 | Q-K3 |
| 16 N-Q3 | B-Q3 |
| 17 PxP | PxP |

**18 P-K3**

White is slowly forfeiting the initiative. Black's hanging pawns on QB4 and Q4 control a lot of space and his development is more efficient.

White could not of course play 18 BxN QxB 19 NxP? because of 19 . . . BxN 20 RxB P-Q5 21 P-B3 Q-K6+ followed by 22 . . . P-Q6 winning.

| 18 . . . | P-R5 |
| 19 PxP | B-R3 |
| 20 R-K1 | BxN? |

White was faced by a number of tactical threats but this hasty decision releases most of them. Best was 20 . . . Q-B4 21 R-B2 B-B5 increasing the pressure.

| 21 QxB | RxP |
| 22 Q-N3 | |

Objectively White should have no difficulty in drawing now, but Korchnoi only had twenty minutes (against Karpov's fifty) in which to reach the time control at move 40.

| 22 . . . | R(R5)-R1 |
| 23 BxN | PxB |

20 . . . QxB 21 R(K1)-Q1 P-B5 leads to liquidation and an early draw. Karpov probably decided to chance his arm on Korchnoi's clock.

| 24 QxQ | RxQ |
| 25 P-QR3 | R-R5 |
| 26 KR-Q1 | P-B3 |
| 27 K-B1? | |

Better was 27 R-B3 followed by 28 R-N3 when White's active rooks leave him with nothing to fear.

| 27 . . . | K-B2 |
| 28 R-B2 | B-K2 |

| 29 R-Q7 | R-N3 |
| 30 P-N4 | |

A more dignified way of drawing was 30 RxP (threatening to double on the seventh) 30 . . . K-K1 31 R(B5)-B7 B-Q3 32 RxB RxR 33 RxP and White is slightly better, although he cannot win.

| 30 . . . | K-K3 |
| 31 R-B7 | R-R1 |

Now White's adventurous rook is in some danger but in trying to find a way to trap it Karpov also got into time trouble and I noticed that the world champion was becoming flustered.

| 32 R-Q2 | P-N3 |

32 . . . R-Q1 would have given White some problem.

| 33 K-N2 | P-B4 |
| 34 P-N5! | |

Now White has nothing to worry about. If necessary he can bale out with B-B6. Soon Karpov is reduced to trying to exchange the rook he wanted to trap.

| 34 . . . | R-Q3 |
| 35 R-B2 | R(Q3)-R3 |
| 36 P-KR4 | R-(R1)-R2 |
| 37 R-B8 | R-R1 |
| 38 R-B7 | R-(R1)-R2 |
| 39 R-B8 | |

**Draw agreed**

(Times: 2.26  2.27)

# GAME TWENTY

At 10.45 on the morning of the twentieth game I was dragged out of bed by Camponanes and summoned to a meeting of the jury at which the future of the two Ananda Margas was discussed. I promised that they would watch the games in civilian clothes (i.e. without their saffron robes and turbans) and also that they would maintain a low profile by abandoning the lotus position. It was decided to leave the whole matter to Camponanes, who resolved only one hour before the game was due to start that the Ananda Margas would not be allowed to enter. I then explained to him that this decision was unfair and it was duly modified by providing that people with criminal records (no names mentioned!) should be banned from the auditorium as from game twenty-one. The Ananda Margas were allowed in for the last time to watch game twenty on condition they behaved normally.

Meanwhile Korchnoi had been receiving support from various interesting quarters. A telegram from France saying *"Avec nous en coeur"* purported to come from an eminent literary quartet Arrabal, Becket, Ionesco and Sartre. We were not sure whether it was genuine but we certainly hoped so. The backing of Fernando Arrabal, as originator of the *Theatre of Panic*, seemed especially appropriate!

Korchnoi also received a telegram from Donald Woods, whose outspoken criticisms of *apartheid* had caused him to be banned in South Africa and who now lives in England. His message was: "Have African witch doctor casting spells for you. Free world hopes for your victory." Was one of these spells resposible for Karpov's forty-second move in the twentieth game?

In game twenty Korchnoi defended with a line of the Caro Kann which I recently examined in *Modern Chess Theory*. Although it is unpopular I have a lot of faith in it and managed to convert Korchnoi. The opening was a surprise to Karpov and he was unable to obtain any real advantage. But in the middlegame Korchnoi faltered seriously, wasting time with inane knight manoeuvres, and eventually he allowed his queenside to collapse. At adjournment his position was hopeless but then a miracle occurred. Karpov had not sealed the obvious and immediately decisive move. Karpov should still have won but further mistakes allowed Kochnoi to escape with a totally unexpected draw.

After the game Korchnoi said: 'No amount of gurus will help me if I play bad moves". This sober admission I took as a good sign.

Karpov now led 4-1 with 15 draws.

**White: Karpov**
**Black: Korchnoi**

### Caro Kann Defence

| | |
|---|---|
| 1 P-K4 | P-QB3 |
| 2 P-Q4 | P-Q4 |
| 3 N-Q2 | PxP |
| 4 NxP | N-B3 |
| 5 NxN+ | KPxN |

This move has often been condemned but the situation is deceptive and Golombek, Bronstein and Flohr have all used the move to good effect. White obtains the long-term advantage of a potential queenside pawn majority, but, despite the doubled KBP, Black's mass of kingside pawns offer good compensation, since the front KBP can advance while the rear KBP stays at home to shelter the Black king. As the game proceeds all these themes are illustrated.

| | |
|---|---|
| 6 B-QB4 | N-Q2 |

Korchnoi's theoretical novelty. The idea is to save a tempo on such lines as 6 . . . B-Q3 7 Q-K2+ B-K2

| | |
|---|---|
| 7 N-K2 | B-Q3 |
| 8 0-0 | 0-0 |

8 . . . Q-B2 is also possible

| | |
|---|---|
| 9 B-B4 | N-N3 |
| 10 B-Q3 | |

An interesting decision. The natural move would be 10 B-QN3 to keep the bishop aimed at KB7 but Karpov appreciates that the bishop will ultimately be more useful on the KR1-QR8 diagonal supporting the advance of his queenside pawn majority.

| | |
|---|---|
| 10 . . . | B-K3 |
| 11 P-QB3 | N-Q4 |
| 12 BxB | QxB |
| 13 Q-Q2 | QR-Q1 |

Keeping a watchful eye on the prospective passed pawn.

| | |
|---|---|
| 14 KR-K1 | P-KN3 |
| 15 QR-Q1 | K-N2 |
| 16 B-K4 | N-B2 |
| 17 P-QN3 | KR-K1 |
| 18 B-N1 | |

It looks strange to abandon the ideal diagonal but there were tactical threats against the bishop. If instead 18 B-B3 Korchnoi was planning the complicated manoeuvre 18 . . . P--R4 (threatening 19 . . . B-N5) 19 P-KR3 B-B1 followed by . . . N-K3 and . . . N-N4 molesting the bishop.

| | |
|---|---|
| 18 . . . | B-N5 |
| 19 P-KR3 | BxN |
| 20 RxB | RxR |
| 21 QxR | N-Q4 |
| 22 Q-Q2 | |

| | |
|---|---|
| 22 . . . | N-B5? |

Korchnoi's opening has been a success but now he throws away the fruits of his good play. After the obvious 22 . . . P-KB4 White's

bishop is deprived of any immediate possibility of returning to the
key KR1-QR8 diagonal and Black
could then manoeuvre his knight
to K5 via KB3 or carry out a
general advance of his kingside
pawns in more favourable circumstances than later occurs in the
game.

**23 B-K4**

Of course. Now Black has to
struggle for survival.

**23 ...                P-KB4**

'Too late. Too late she cried,
waving her wooden leg'.

**24 B-B3              P-KR3**
**25 P-KR4**

Planning to cut off the knight,
which involves Black in a general
retreat. Still the pawn on KR4
does become a target.

Also dangerous was 25 P-Q5 PxP
26 Q-Q4 with moves like QxRP
and PxP in the offing.

Karpov had now spent one hour
twenty-five minutes and Korchnoi
one hour fifty minutes.

**25 ...                N-K3**
**26 Q-K3             N-B2**
**27 P-B4             P-B5?**

I believe this was a blunder over-
looking White's 29th move. Correct was 27 ... Q-B3

**28 Q-B3            Q-B3**
**29 Q-R5**

### DIAGRAM

Exceedingly strong. Korchnoi's
now used up fifteen of his remaining thirty-five minutes, but then
proceeded to move at blitz speed.
Since 29 Q-R5 wipes out Black's
queen side the situation is fast becoming critical for Korchnoi.

**29 ...                N-K3**

**30 P-Q5             PxP**
**31 PxP              P-N3**

Not 31 ... N-Q5? 32 RxN.

**32 Q-R4**

A powerful *intermezzo* again
preventing ... N-Q5.

**32 ...                N-B4**
**33 QxRP            N-Q2**
**34 P-Q6             QxRP**
**35 Q-B7             Q-B3**
**36 P-QN4           P-R4**

A last desperate attempt to exploit his kingside majority with a
rush of his peasant army.

**37 P-R4             K-R3**
**38 P-N5**

Of course 38 P-R5 was also possible but I suppose Karpov did not
want to eliminate the weak Black
QNP.

**38 ...                P-N4**
**39 B-B6             N-B4**
**40 P-Q7             K-N2**

40 ... N-K3 at once would have
saved a tempo.

**41 R-K1             N-K3**
### DIAGRAM

**42 Q-Q6??**

The disastrous sealed move over
which Karpov thought for thirty
minutes. After the expected 42
QxNP Black's kingside counterplay

soon fizzles out e.g. 42 . . . P-N5 43 P-R5 P-N6 44 PxP PxP 45 Q-K3 Q-R5 46 R-Q1 and Black can do nothing. 43 . . . P-B6 is a better chance but it is still extremely forlorn.

Our analysis lasted through the night but it was haunted by the knowledge that 42 QxP was murderous. Murei did not even dare to watch the resumption of play since he could not bear to face the prospect of 42 QxP being played. There were sighs of relief all round from the rats who had not left the sinking ship when the queen appeared on Q6 not QN6.

42 . . . P-N5
43 K-B1

A typical Karpov safety precaution. If 43 R-K5 P-N6 44 P-R5 PxRP 45 P-N6 P-B6! exploiting the theme of Black's opening variation in a particularly striking way e.g. 46 PxNP PxP 47 BxP RxP 48 QxR QxR and Black can hold on since the White king is exposed. Or 46 PxBP Q-R5 47 PxP QxP+ and again Black will probably obtain a perpetual. Finally 46 BxP allows 46 . . . PxP+ 47 KxP RxP etc.

43 . . . P-N6?
Overcome with relief Korchnoi

moved too hastily. 43 . . . P-R5 would have saved an important tempo.

44 Q-K5 P-R5
45 P-R5

This pawn sacrifice keeps White's chances alive.

45 . . . PxP
46 P-N6 QxQ
47 RxQ R-QN1
48 P-N7 N-Q1

Black's only chance is a last-ditch Nimzowitschian blockade. His pieces are now spectacularly paralysed.

After the game Murei commented that Black's position was now reminiscent of Korchnoi's situation during the Nazi blockade of Lenningrad.

49 R-K8 K-B3

Of course 49 . . . NxB loses to 50 PxR NxR 51 P-Q8=Q.

50 PxP BPxP
51 K-K2 K-N2
52 B-B3?

This allows the Black QRP to become a menace and White has to suspend his grip. Correct was the manoeuvre 52 K-B3 P-B4 53 B-R4 followed by 54 B-B2 and 55 BxP which should win for White.

52 . . . P-R5
53 R-K4

If 53 K-Q3 P-B4 54 K-B3 P-B5 55 K-N4 RxP+ 56 BxR NxB and Black should not lose.

53 . . . K-B3
54 RxQRP K-K2
55 RxP

If 55 R-R8 RxP 56 BxR NxB draws. White cannot win the exchange ahead if Black can pick up White's QP and retain his own

KBP and here he can achieve both objectives.

| 55 . . . | KxP |
|---|---|
| 56 R-KB4? | |

The last chance was 56 R-R8. Now it is a draw.

| 56 . . . | K-Q3 |
|---|---|
| 57 R-QN4 | K-B2 |
| 58 R-B4+ | K-Q2 |
| 59 B-N4+ | K-K1 |
| 60 R-K4+ | K-B1 |
| 61 B-Q7 | RxP |

Not 61 . . . NxP? allowing the pin 62 R-QN4 followed by 63 B-B6.

| 62 R-K8+ | K-N2 |
|---|---|
| 63 RxN | R-N7+ |

### DIAGRAM

**Draw agreed.**

White must defend his last pawn by 64 K-B3 but then Black draws

by the pin 64 . . . R-Q7 with the unanswerable threat of 65 . . . K-B3 and 66 . . . K-K2

A difficult, fascinating but flawed game.

(Times: 3.29 — 3.35)

Note these are the times after move 60. No official record exists of the times at the end of the game.

# GAME TWENTY-ONE

## 12th and 13th September

In accordance with Camponanes' edict the Anada Margas absented themselves from the Playing Hall and it looked as though the match might be about to enter a sane phase. But students of sensation need not worry. Our mystical friends will shortly return to enliven these pages!

The twenty-first game featured a great come-back by Korchnoi. He reverted to the variation of the Queen's Gambit Declined he had played in the ninth game — partly out of devilry since Tal had written in *64* that the variation was harmless . The Russians had a startling innovation ready which most observers assumed had been fed to Karpov by his more risk-prone seconds Tal and Zaitsev. Korchnoi calmly demonstrated that Black's violence was premature and emerged from the complications with an extra pawn. Careless play allowed Karpov to regain the pawn but then the champion returned the favour and allowed the challenger to adjourn a pawn up. Although we started on the wrong track we eventurally analysed the adjourned position more efficently than the Russians. The position was not clearly won for Korchnoi but it required more accurate defence from Karpov than it received. After the champion fell into a neat trap the challenger made no mistake and finished off with an elegant piece sacrifice.

After the game Korchnoi commented to the assembled press "Lord forgive them. They know not what they do." This was presumably a reference to the Russians' adjournment analysis which for the first time was substantially inferior to our own — an encouraging sign.

Despite mistakes on both sides this game was generally considered the best of the match so far. Both players played creatively and it was the first decisive game in which the result could be attributed more to good play by the winner than unforced errors by the loser.

Karpov remained hot favourite but this game made it clear that Korchnoi was not going to surrender without a fight, as many had feared after his debacle in the seventeenth game.

Karpov now led 4-2 with 15 draws.

| | | | |
|---|---|---|---|
| **White: Korchnoi** | | 1 P-QB4 | N-KB3 |
| **Black: Karpov** | | 2 N-QB3 | P-K3 |
| | | 3 N-B3 | P-Q4 |
| Queen's Gambit Declined | | 4 P-Q4 | B-K2 |

101

| 5 B-B4 | 0-0 |
| 6 P-K3 | P-B4 |
| 7 QPxP | BxP |
| 8 Q-B2 | N-B3 |
| 9 R-Q1 | Q-R4 |
| 10 P-QR3 | |

All so far as in the ninth game.

10 . . .                R-K1

A new move, varying from 10 . . . B-K2 played in the ninth game.

| 11 N-Q2 | P-K4 |
| 12 B-N5 | |

12 . . .                N-Q5

The point of Black's tenth move. Although the move came as a terrible shock, analysis convinced Korchnoi that the positon did not justify such violence and he fell back in good Steinitzian order.

13 Q-N1

Karpov now stopped moving instantaneously and the Russians trooped off to the press room to analyse. Since Karpov's innovation turns out badly the Russian prepared analysis must have overlooked something but can it really have been this natural retreat?

Korchnoi is renowned for grabbing material and trying to weather the ensuing storm but, as in the tenth game, he now decides that discretion is the better part of valour. His caution was justified e.g. (A) 13 PxN PxP+ 14 N-K2 N-N5 (threatening 15 . . . P-Q6 and 16 . . . BxP mate) 15 B-R4 PxP 16 QxP N-K4 with . . . P-Q6 and . . . N-Q6 in the offing.
(B) 13 PxN PxP+ 15 B—K2 PxN 16 N-N3 Q-N3 17 NxB QxN 18 BxN PxB does not accomphish anything for White.

13 . . .                B-B4

If 13 . . . B-KN5 14 BxN PxB 15 NxP! BxR 16 KxB leaves Black exposed to a multitude of threats such as 16 P-QN4, 16 PxN and 16 NxP+.

| 14 B-Q3 | P-K5 |
| 15 B-B2 | |

15 BxN PxB(Q6) 16 BxN BxB 17 NxP P-QN4 is unclear. It is possible that the cynical 15 B-B1 would have refuted Black's conception entirely, but Korchnoi feared this might be going slightly too far on the Steinitzian path.

The text has the disadvantage that it allows Black to exchange his errant knight but at least Black's centre remains a target for Korchnoi to tilt at.

15 . . .                NxB+
16 QxN                Q-R3

If 16 . . . PxP, 17 BxN PxB 18 P-QN4 PxP e.p. 19 NxP QxP 20 R-R1 Q-N5 21 R-R4 Q-N3 22 N-Q5 looks good for White and so Karpov decides to sacrifice a pawn for reasonable counterplay.

| 17 BxN | QxB |
| 18 N-N3 | B-Q3 |
| 19 RxP | R-K4 |
| 20 N-Q4 | R-QB1 |

DIAGRAM

**21 RxR?**

A careless move which loses the extra pawn. Correct was 21 NxB.

| 21 . . . | QxR |
| 22 NxB | QxN(B4) |
| 23 0-0 | RxP |
| 24 R-Q1 | Q-K4? |

A plausible blunder which Karpov played after only a few minutes thought. Best was 24 . . . B-K2 25 Q-N3 Q-B1 and Black has little to fear.

| 25 P-KN3 | P-QR3 |
| 26 Q-N3 | P-QN4 |
| 27 P-QR4 | |

Now Black cannot satisfactorily defend his queenside. Karpov finds the best chance but it is not very impressive.

| 27 . . . | R-N5 |
| 28 Q-Q5 | QxQ |
| 29 RxQ | B-B1 |
| 30 PxP | P-QR4 |
| 31 R-Q8 | RxP(N7) |
| 32 R-R8 | P-B4 |
| 33 RxP | B-N5 |
| 34 R-R8+ | K-B2 |
| 35 N-R4 | R-N8+ |
| 36 K-N2 | B-Q3 |
| 37 R-R7+ | K-B3 |
| 38 P-N6 | B-N1 |
| 39 R-R8 | |

Panno pointed out the ingenious

39 R-B7! threatening 40 R-B8. Black cannot then play 39 . . . BxR 40 PxB R-B8 41 N-N6 RxP 42 N-Q5+ or 39 . . . R-N5 40 N-B5 RxP 41 N-Q7+ K-N3 42 R-B8 winning.

| 39 . . . | B-K4 |
| 40 N-B5 | B-Q3 |
| 41 P-N7 | K-K2 |
| 42 R-KN8 | B-K4 |

**43 P-B4**

The sealed move which is White's only way of making progress. The point is to free White's king and open up Q3 for the knight.

| 43 . . . | PxP e.p. + |
| 44 KxP | K-B2 |
| 45 R-B8 | |

We had analysed the adjouned position until the last hour. We wasted a lot of time considering the unnecessary piece sacrifice 45 R-Q8 K-K2 46 R-Q7+ K-K1 47 P-K4 R-N4 48 PxP RxN 49 RxP but we finally decided that 49 . . . P-R3! refutes the whole idea since White needs KN5 for his rook while rook endings with an extra pawn are drawn. An hour before the second session Korchnoi abandoned the whole unsound idea and we frantically started analysing the text move.

| 45 . . . | K-K2 |
| --- | --- |
| 46 P-R3! | |

A subtle trap which the Russians overlooked.

| 46 . . . | P-R4? |
| --- | --- |

Correct was 46 . . . R-N4 when White still has chances but there is no clear win. After the text all Black's pawns are exposed along the fourth rank.

| 47 R-KN8 | K-B2 |
| --- | --- |
| 48 R-Q8 | P-N4 |

The point of the trap is that the intended 48 . . . K-K2 loses to 49 R-Q7+ K-K1 50 R-Q5 B-B3 51 RxP since Black's KRP is attached and so he has no time to pick up White's QNP.

49 P-N4!

A very good move. 49 N-Q7 wins a piece but probably not the game after 49 . . . P-N5+ 50PxP RPxP+ 51 K-K2 BxP.

49 N-Q3 also only draws after 49 . . . P-N5+ 50 PxP RPxP+ 51 K-B2 K-K2 52 NxB KxR 53 P-N8=Q+ RxQ 54 N-B6+ K-B2 55 NxR KxN 56 P-K4 K-B2!.

| 49 . . . | RPxP+ |
| --- | --- |
| 50 PxP | K-K2 |
| 51 R-KN8 | PxP+ |

If now 51 . . . B-Q3 52 N-R6 RxP 53 R-N7+ wins.

| 52 KxP | K-B2 |
| --- | --- |
| 53 R-B8 | B-Q3 |
| 54 P-K4 | |

Not at once 54 KxP BxN 55 P-N8=Q RxQ 56 RxR BxP+ winning White's last pawn and leaving a drawn R v B ending. But now 55 KxP is a threat.

| 54 . . . | R-N8+ |
| --- | --- |
| 55 K-B5 | P-N5 |
| 56 P-K5 | R-B8+ |
| 57 K-K4 | R-K8+ |
| 58 K-Q5 | R-Q8+ |

If 58 . . . BxP 59 N-Q3 wins.

59 N-Q3!

An elegant piece sacrifice with which to round off the game.

| 59 . . . | RxN+ |
| --- | --- |
| 60 K-B4 | |

Schmid was now hovering with a White queen ready for the expected promotion of White's QNP. Korchnoi skittishly requested that he have a rook knight and bishop ready as well in case he decided to underpromote. **Karpov** took the hint and **resigned** to the accompaniment of loud cheers and chapping.

A fascinating, difficult but flawed game.

(Times: 3.39 —3.31)

# GAME TWENTY-TWO

After the Ananda Margas first appeared on the scene Camponanes ordered a summary of their trial and before the twenty-second game he distributed the fruits of his research. The report on the trial proved to be a very damning document which put both the individuals, Dwyer and Shepperd, the the Ananda Marga organisation as a whole in a very bad light.

The report filed by provincial fiscal B. Jose Castillo stated that in the case of The People of The Philippines vs. Steven Michael Dwyer and Victoria Shepperd (Seventh Judicial District of the Circuit Criminal Court) the accused had been convicted of the fustrated murder of an Indian Embassy official, Jyoti Suarap Vaid in February 1978 in Makati Metro Manila. The summary of the trial appears to be full of inconsistencies and even accuses Ananda Marga of being communist inspired! Rather oddly for a legal document it contains a general condemnation of Ananda Marga which I quote:

"The fact that the Ananda Marga does not stop at anything to achieve its diabolical ends unmistakably makes its followers not only threats to individual lives but also to national security. The symptom and the warning on this particular occasion had surfaced: the Ananda Marga considers government officials as fair game in their missions of assassination."

Whether or not the Ananda Margas were rightly convicted, it is not surprising that their association with the match gave rise to concern. The issues involved (especially the importance to be attached to the existence of a serious criminal charge before the truth of the charge has been finally determined) bore a striking similarity to those which were simultaneously dogging the Liberal Party Conference in England.

The day the report of the trial was released there was an exchange of letters between Lim Kok Ann and Camponanes extracts from which follow. (Italics mine).


Lim Kok Ann to Camponanes
"I hope I am not being alarmist but I cannot help being concerned by the intrusion of the Ananda Marga people into our proceedings. Although it has been reported that the members of

the sect are not authorised to undertake acts of violence by their leader it is also reported that such acts have been performed, e.g. suicide by burning in the name of love for all humanity. I hardly need point out that all manner of atrocities have been performed in the same name in human history down the ages."

. . . . .

"I am sorry to trouble you with these groundless fears, perhaps, and *I am sure you will take care of the matter* in the appropriate manner."

Camponanes to Lim Kok Ann

"[The Ananda Margas'] continued association with its implications and consequences will compel us to ask for a technical recess of the match *until this question is resolved by the jury*. This failing, we are left with no alternative but to terminate the match for reasons of general and personal security."

So once again the match was in danger of ending prematurely and the Chairman of the Jury and the Match Organiser were each hoping the other would do something about it. The Korchnoi camp had already conceded one point when we acquiesced in the decision that the Ananda Margas should not enter the Playing Hall itself. We now made another concession by persuading the Ananda Margas to move from the Pines Hotel to the private villa which had been supplied for Korchnoi's use during the match. The agreement that their activities should in future be confined to consenting yogis in private assuaged the fears of the organisers and the match was on again. A few days later the dismissal of the Ananda Margas to the shadows was confirmed by my announcement that they should no longer be considered part of the Korchnoi delegation.

Having quoted the views of so many other people, I had better express my own views on the Ananda Margas. Perched firmly on my fence all I can say is that it is possible they were a genuine security risk. It is also possible that they were framed and the whole issue blown up out of all proportion. It is possible they were basically publicity seekers for their own cause. It is also possible that they were good hearted people who just wanted to help Korchnoi. It is almost impossible to decide.

The Ananda Marga dispute was merely concerned with their public manifestation. Although personally I did not find some of their antics exactly to my taste, I cannot deny that in their private capacity they appeared to be helpful to Korchnoi. He had appeared much calmer since his return from Manila where he met the Ananda Margas in the interval between the seventeenth and eighteenth games. It is true that his recovery could also be attributed to the settlement of the Zukhar dispute at the same time but I think it would be churlish to deny that, through the medium of their spiritual exercises, the Ananda Margas played an important part.

Returning at last to the chess, the twenty-second was in a way a disappointment for both players.

Korchnoi, playing the French Defence again, obtained an uncomfortable middlegame in which he was thoroughly outplayed by Karpov. It was clear that he had still not found a satisfactory defence with Black.

Karpov had even more reason to be disappointed. He wasted his earlier fine play by mistakes *after* the time control. When the game was adjourned on the forty-seventh move his opportunity had gone. In the second session Korchnoi secured a draw though it took some very accurate endgame play to do so. Karpov's disappointment must have been increased by the knowledge that his missed opportunity was so unnecessary. He could have made virtually certain of the win by sealing as soon as he reached the time control.

Golombek cited the game as evidence for the existence of life after death.

Karpov now led 4-2 with 16 draws.

**White: Karpov**
**Black: Korchnoi**

### French Defence

| 1 P-K4 | P-K3 |
|--------|------|
| 2 P-Q4 | P-Q4 |
| 3 N-Q2 | P-QB4 |
| 4 KPxP | KPxP |
| 5 B-N5+ | B-Q2 |
| 6 Q-K2+ | B-K2 |

Varying from 6 ... Q-K2 played in the sixteenth game.

| 7 PxP | N-KB3 |
|-------|-------|
| 8 N-N3 | 0-0 |
| 9 B-K3 | R-K1 |
| 10 N-B3 | |

An unusual move which Karpov played at blitz speed. Korchnoi, after long thought, now decides to regain the pawn with a pseudo-combination but White retains the initiative in the opposite bishops middle game.

| 10 ... | BxP |
|--------|-----|
| 11 NxB | Q-R4+ |
| 12 Q-Q2 | QxB |
| 13 0-0-0 | P-QN3 |

Better was 13 ... B-N5, to inflict counter-weaknesses on White's position.

| 14 NxB | QNxN |
|--------|------|
| 15 K-N1 | N-K5 |
| 16 Q-Q3 | QxQ |
| 17 RxQ | N(Q2)-B3 |
| 18 P-KR3 | |

This is just the kind of position not to have against Karpov, who can develope his offensive against White's isolated queen pawn virtually unmolested.

| 18 ... | N-B4 |
|--------|------|
| 19 R(Q3)-Q1 | N-K3 |

| 20 P-B3 | P-QN4 |

In search of counterplay, Korchnoi exposes his pawns.

| 21 N-Q4 | P-QR3 |
| 22 N-B2 | P-QR4 |
| 23 R-Q3 | QR-N1 |
| 24 R(R1)-Q1 | P-R3 |
| 25 P-KB4 | QR-B1 |
| 26 P-KN4 | |

| 26 ... | P-Q5 |

Karpov has played with great skill and Black's position is now critical. Nobody could see an answer to White's projected P-KN5. Korchnoi solves (well - not quite solves) his problems by sacrificing the weakling QP to obtain good squares for his knights. This is an imaginative solution but not quite adequate.

26 ... P-Q5 is pure Nimzowitsch and the following quotation from *My System* could easily apply to it:

"So powerful is the pawn's desire to press on here to expand (of which fact indeed visible recognition is given in the way the officers, laying aside all pride of cast, picturesquely group themsleves round this simple foot soldier), that our pawn often seems

ready to advance on his own account, when to do so will cost him his life — and now all of a sudden the forces in the rear come to life".

| 27 PxP | N-Q4 |
| 28 R-KB1 | P-N5 |

Korchnoi opined that he would have sufficient compensation if his pawns were still on QR2 and QN3 — but they aren't.

| 29 B-Q2 | R-K2 |
| 30 P-B5 | |

If 30 N-K3 N(K3)xP 31 RxN NxR 32 N-B5 R-K7 and the knight on KB5 is immune.

| 30 ... | N-N4 |
| 31 N-K3 | N-B3 |
| 32 P-Q5 | |

Sensibly returning the sacrificed pawn in order to envigorate his own queen pawn and attack Black's queenside.

| 32 ... | NxRP |

32 ... N(N4)-K5 offered better practical chances.

| 33 P-Q6 | R-Q2 |
| 34 N-Q5 | NxN |
| 35 RxN | R-R1 |
| 36 B-K3 | N-N4 |

In desperate time trouble Korchnoi misses the last real chance, which lay in 36 ... R-R3.

| 37 B-N6 | N-K5 |
| 38 R(B1)-Q1 | P-R5 |
| 39 R(Q5)-Q4 | R-K1 |
| 40 RxP | RxP |
| 41 RxR | NxR |

DIAGRAM

42 B-B7??

Why on earth did not Karpov seal the simple 42 RxP? He had

108

plenty of time and was in any case already past the time control.

| | |
|---|---|
| 42 ... | R-K8+ |
| 43 K-B2 | N-K1 |
| 44 B-R5 | P-R6 |
| 45 R-N8 | R-K2 |
| 46 B N4? | |

46 PxP must be superior. Did he overlook that Black's next move or what??

| | |
|---|---|
| 46 ... | R-K7+ |
| 47 K-Q3 | PxP |

The sealed move over which Korchnoi pondered for forty minutes. It later transpired that 47 . . . RxP 48 RxN+ K-R2 49 BxP RxP leads to a position where Black has time for . . . P-KB3, when the perpetual threat of . . . P-R4 means White cannot win. But who would dare seal a move like 47 . . . RxP?

On resumption — after many hours of analysis — we believed that Black could still draw, in spite of White's outside passed pawn supported by a bishop. The Russians had announced that 47 . . . RxP was a draw but that 47 . . . PxP lost but, as in the previous game, our adjournment analysis proved superior to theirs. It was Korchnoi who moved at

lightning speed in the second session while Karpov had to wrack his brains trying to find a win which wasn't there.

**48 B-Q2**

48 B-B3 P-N8=Q+ 49 RxQ RxP 50 R-N8 transposes into the drawn piece sacrifice line referred to in the previous note.

| | |
|---|---|
| 48 ... | R-K2 |
| 49 P-R4 | R-Q2+ |
| 50 K-B2 | K-R2 |
| 51 RxP | P-R4! |

Necessary, in order to create targets for the knight.

| | |
|---|---|
| 52 PxP | N-Q3 |
| 53 R-R2 | |

Another key variation is 53 R N4 NxP 54 P-R5 N-Q5+ followed by . . . N-B3 and . . . NxP when White cannot win despite his extra piece.

| | |
|---|---|
| 53 ... | NxP |
| 54 P-R5 | N-Q5+ |
| 55 K-B3 | N-B3 |
| 56 P-R6 | R-Q4 |

After this Karpov stopped for a long think. Black wipes out White's kingside and White cannot shift the knight on Black's QB3.

**57 B-B4**

57 P-R6 may be a better try but it doesn't work either.

| | |
|---|---|
| 57 ... | R-B4 |
| 58 B-Q6 | R-Q4 |
| 59 B-N3 | R-KN4 |
| 60 B-B2 | RxP |
| 61 K-B4 | N-R4+ |
| 62 K-B3 | N-B3 |
| 63 R-R4 | K-N1 |

This move, over which Korchnoi thought for half an hour draws, since White cannot prevent the Black king reaching Q2 and defending the knight on QB3. Karpov now resigns himself to the draw.

**64 K-B4          N-R4+**
**Draw agreed.**

(Times: 3.34 — 4.00)

# GAME TWENTY-THREE

### 16th September

Korchnoi's villa had now turned into a mystics playground with gurus levitating in and out at will. Some even levitated into my room which meant I had to move to the Pines Hotel permanently.

One group of gurus was of course the celebrated Ananda Margas, who now had nowhere else to go, poor things, having been banished from both the Playing Hall and the Pines Hotel. The other group comprised the parapsychological posse of Father Bulatao's decorous disciples who were free to roam at will — and did so. They were now led by one Lun, a Belgian.

I was having coffee with Ms. Leeuwerik one day when the phone rang and a waiter informed her that a Mr. Rasputin wanted to speak to her. I managed to maintain a stiff upper lip at this startling intelligence and merely uttered a silent prayer that Korchnoi and Ms. Leeuwerik would not suffer from the Red Army the fate which befell two earlier adherents of the mad monk, Nicholas and Alexandra. I was reassured when Ms. Leeuwerik explained that Rasputin was merely the code name for the aforementioned Lun. I do not think he really deserves such an illustrious sobriquet and would tentatively suggest as an alternative "The Wild Bore".

The twenty-third game was a high-class encounter, though not a particularly sensational one. Korchnoi quietly built up an advantage but Karpov defended skilfully and the game petered out into a draw shortly before the end of the first session.

The draw was accomplished in yet another new manner. Korchnoi simply wrote ½-½ and signed his score sheet and waited for Karpov to do likewise. An interesting situation would have arisen if Karpov had declined to do so!

Karpov now led 4-2 with 17 draws.

**White: Korchnoi**
**Black: Karpov**

Queen's Gambit Declined

| | | | |
|---|---|---|---|
| 1 P-QB4 | N-KB3 | 4 P-Q4 | B-K2 |
| 2 N-QB3 | P-K3 | 5 B-B4 | 0-0 |
| 3 N-B3 | P-Q4 | 6 P-K3 | P-B4 |
| | | 7 QPxP | BxP |
| | | 8 Q-B2 | N-B3 |
| | | 9 R-Q1 | Q-R4 |
| | | 10 P-QR3 | B-K2 |

111

Karpov abandons the line 10 ...
R-K1 11 N-Q2 P-K4 12 B-N5
N-Q5 which was a glorious failure
in the twenty-first game.

| 11 N-Q2 | P-K4 |
| 12 B-N5 | P-Q5 |
| 13 N-N3 | Q-N3 |

Karpov's improvement on 13 ...
Q-Q1 played in the ninth game.
We had analysed it in some detail
and concluded that White could
maintain a slight edge.

| 14 BxN | BxB |
| 15 N-Q5 | Q-Q1 |
| 16 B-Q3 | P-KN3 |

Considerably better than 16 ...
P-KR3 when the weakening of the
White squares means that White
can retain his knight on Q5. The
text also threatens 17 ... B-N2.

| 17 PxP | NxP |
| 18 NxN | PxN |
| 19 NxB+ | QxN |
| 20 0-0 | |

The position is simplified, but
White has some advantage based
on the mobility of his queenside
pawns. Objectively, though,
Black's QP should always hold the
balance.

| 20 ... | B-K3 |
| 21 KR-K1 | |

More promising is 21 P-B4 B-B4
22 BxB PxB 23 Q-N3 entertaining
such ideas as Q-N3+ followed by
Q-N5. After the game Korchnoi
described 21 P-B4 as "not the sort
of move I play", but what about
the third game of this match?

| 21 ... | QR-B1 |
| 22 P-QN3 | |

Korchnoi consolidates his position. It was also possible to try to
molest Black's queenside by 22
Q-R4.

| 22 ... | KR-Q1 |
| 23 B-K4 | R-B2 |
| 24 Q-Q2 | B-N5 |
| 25 P-B3 | |

Although he had played the
opening very quickly, Korchnoi
only had forty-five minutes left
after this move, while Karpov —
incredibly — had only used about
forty minutes thinking time. Anyway Korchnoi's thought now begins to bear fruit and he obtains a
tangible initiative.

| 25 ... | B-K3 |
| 26 P-QR4 | P-N3 |
| 27 P-R5 | P-QN4 |

Karpov could have played possum
but he generally chose to become
active when Korchnoi had less
than an hour left on his clock.

| 28 PxP | BxP |
| 29 R-N1 | B-Q4 |

29 ... R-B6 may be stronger.

| 30 P-N6 | PxP |
| 31 RxP | |

31 PxP is also dangerous for
Black, but our investigations re-
vealed that Black could still draw.

| 31 ... | R-B3 |
| 32 RxR | |

It looks good to try 32 BxB RxB

33 R-K8+ K-N2 34 R(N6)-N8 but
after 34 . . . Q-N4 it is White who
has problems.

| 32 ... | BxR |
| 33 B-Q3 | |

White still has some pull with his
distant passed pawn but Karpov
finds a clever manoeuvre to neutra-
lise it. His . . . B-Q2 followed by
. . . B-B4 is an excellent idea.

| 33 ... | B-Q2 |
| 34 P-R6 | B-B4 |
| 35 Q-B4 | |

I would prefer 35 R-R1, but
Korchnoi has a neat tactical point
in mind.

| 35 ... | K-N2 |

**36 BxB**

Now the game burns out to a
draw. Korchnoi had been planning
36 P-R7 BxB 37 Q-N8 B-B7 38
R-K8 winning but at the last
minute he saw the brilliant
counterstroke 37 . . . B-K7!! 38
RxB P-Q6 and Black draws e.g.
39 R-K8 Q-R8+.

| 36 ... | QxB |
| 37 QxQ | PxQ |
| 38 R-R1 | |

Immediately after the game
Korchnoi thought 38 K-B2 was a
significant improvement, but it
still leads to a draw.

| 38 ... | P-Q6 |
| 39 K-B2 | R-K1 |
| 40 R-R2 | R K2 |
| 41 R-Q2 | R-K3 |
| Draw agreed. | |

After the game Korchnoi sat
staring at the board for five
minutes, unable to believe his
position had not been winning at
some stage.

(Times: 2.30 — 1.53)

# GAME TWENTY-FOUR

19th September

Korchnoi prepared for the twenty-fourth game in a somewhat unconventional manner. The evening before the game an assortment of seeventeen parapsychologists, gurus, grandmasters and respectable girls and matrons assembled at Korchnoi's villa for a meditation session. Seated, of course, in the lotus position and forming a mystic circle we proceeded to chant the universal mantra *baba nam ke walam* for twenty minutes. After this spiritual cleansing our bodies were refreshed by a delicious meal of holy fruits and vegetables (meat being taboo to the Ananda Margas). Ananda Marga means 'Path of Bliss' and it now seemed to be living up to its name.

Korchnoi was so uplifted by this experience that he treated us to a spirited rendition of 'There's a Tavern in the Town' in Russian.

Whatever other effects this occasion had on Korchnoi's morale it must at least have made up for his cold, which he attributed to following the Ananda Margas' advice by sprinkling cold water on his eyes to soothe his nerves.

Korchnoi appeared to be in a daredevil mood in the twenty-fourth since he again defended with the Open Ruy Lopez which he had abandonned (for good reason) earlier in the match. Karpov seemed puzzled by the choice of opening, which was in fact largely bluff. He missed two opportunities of testing the soundness of Korchnoi's opening and drifted into an inferior middle game as a result of too automatic play. But Korchnoi was by then short of time and rejected the most forceful continuation (which he saw) in favour of one that led to a slight endgame advantage. Thereafter Karpov had no difficulty in defending and, although the game was adjourned, the second session was a formality. A draw was agreed after only four more moves.

Karpov now led 4-2 with 18 draws.

White: Karpov
Black: Korchnoi

Ruy Lopez

| | | | |
|---|---|---|---|
| 1 P-K4 | P-K4 | 5 0-0 | NxP |
| 2 N-KB3 | N-QB3 | 6 P-Q4 | P-QN4 |
| 3 B-N5 | P-QR3 | 7 B-N3 | P-Q4 |
| 4 B-R4 | N-B3 | 8 PxP | B-K3 |
| | | 9 P-B3 | B-K2 |

Varying from 9 . . . B-QB4 played in earlier games.

| | |
|---|---|
| 10 B-B2 | N-B4 |

114

**11 P-KR3**

Karpov spent fifteen minutes on this move but it is not the best. More dangerous for Black is the pawn sacrifice 11 N-Q4 (a common motif in this variation — compare game eight) 11 ... NxP 12 P-KB4 persecuting Black's minor pieces.

| 11 ... | 0-0 |

**12 R-K1**

Again 12 N-Q4 NxP 13 P-KB4 was unpleasant for Black. Korchnoi was even considering the humble 12 ... Q-Q2 in reply.

| 12 ... | Q-Q2 |
| 13 N-Q4 | NxN |
| 14 PxN | N-N2 |

**15 N-Q2**

Rather tame. Why not 15 N-B3 P-QB4 16 PxP NxP 17 B-K3 planning 18 B-Q4?

| 15 ... | P-QB4 |
| 16 PxP | NxP |
| 17 N-B3 | B-B4 |

This clears up most of Black's problems. Of course White cannot accept the pawn e.g. 18 BxB QxB 19 QxP KR-Q1 20 Q-B6 QR-B1 21 Q-N6 N-Q6 22 R-B1 NxBP 23 RxN R-Q8+ etc

| 18 B-K3 | QR-B1 |
| 19 R-QB1 | BxB |

| 20 RxB | N-K3 |
| 21 R-Q2 | KR-Q1 |
| 22 Q-N3? | |

This weak move hands over the initiative to Black. 22 B-N6 B-N5 achieves nothing but 22 R-Q3 keeps up a little pressure. Now White's queen is pushed out of play.

| 22 ... | R-B5 |

Bold but strong.

| 23 R(K1)-Q1 | Q-N2 |
| 24 P-R3 | P-N3 |

Korchnoi now only had about half an hour left and he was moving with excruciating slowness. He was considering here 24 ... P-R3 with the positional threat 25 ... B-N4 but he did not want to weaken his KB4. Nevertheless 24 ... P-R3 has probably the best move.

**25 Q-R2**

This indicates the bankruptcy of White's middlegame strategy and suggests that the blind piling up on Black's QP was insufficently subtle. The queen can do nothing from this remote square but White had to try to regroup somehow.

| 25 ... | P-QR4 |
| 26 P-QN3 | R-B6 |
| 27 P-QR4 | |

**27 . . .**                    **PxP**

Objectively the best move is 27
. . . P-N5 e.g. 28 B-Q4? RxN! 29
PxR B-N4 30 B-K3 P-Q5 and
White's position collapses. Korchnoi saw this variation but, with
only twenty minutes left on his
clock, opted for a slightly advantageous endgame rather than a
complicated middlegame — an
understandable decision.

**28 PxP**

Not 28 QxP? RxP 29 QxP R-R1
trapping the queen.

**28 . . .**                    **R-B5**

28 . . . R-R6 29 Q-B2 R-QB1 30
Q-N1 also results in the exchange
of Black's QP for Whites QRP.

| | |
|---|---|
| 29 R-Q3 | K-N2 |
| 30 Q-Q2 | RxP |
| 31 B-R6+ | K-N1 |
| 32 RxP | RxR |
| 33 QxR | QxQ |
| 34 RxQ | B-B1 |
| 35 BxB | KxB |

Black's outside passed pawn
merely constitutes a nominal
advantage. White has no difficulty
in drawing.

| | |
|---|---|
| 36 P-N3 | K-K2 |
| 37 R-N5 | N-B2 |
| 38 R-B5 | N-K3 |
| 39 R-N5 | N-Q1 |
| 40 K-N2 | P-R3 |
| 41 N-Q2 | R-R8 |
| 42 N-B4 | |

The sealed move. The second
session only lasted about five
minutes.

| | |
|---|---|
| 42 . . . | N-B3 |
| 43 R-B5 | K-Q2 |
| 44 N-N6+ | K-B2 |
| 45 N-B8 | KxN |

The players now looked at each
other with a mild surmise and
**agreed a draw** — silent, upon a
peak in Baguio.

(Times: 2.23 — 2.49)

# GAME TWENTY-FIVE

## 23rd and 24th September

Dr Max Euwe, FIDE President, arrived in Baguio after the twenty-fourth game — just in time to witness another row blow up over the Ananda Margas.

I was summoned to a meeting of the jury at which the Chairman Lim Kok Ann read out a letter complaining that he had seen two members of the Ananda Marga in the lobby of the Pines Hotel and stating: "In my opinion this negates the undertaking given by Mr Keene." I was very annoyed for various reasons.

1. It was simply not true that the presence of the Ananda Margas in the Pines Lobby negated any undertaking I had given. I had said that the Ananda Margas would move from the Pines to Korchnoi's villa and this they had done. I had not said that they would not *visit* the Pines Hotel in their capacity as friends of Korchnoi who was resident at the hotel.

2. It seemed to be assumed that, as head of the Korchnoi delegation, I was in a position to direct the movements of the Ananda Margas. There *might* have been something in this if they had remained official members of the Korchnoi delegation with the various rights and obligations that status entailed. But, at the insistence of the organisers and much against Korchnoi's will, it had been agreed they should not be members of the delegation. So how could I or anyone else direct the movement of private individuals in a free country?

3. The complaint came not from the Russian delegation or the organisers but from the chairman of the jury. I have been brought up in a system in which the roles of judge and prosecutor are not combined and I believe this to be the best system. I was disappointed in Lim Kok Ann whom I have always regarded as a pillar of wisdom and good sense. On this occasion it appeared to be a case of "The Chairman doth protest too much".

4. Although I knew roughly what was in the offing I was not given an advance copy of Lim Kok Ann's letter (as the letter itself indicated) and the meeting was summoned at too short notice for me to prepare my defence properly.

Having had time to collect my thoughts, I have presented my case in (I hope) a dispassionate and cogent manner. But at the time I was simply furious and left the meeting in case I exploded. The meeting continued in my absence and reached no conclusions. The following day I wrote to Campomanes explaining my position as outlined above.

The matter was then allowed to drop. A few days later Lim Kok Ann offered an olive branch which I was happy to accept. We are now again good friends.

Perhaps I have devoted too much space to a petty incident which in the end led nowhere. But it does illustrate the trivia which in this match so often diverted attention from the chess and wasted everyone's time and nervous energy.

With the twenty-fifth game the match moved into extra time. All other world championship matches since the Second World War have been limited to twenty-four games and under the old rules Karpov would by now have won the match. As it was he was no nearer winning than he had been three weeks before when he scored his fourth victory in the seventeenth game.

The two contestants did not agree on many things during the match and the rule governing its duration was not one of them. Karpov disliked the open-ended system because, he said, he preferred to play for draws when in the lead, rather than have to try to increase his lead. Korchnoi favoured the new system for precisely that reason. He also said he believed he was better prepared for a long match (despite his age) and that Karpov was only programmed for a twenty-four game series.

My own view was that the open-ended system was fairer even though it did place an excessive premium on stamina. But the fact that nobody knew when the match would end was very inconvenient for all those connected with the match, especially for the organisers who were in effect required to write out a blank cheque for hotel bills etc.

Each player was entitled to three postponements before the twenty-fifth game. Korchnoi had already used all his and Karpov now claimed his third postponement. From now on each player was entitled to one more postponement for each additional eight games.

The twenty-fifth game was a dramatic encounter. Karpov gradually outplayed Korchnoi with Black but just before the time control he overlooked a tactical *coup*. Korchnoi displayed superb opportunism in playing the combination at all, with only seconds left on his clock, but he almost spoilt his chance by playing the moves of the combination in the wrong order. However, Karpov failed to exploit this slip. Once again his error came *after* the time control. Korchnoi adjourned with some advantage but although the game lasted until move eighty the draw was never in real doubt.

This was another lucky escape for Korchnoi. Stean likened his desperate combination to the act of a drunk jumping out of a plane with something strapped to his back, not sure whether it was a parachute or a rucksack. Fortunately it turned out to be a parachute.

Karpov now led 4-2 with 19 draws.

| White  Korchnoi | **English Opening** | |
|---|---|---|
| **Black: Karpov** | | |
| | 1 P-QB4 | N-KB3 |

**2 N-QB3          P-K4**

For the first time Karpov varies from his solid 2...P-K3 set up. Presumably he was dissatisfied with the positions he had been obtaining defending the Queen's Gambit.

**3 P-KN3          B-N5**
**4 Q-N3**

An unusual move which puzzled Karpov, who handled the opening slowly.

**4 . . .          N-B3**

Another idea was 4 . . . BxN 5QxB N-B3 planning ...P-Q4 to hound White's queen.

**5 N-Q5**

Avoiding ...BxN. Any capture of the knight now will grant White pressure on the QB file.

**5 . . .          B-B4**
**6 P-K3**

White adopts a Stauntonesque formation!

**6 . . .          0-0**
**7 B-N2          NxN**
**8 PxN          N-K2**
**9 N-K2          P-Q3**

Korchnoi considered the immediate 9...P-QB3 superior.

**10 0-0          P-QB3**
**11 P-Q4          KPxP**
**12 KPxP          B-N3**
**13 B-N5          B-Q2**
**14 P-QR4**

Up to now Korchnoi had moved quickly (having used half an hour against Karpov's hour), but he used forty minutes over this move and seemed to be losing the thread. The plan of driving back Black's KB is a good one but why spend forty minutes on it?

**14 . . .          P-KR3**
**15 BxN          QxB**
**16 B-B3**

A curious move. Better was 16KR-K1 or 16P-R5 QxN 17 PxB RPxP 18 QxP Q-N4 when the position is drawn since White's KB is not participating in the struggle.

**16 . . .          QR-N1**
**17 P-R5          B-B2**
**18 Q-B3**

Better was 18 KR-B1

**18 . . .          KR-B1**

**19 N-B4?**

White should have baled out with 19 P-R6 leading to a drawish position after 19...B-N3. 20 RPxP RxP 21 PxP BxP 22 BxB R(N2)-B2 threatening the bishop on QB3 and the knight on K7.

**19 . . .          B-Q1**
**20 KR-K1          Q-B1**

Karpov's subtle defence gradually gains him the upper hand. Soon White starts a full scale retreat.

**21 Q-N3          B-N4**
**22 N-K2**

Korchnoi thought for fifteen minutes over this move, leaving himself with only fourteen minutes for eighteen moves — horrendous time trouble.

| 22 . . . | B-B3 |
| 23 QR-Q1 | P-B4 |
| 24 B-K4 | Q-Q1 |
| 25 Q-R2 | B-N5 |

Now White is strategically busted. The position resembles a Modern Benoni in which everything has gone wrong for White.

| 26 PxP | RxP |
| 27 P-N4 | R-B2 |
| 28 Q-N3 | QR-B1 |
| 29 P-B3 | B-Q2 |
| 30 Q-K3 | P-R3 |
| 31 B-Q3 | B-N7 |
| 32 K-N2 | |

Korchnoi does his best to patch together the tattered shreds of his position, but the following spectacular bishop invasion should have been decisive.

| 32 . . . | Q-B3 |
| 33 R-QN1 | B-R5 |
| 34 N-B4 | P-KN3 |
| 35 R-K2 | B-B8 |
| 36 Q-K4 | K-B1 |

Black could have won White's queen for rook and bishop by 36...R-K1. The resulting position would have been technically won for Black, though difficult. Could Karpov really have overlooked this, or was he playing for more?

| 37 P-N5 | PxP |
| 38 Q-N4 | R-B4?? |

Karpov overlooks a brilliant tactical point. The simple 38...BxN would have left White positionally crushed.

### DIAGRAM

**39 RxB?**

With only seconds on his clock Korchnoi sees the right idea but gets the moves in the wrong order. Correct was the immediate

39 NxP+ when Black must accept the sacrifice and after 39...PxN 40 RxB RxR 41 R-K6 Q-N4 42 QxP+ K-N2 43 Q-Q7+ K-B1 44 Q-Q6+ leads to perpetual check.

| 39 . . . | RxR |
| 40 NxP+! | K-N2! |

Now Black does not have to accept the knight.

| 41 N-K7 | R(B1)-B5? |

After 41...R-Q1 Black would still have had winning chances.

**42 BxR**

The sealed move 42 QxQP was also possible but it does not make much difference. White now stands better but analysis convinced us that he could not win against the most accurate defence.

| 42 . . . | RxB |

If 42...B-Q8 43 N-B5+ K-B1 44 Q-N2 QxQ 45 RxQ BxR 46 P-R6 wins for White.

**43 QxQP**

43 Q-N1 fails to 43...P-N5 44 N-B5+ K-R1 45 N-K3 Q-K4 46 Q-K1 (or 46 K-B2 Q-Q5) R-B6 47 N-Q1 R-B7. The text wins a pawn but the position remains an easy draw.

| 43 . . . | R-B6 |

A good move which obliges White to weaken himself with 44 P-B4, after which White has no winning chances.

| | |
|---|---|
| 44 P-B4 | QxQ |
| 45 N-B5+ | K-N3 |
| 46 NxQ | B-N6 |
| 47 P-B5+ | K-N2 |
| 48 N-K8+ | K-B1 |
| 49 N-B6 | K-N2 |
| 50 N-R5+ | K-B1 |
| 51 N-B4 | B-B5 |
| 52 R-K5 | R-R6 |
| 53 P-Q6 | R-R7+ |
| 54 K-B3 | R-Q7 |
| 55 R-K7 | RxQP |
| 56 RxNP | R-R3 |
| 57 R-N6 | RxP |
| 58 RxRP | P-N5 |
| 59 R-QB6 | B-N4 |
| 60 R-B1 | P-N6 |
| 61 R-QN1 | B-B5 |
| 62 K-K4 | R-R7 |
| 63 K-Q4 | R-QB7 |
| 64 N-Q3 | BxN |
| 65 KxB | RxP |
| 66 RxP | |

The position is now a book draw but, unperturbed by snoring from the audience, Korchnoi plays on for another fourteen moves before bowing to the inevitable.

I was interested to learn that on BBC television Bill Hartston (the learned author of *How to Cheat at Chess*) was asked whether one should make one's opponents suffer by playing on in positions such as this. He replied with an emphatic "Yes".

| | |
|---|---|
| 66 ... | K-N2 |
| 67 K-K4 | R-R7 |
| 68 K-B4 | R-R5+ |
| 69 K-N5 | R-R4 |
| 70 P-N4 | R-B4 |
| 71 K-R5 | R-R4 |
| 72 R-KB3 | R-N4 |
| 73 P-N5 | R-N8 |
| 74 P-B6+ | K-R2 |
| 75 R-KR3 | R-KN8 |
| 76 R-R2 | R-N6 |
| 77 R-R1 | R-N7 |
| 78 R-R1 | R-R7+ |
| 79 K-N4 | K-N3 |
| 80 R-R8 | R-N7+ |

Now, at last, a **draw** was agreed.

(Time: 5.17 — 3.27)

# GAME TWENTY-SIX

## 26th September

Karpov had apparently been sleeping badly of late and he briefly moved from the Terraces Plaza Hotel to the Baguio Country Club and back again. He was certainly looking tired during the twenty-sixth game and this may explain his choice of the English Opening. He sometimes chooses this opening when he needs a rest. The only other occasion he had played this opening was in the sixth game which was played in the interval between the second and third sessions of the marathon fifth game.

Korchnoi defended with an inferior variation against the English. His excuse was that he did not want to give anything away when confronted by his own favourite opening. Karpov failed to capitalize on his opening advantage and Korchnoi found a neat way of forcing a drawn ending.

Karpov now led 4-2 with 20 draws.

White: Karpov
Black: Korchnoi

### English Opening

| | |
|---|---|
| 1 P-QB4 | P-K4 |
| 2 N-QB3 | P-Q3 |
| 3 P-KN3 | P-KB4 |
| 4 B-N2 | N-QB3 |
| 5 P-Q3 | N-B3 |
| 6 P-K3 | B-K2 |
| 7 KN-K2 | 0-0 |
| 8 0-0 | Q-K1 |
| 9 P-B4 | B-Q1 |
| 10 P-QR3 | R-N1 |
| 11 P-QN4 | B-K3 |
| 12 N-Q5 | P-QN4 |

Black has played an inferior defence to the English Opening. The risky text move was prompted by the knowledge that with normal methods Black stood badly.

| | |
|---|---|
| 13 B-N2 | NPxP |
| 14 QPxP | P-K5 |

**15 NxN+**

Instead of the general liquidation inaugurated with this move

122

White should have played 15
R-B1 with an enduring positional
grip. Now the position is equal.

| | |
|---|---|
| 15 ... | BxN |
| 16 BxB | RxB |
| 17 R-B1 | P-QR4 |
| 18 P-N5 | N-Q1 |
| 19 R-KB2 | N-N2 |
| 20 B-B1 | N-B4 |
| 21 N-B3 | B-B2 |
| 22 N-Q5 | |

If 22 N-R4 Black replies 22...
B-R4 and then plays possum with
23...R-Q1 when White cannot
break through.

| | |
|---|---|
| 22 ... | BxN |
| 23 PxB | |

### DIAGRAM

| | |
|---|---|
| 23 ... | N-Q6! |

An unexpected but efficient
way of enforcing the draw. If
Black does nothing and relies
on the strength of his knight
on QB4 White may be able to

organise a profitable exchange
sacrifice.

| | |
|---|---|
| 24 BxN | PxB |
| 25 QxP | QxNP |
| 26 QxQ | RxQ |
| 27 RxP | R-B2 |

Draw agreed.

After 28 R-B8! R-B1 29
R-B6 Blacks best way to draw is
29...RxP 30 R-N2 P-N3.

(Time: 1.34 — 2.00)

# GAME TWENTY-SEVEN

28th and 29th September

The duties of a world championship delegation head are many and various. On the morning of the twenty-seventh game I was entertained by City Security Chief Major Bugasto at Baguio police H.Q. Three local citizens had been arrested for demanding 15,000 dollars from Korchnoi for (unsolicited!) black magic services to help him win. The problem was that they threatened to ensure his loss if he failed to pay up. This sounded to the Baguio police more like blackmail than black magic and they decided to refer the matter to the local magistrates for a second opinion.

Before the twenty-seventh game Karpov had gone ten games without a win. Most commentators were predicting a long match and the record of thirty-five games held by Capablanca v Alekhine 1927 appeared in danger. Some critics were even claiming that Karpov had now completely run out of steam and that Korchnoi could still turn the match in his favour. I was not so optimistic. Although Korchnoi had not lost for ten games he had had three totally lost positions and he could not rely on Karpov continuing to let him of the hook.

In the twenty-seventh game Korchnoi's luck finally ran out. He obtained a good position but allowed this to deteriorate and blundered away a vital pawn in his inevitable time trouble. Korchnoi adjourned in a hopeless position and he informed me that he intended to resign on resumption. I turned up to watch the funeral rites but Korchnoi did not arrive. We were unable to contact him by telephone and so Stean drove to Korchnoi's villa to find out what had happened. He returned, brakes screeching, just in time to hand over a formal note of resignation signed by Korchnoi before Korchnoi lost on time. Apparently Korchnoi assumed I would resign on his behalf but without specific instructions I felt unable to do so. It was a little embarrassing at the time, but Korchnoi's note made it clear that there had merely been a misunderstanding and no impoliteness was intended.

Karpov now led 5-2 with 20 draws.

| White: Korchnoi | | 2 N-QB3 | P-K4 |
| Black: Karpov | | 3 N-B3 | N-B3 |
| | | 4 P-KN3 | B-N5 |
| **English Opening** | | 5 N-Q5 | NxN |
| 1 P-QB4 | N-KB3 | Insufficiently | subtle. A better |

alternative for Black is 5 . . . B-B4 played in the fifth Korchnoi Petrosian match game 1977.

A popular but less satisfactory alternative for Black is 5 . . . P-K5 6 N-R4 B-B4 7 B-N2 e.g. A) 7 . . . P-Q3 8 0-0 B-K3 (Ghitescu-Browne Wijk aan See 1974) and now 9 NxN+ QxN 10 BxP BxP 11 Q-R4 is good for White. B) 7 . . . 0-0 8 0-0 R-K1 9 P-Q3 PxP 10 QxP N-K4 11 Q-B2 P-B3 (Smyslov-Mecking Petropolis 1973) and now 12 NxN+ QxN 13 P-N3! is a promising sacrifice for White.

| | |
|---|---|
| 6 PxN | N-Q5 |
| 7 NxN | PxN |
| 8 Q-B2 | Q-K2 |
| 9 R-N2 | |

Not 9 QxP Q-K5! Now White enjoys a slight plus since his advanced QP is stronger than Black's.

| | |
|---|---|
| 9 . . . | B-B4 |
| 10 0-0 | |

The natural move but the forcing 10 P-QN4 may be stronger e.g. A) 10 . . . BxP 11 QxP and White has the superior pawn structure and his queen is a thorn in Black's flesh. B) 10 . . . P-Q6 11 QxP Q-B3 12 PxB QxR and White has great compensation for the sacrificed exchange. C) 10 . . . B-N3 11 P-QR4 P-Q6 (If 11 . . . P-QR4 12 PxP) 12 QxQP Q-B3 13 Q-K4+ K-Q1 14 R-R3 QxP+ 15 K-Q1 and White stands better in view of his central pawn mass and the superior co-ordination of his pieces.

| | |
|---|---|
| 10 . . . | 0-0 |
| 11 P-K3 | |

A good move blocking the diagonal of Black's KB — a theme which also occurred in the twenty-fifth game.

| | |
|---|---|
| 11 . . . | B-N3 |
| 12 P-QR4 | PxP? |

Black mistakenly abandons control of his Q5 and brings White's position to life. Presumably his idea was to remove obstructions from the path of his KB with all possible speed, but this is strategically dubious. Better was 12 . . . P-QR4.

**13 QPxP**

Not a bad move but even stronger was 13 BPxP opening the KB file and envisaging a fianchetto of the QB. That would have refuted Karpov's strategy.

| | |
|---|---|
| 13 . . . | P-QR4 |
| 14 B-Q2 | B-B4 |
| 15 B-QB3 | P-Q3 |
| 16 Q-Q2 | P-QN3 |
| 17 KR-K1 | B-Q2 |
| 18 P-K4? | |

White naturally wishes to advance his central pawn majority but he should have prepared the advance slowly by P-KR3 followed by K-R2 when Black can undertake nothing and must simply wait and see whether White can convert his space advantage. The disadvantage of the text is that is prematurely opens the diagonal of Black's bishop on QB4.

| 18 ... | KR-K1 |
| 19 K-R1? | |

Also weak, partly because it undefends White's KBP and partly because the idea of a pawn push with P-KB4 and P-K5 is now out of place as Karpov demonstrates with his next move.

White could have retained some advantage by 19 B-B1 intending to go to QN5 or QB4 and to consolidate his kingside with K-N2.

| 19 ... | P-QB3! |

An excellent move which blunts White's offensive and reaches clear equality. The apparent weakening of Black's QP is illusory in view of Black's bishop entrenched on QB4.

**20 P-K5**

Before this move Karpov had consumed one hour and twenty-five minutes while Korchnoi had only used one hour and fifteen minutes. But now Korchnoi drove his supporters berserk by thinking for forty-five minutes about — what? When we discussed the position after the game Korchnoi seemed to be suffering from the illusion that he now stood worse. But after, say, 20 P-N3 the position

is dead level. One eminent commentator (my wife!) suggested 20 B-B3 and this is also quite adequate.

| 20 ... | BPxP |
| 21 BxQP | QR-Q1 |
| 22 Q-B4 | Q-B1 |

A pretty obvious move but it seems to have baffled Korchnoi who thought for a further fifteen minutes over his reply. This left him only fifteen minutes for his next eighteen moves. The position is still drawn but Black is gaining a slight advantage due to his superior development and co-ordination.

| 23 Q-B3 | PxP |
| 24 BxKP | B-KN5 |
| 25 QxB | R(Q1)xB |
| 26 B-B3 | |

Of course 26 BxP? fails to 26 ... RxR+ 27 RxR QxB 28 R-K8+ B-B1. Korchnoi now only had five minutes left.

| 26 ... | R(K1)-Q1! |

Quite right! Black avoids simplifications and emphasises his grip on the position.

| 27 K-N2 | B-Q5 |
| 28 QR-B1 | P-N3 |
| 29 Q-K2 | Q-Q3 |
| 30 BxB | RxB |

**31 Q-N5??**

A time trouble blunder losing a pawn. After 30 Q-B3 he could still hang on.

| 31 ... | R-QN5 |
|--------|-------|
| 32 R-K8+ | K-N2 |
| 33 RxR | QxR |
| 34 Q-K2 | Q-Q4+ |
| 35 P-B3 | |

35 Q-B3 would have led to a lost rook and pawn ending.

| 35 ... | RxRP |
|--------|------|
| 36 R-B2 | R-Q5 |
| 37 Q-K3 | P-QN4 |
| 38 P-R4 | P-R4 |
| 39 Q-K2 | P-R5 |
| 40 Q-K3 | P-N5 |
| 41 R-B2 | R-Q6 |

The sealed move. **Korchnoi resigned** without waiting to see what it was. White's position is palpably lost.

(Times: 3.20 — 2.15)

# GAME TWENTY-EIGHT

30th September and 1st October

With Karpov now only needing one more win, the vultures (who had been having a lean time since game seventeen) reassembled expectantly for the twenty-eigth game. But a defiant Korchnoi sent them away hungry.

Karpov played insipidly, as if hoping for Korchnoi to dig his own grave. But the challenger failed to oblige and until his sealed move conducted the whole of the first session in fine style. However Korchnoi jeopardised his chances of victory by sealing an inferior move. The adjourned position, although clearly favourable for Korchnoi, was extremely difficult to analyse exhaustively. We analysed furiously (without stopping for breakfast or lunch) but when we finished our analysis twenty minutes before the game was due to resume, we were still not sure whether Korchnoi had a clear win.

I could not bear to watch the first hour of the second session and stayed in my hotel room to rest. I was just preparing to set out for the playing hall when I heard familiar laughter emanating from the lift. Korchnoi had won already! Karpov had bashed out moves like a machine gun (according to Korchnoi) and contrived to lose in one hour a positon we had not been able to solve in nine hours' analysis. Korchnoi's description of how he had beaten the world champion from a possibly drawn adjourned position was: 'I simply played to get through my time trouble. When I accomplished this I relaxed, made a couple of moves and Karpov resigned.'

Karpov's conduct of the second session was amazing. If the position had been clearly lost one could have understood him invoking his old ally the clock as his last desperate hope. But the adjourned position was in fact unclear and, as it turned out, Karpov missed at least two draws in the second session. It is possible that Karpov decided on his blitz tactics on the assumption that Korchnoi had sealed one of the clearly winning moves at his disposal. Even so he should have had the presence of mind to change his tactics when confronted by an inferior sealed move.

When asked by journalists after the game if this victory signalled the start of a revival Korchnoi replied sarcastically 'Well, I won one game in a row'.

The game was widely claimed to be Korchnoi's first victory over Karpov with Black. This was not strictly true as Korchnoi had beaten Karpov twice with Black in their secret training match in 1971. It was at least his first Black win in an 'official' game.

After the game it was rumoured that Karpov's Toyota Crown official match car was involved in a minor crash on the way to his hotel at the end of the first session. Baturinsky denied that Karpov was inside but some witnesses said they saw him get out of the damaged vehicle and proceed in the police escort. Curious.

Karpov now led 5-4 with 20 draws.

**White: Karpov**
**Black: Korchnoi**

### Ruy Lopez

| | |
|---|---|
| 1 P-K4 | P-K4 |
| 2 N-KB3 | N-QB3 |
| 3 B-N5 | P-QR3 |
| 4 B-R4 | N-B3 |
| 5 0-0 | NxP |
| 6 P-Q4 | P-QN4 |
| 7 B-N3 | P-Q4 |
| 8 PxP | B-K3 |
| 9 P-B3 | N-B4 |
| 10 B-B2 | B-N5 |

I prefer this plan to the other lines Korchnoi had adopted in this opening since it puts more pressure on White. Black may be able to play . . . BxN at some moment forcing doubled pawns which would give him real counter-chances. The drawback of Black's plan is that his QP is rather vulnerable.

**11 R-K1**

More dangerous for Black is 11 Q-K2 intending R-Q1 followed by P-QN4 and B-N3 or B-K4.

| | |
|---|---|
| 11 . . . | B-K2 |
| 12 QN-Q2 | |

An interesting try is 12 P-N4 N-K3 13 P-QR4 but that would have been rather sharp for a tired Karpov at this stage in the match.

| | |
|---|---|
| 12 . . . | Q-Q2 |

12 . . . P-Q5 was also playable but Korchnoi, ambitiously wanted to maintain the tension and avoid exchanges.

**13 N-N3**

Another possible grouping of White's pieces is 13 N-B1 R-Q1 14 N-K3 B-R4 15 N-B5 0-0 and Black has a solid position to compensate for White's strong knight on KB5.

| | |
|---|---|
| 13 . . . | N-K3 |

In keeping with policy indicated by Black's twelfth move.

| | |
|---|---|
| 14 P-KR3 | B-R4 |
| 15 B-B5 | |

The pin looks annoying, but it can always be broken by . . . B-N3 or even . . . P-N3 as Korchnoi in fact later plays.

| | |
|---|---|
| 15 . . . | QN-Q1 |

Supporting the other knight and also planning . . . P-QB4 at an opportune moment. Black's position is a little congested but Korchnoi has at any rate succeeded in his objective of provoking a complex struggle.

| | |
|---|---|
| 16 B-K3 | P-R4 |

A good move, preparing to force White to declare his intentions regarding the alignment of his minor pieces.

| | |
|---|---|
| 17 B-B5 | P-R5 |
| 18 BxB | QxB |

### DIAGRAM

**19 QN-Q2?**

Feeble. White could not of course play 19 QxP? because of 19 . . . P-QB3. Best was 19 N(N3)-Q4

129

when White has a slight advantage.

**19 ...**          **P-QB3**

Consolidation at last.

**20 P-QN4**        **N-N4**

Finally exploiting the pin on White's KN. It is interesting that Black's reserve knight can also gallop from Q1 via K3 to KN4.

**21 Q-K2**          **P-N3**
**22 B-N4**

This allows Black to gain the better ending by taking the KR file. Better was 22 B-B2 NxN+ 23 NxN N-K3 24 Q-K3 BxN 25 QxB Q-R5 when the position is equal since White's KB is restricted by the network of Black pawns on the light squares.

| 22 ... | BxB |
|--------|-----|
| 23 PxB | QN-K3 |
| 24 Q-K3 | P-R4 |
| 25 NxN | QxN |
| 26 QxQ | NxQ |
| 27 PxP | RxP |

Korchnoi had played well so far and managed to obtain a slightly better positon. This was nothing new. What was new was that he now managed to continue to play well in the crucial final hour of the first session despite being in time trouble.

| 28 N-B1 | R-R5 |
|---------|------|
| 29 QR-Q1 | K-K2 |

| 30 P-B3 | N-K3 |
|---------|------|
| 31 N-K3 | R-Q1 |

Black finally abandons any intention of castling.

| 32 N-N4 | N-N2 |
|---------|------|
| 33 N-K3 | N-K3 |
| 34 N-N4 | N-N2 |
| 35 N-K3 | N-B4 |

Although short of time (he had about five minutes left) Korchnoi spurns repetition. He has a long-term advantage based on the superior compactness of Black's queenside pawns and Whites dead point at K5, which looks aggressive but turns out to be a liability.

**36 N-B2?**

Why not 36 N-N4? The text (and 36 NxN+ which would also be a mistake) allows Black's rook to reach an ideal square on his QB5.

| 36 ... | R-QB5 |
|--------|-------|
| 37 R-Q3 | P-Q5!! |

A very deep move played in high time trouble. Korchnoi was twitching and fidgeting in his seat before playing this move and I thought he had overlooked White's next move. But, although Korchnoi had less than a minute left, everything was under control.

| 38 P-N4 | N-N2 |
|---------|------|
| 39 NxP | N-K3! |

Now everything becomes clear. Black will obtain a vastly superior ending in which White is burdened with weak points.

| 40 KR-Q1 | NxN |
|----------|-----|
| 41 PxN | RxNP |
| 42 K-B2 | |

DIAGRAM

**42 ...**          **P-QB4?**

The sealed move which is a

# GAME TWENTY-EIGHT

mistake although Korchnoi took thirty-eight minutes over it. Stronger was either 42 ... K-K3 or 42 ... R-N7+ 43 R(Q1)-Q2 RxR+ 44 RxR P-N5 when White has no counterchances as Black's king has a free path to K3 and Q4.

**43 P-Q5**

Probably not best. Our analysis also considered the following possibilities:

A) 43 PxP RxR 44 RxR R-N7+ and 45 ... RxRP winning.

B1) 43 K-K3 R(Q1)xP? 44 RxR PxR+ 45 RxP R-N7 46 K-K4 P-R6 (If 46 ... RxP 47 R-N4 is equal) 47 R-Q5 P-N5 48 R-N5 K-Q2 49 K-Q5 RxP 50 R-N7+ K-Q1 51 RxNP R-R8 52 R-Q4 P-R7 53 R-Q2 P-N4 (otherwise 54 P-B4 draws) 54 P-K6 (54 K-K4+ K-K2 55 K-B5 also draws) K-K2 55 PxP KxP 56 K-Q6 with a draw.

B2) 43 K-K3 P-B5! and now Black has winning chances though we had not sorted out all the possibilities before resumption. If 44 R-B3 R-N7 wins for Black. The position is not so clear after 44 R(Q3)-Q2 but Black still has chances after 46 ... P-R6 planning 47 ... R-N7.

**43 ...          R-N7+**
**44 K-N3**

The king would be exposed on K3 and anyway Black wants that square for his rook.

**44 ...          RxRP?**

Korchnoi forgot our analysis! The correct move was 44 ... P-N4! dislocating White's kingside pawns and threatening 45 ... R-KR1 with a mating net. One variation is 44 ... P-N4 45 P-K6 PxP 46 R-K3 R-Q3 and Black should win.

**45 R-K3          P-N5**
**46 P-K6**

White should now draw and he is even threatening to win by 47 P-Q6+.

**46 ...          R-R6**
**47 R-K2?**

Also bad was 47 P-Q6+ RxP 48 RxR(Q6) RxR and Black wins but White could have drawn by 47 RxR! PxR 48 PxP+ KxP 49 K-B4 and Black will not be able to hold his split queenside pawns.

**47 ...          PxP**
**48 RxP+          K-B2**
**49 R(Q1)-K1**

Karpov, still playing at full speed, misses his last chance which was 49 P-N5 threatening a series of checks starting with 50 R-B6+. It is possible White could then still draw.

| 49 ... | R-Q2 |
|---|---|
| 50 R-N6 | R-Q6 |
| 51 R(K1)-K6 | R(Q6)xP |
| 52 RxKNP | P-R6 |
| 53 R(N6)-B6+ | K-K2 |
| 54 R(B6)-K6+ | K-B1 |
| 55 R-B6+ | K-K2 |
| 56 R(N6)-K6+ | K-Q1 |
| 57 R-QR6 | R-QN2 |
| 58 R-B8+ | K-B2 |

| 59 R-B7+ | R-Q2 |
|----------|------|
| 60 R-B5 | P-N6 |
| 61 RxP(B5)+ | K-N1 |

### DIAGRAM

White has run out of checks and he cannot prevent one of Black's advanced pawns queening. **Karpov** therefore **resigned**.
(Approximate times: 2.45 — 3.35. The deputy chief arbiter forgot to record the exact times!)

# GAME TWENTY-NINE

## 7th and 8th October

Korchnoi's win in game twenty-eight showed that he was not prepared to surrender the match without a fight. But the sword of Damocles remained suspended precariously over his head. However many games the match might continue he knew that in every remaining game one blunder (and he had made all too many so far) could bring the match to an abrupt end.

The tension increased when the twenty-ninth game was twice postponed. On the Tuesday that the game was originally due to be played an explosion in the generator plunged the Playing Hall into darkness only one hour before the game was due to start. The generator was known to be a sickly specimen and so foul play was not suspected. The frantic application of smelling salts, spanners and glue resuscitated the generator in time for play to start of the Thursday.

But in the meantime there had been another casualty. Korchnoi had spent his free day on the beach. Alas he stayed too long. He returned badly sunburnt and had to postpone the game from Thursday to Saturday. On Saturday he had still not recovered from his sunburn and had caught a cold as well. But he was not entitled to any more postponements and so he had to play.

When Korchnoi arrived for the postponed twenty-ninth game someone remarked that he looked like a fluorescent carrot. But his play did not appear to be affected and after nurturing a slight positional advantage he adjourned with a small plus. This should not have been enough to win but once again Karpov tried to blitz him in time trouble and it was the champion who produced the decisive errors. Korchnoi's conduct of the game was well-nigh flawless but the same cannot be said of Karpov. After the game Korchnoi attributed his victory to Karpov's mistakes but added that he was proud of his own fighting spirit. He said to Edmondson 'Fischer respects me because of this. Everyone else he can intimidate with his own fighting spirit, but not me.'

Karpov's defeat must have been all the more galling because Vasyukov had arrived to help him accompanied by the USSR Chess Federation President, Sebastianov, an ex-cosmonaut. Presumably Sebastianov had arrived for the supposedly imminent closing ceremony!

Karpov now led 5-4, with 20 draws.

White: Korchnoi
Black: Karpov

### English Opening

| | |
|---|---|
| 1 P-QB4 | N-KB3 |
| 2 N-QB3 | P-K3 |
| 3 P-K4 | P-B4 |
| 4 P-K5 | N-N1 |
| 5 P-Q4 | |

Korchnoi has adopted a line of the English Opening favoured by Nimzowitsch, Keene and others, but he now rejects the pawn sacrifice 5 N-B3 N-QB3 6 P-Q4 PxP 7 NxP NxP with which I beat Karpov's late trainer Furman at Bad Lauterberg last year. The move Korchnoi adopts has been dismissed by theory as too drawish but the Korchnoi camp had worked out some improvements.

| | |
|---|---|
| 5 . . . | PxP |
| 6 QxP | N-QB3 |
| 7 Q-K4 | P-Q3 |
| 8 N-B3 | PxP |
| 9 NxP | N-B3 |

Korchnoi's choice of opening has been a success as Karpov had now used almost an hour against Korchnoi's four minutes.

Instead of the text which weakens Black's pawn structure theory regards 9 . . . B-Q2 as best.

| | |
|---|---|
| 10 NxN | Q-N3 |
| 11 Q-B3 | PxN |
| 12 B-K2 | |

12 P-KN3 planning B-N2 to hinder . . . P-QB4 may be an improvement.

| | |
|---|---|
| 12 . . . | B-N2 |
| 13 0-0 | P-B4 |
| 14 Q-R3 | B-K2 |

**DIAGRAM**

15 B-B3

I had expected Korchnoi to play 15 P-QN3 and followed by B-N2 and B-Q3 aiming his bishops at Black's king.

Instead Korchnoi adopts a highly positional plan which aims to leave Black with a bad bishop hemmed in by the pawn on Black's QB4.

| | |
|---|---|
| 15 . . . | 0-0 |
| 16 P-QN3 | KR-Q1 |
| 17 B-K3 | B-B3 |
| 18 N-R4 | Q-B2 |
| 19 BxB | QxB |
| 20 QR-Q1 | QR-B1 |
| 21 Q-N3 | B-Q3 |
| 22 Q-R4 | B-K2 |
| 23 P-B3 | K-B1 |
| 24 Q-B2 | RxR |
| 25 RxR | Q-B2 |
| 26 Q-N3 | |

Exchanging queens does not indicate any pacific intentions on Korchnoi's part. It is consistent with Korchnoi's policy of accentuating the limitations of Black's KB.

| | |
|---|---|
| 26 . . . | QxQ |
| 27 PxQ | P-KR4 |
| 28 K-B2 | K-K1 |
| 29 K-K2 | P-N3 |
| 30 N-B3 | P-R3 |
| 31 N-R4 | R-B3 |
| 32 R-KR1 | B-Q3 |

| 33 B-B2 | N-Q2 |
|---------|------|
| 34 P-KN4 | |

A surprising but fully justified decision. White's doubled pawns tie Black down and White's rook becomes active.

| 34 ... | PxP |
|--------|-----|
| 35 R-R8+ | K-K2 |
| 36 PxP | P-N4 |
| 37 B-K3 | P-B3 |
| 38 N-B3 | K-B2 |
| 39 R-R7+ | K-K1 |
| 40 N-K4 | B-K2 |

**41 R-R6**

The sealed move over which Korchnoi took thirty-six minutes and forty-five seconds. He had already lost his early lead on the clock and he now left himself with only twenty-seven minutes to reach move 56.

It was painful to watch his indecision on the stage. He thought for fifteen minutes, got up and hid in a corner of the stage (to circumvent prying eyes, I imagine). He then wrote down a sealed move, came back and sat slumped over the board. After a further ten minutes he crossed out his move and repeated the performance, finally sealing the text.

Golombek won four bottles of whisky by correctly guessing the sealed move but in fact it is not best! After 41 B-Q2, aiming to transfer the bishop to QB3 as quickly as possible Black is subjected to intolerable pressure.

**41 ...**      **K-B2**

We spent a long time analysing 41 . . . P-R4 which weakens Black's position but is his only chance for active couterplay. We decided it was too risky for Black e.g. 42 R-R8+ N-B1 43 B-Q2 R-R3 44 B-B3 K-B2 45 R-R6 and now:
A) 45 . . . K-N2 46 RxP BxR 47 BxB+ K-N3 48 NxBP and White should win.
B) 45 . . . N-Q2 46 R-R7+ K-K1 (This line shows how Black is squeezed when White's bishop reaches QB3) 47 P-R4 P-B4 48 PxP PxP 49 N-N3 P-B5 50 N-B5 B-B3 51 BxRP and White trickily wins a pawn since Black dare not capture the bishop in view of 52 N-Q6+.

| 42 R-R7+ | K-B1 |
|----------|------|
| 43 R-R8+ | K-B2 |
| 44 B-Q2 | |

The direct method was 44 R-R8 when I had analysed the line 44 . . . N-K4 45 R-R7 K-K1 46 N-B2 P-B4 47 B-Q2 B-B3! (taking White's KNP leaves Black very passive) 48 B-R5 NxP 49 NxN PxN 50 B-B7 and Black is paralysed. One winning idea is K-K3 followed by K-K4 and B-K5. However 48 . . . N-Q2 planning 49 . . . B-Q5 is a much tougher defence to crack.

Instead of adopting the direct approach Korchnoi decides to tack around. Since he only had twenty minutes to reach move 56 I wondered if he was using his time trouble as a kind of provocation to lure Karpov to play incautiously.

| 44 ... | N-B1 |
| 45 R-R1 | |

More tacking.

| 45 ... | K-N3 |
| 46 R-Q1 | P-B4? |

Too risky since it exposes the central White squares. Korchnoi only had ten minutes now but Karpov had been successfully provoked.

| 47 N-B2 | B-Q3 |
| 48 B-B3 | N-Q2 |
| 49 PxP+ | PxP |
| 50 P-KN4! | |

Exchanges help White since both his minor pieces are superior to their opposite numbers and Black's pawns are exposed.

| 50 ... | N-N3 |

Not 50 ... P-B5 51 N-K4!

| 51 K-B3 | B-K2 |
| 52 B-R5 | R-B3 |
| 53 K-N2 | PxP |
| 54 NxP | R-K3 |
| 55 K-B3 | B-B3 |
| 56 NxB | |

On his last move before the second time control Korchnoi makes the right decision. Earlier Black's bishop had been a problem piece but now it was threatening to entrench itself on Q5. After the exchange White's bishop is much stronger than Black's knight.

| 56 ... | RxN+ |
| 57 K-N4 | N-B1 |
| 58 B-Q8 | R-B5+ |
| 59 K-N3 | R-B4 |
| 60 P-R4 | |

White plans P-R5 and B-N6. If White wins a pawn by 60 R-Q7

R-B2 61 RxR KxR 62 BxP Black can draw by rushing his king to QB3. Black should also be able to draw after 60 R-Q5 since after the rook swap White's RP if of the wrong colour for his bishop.

| 60 ... | K-B2 |

Better was 60 ... R-K4.

| 61 R-Q3 | R-K4 |
| 62 K-N4 | K-N3 |

So Black has lost a tempo.

| 63 P-R5 | R-K5+ |
| 64 K-B3 | |

| 64 ... | R-B5+? |

The losing move. 64 ... K-B4 was probably still good enough to draw e.g. 65 BxP N-R2 activating the Black knight or 65 R-Q5+ R-K4 and Black gives up his KNP and rushes his king to QB3. Korchnoi was again in terrible time trouble (for the second time in the session) and Karpov was provoked into another misguided attempt to blitz him.

| 65 K-K3 | R-R5 |
| 66 R-Q5 | R-R6+ |
| 67 K-Q2 | RxP |
| 68 RxP | R-N1 |
| 69 R-B6+ | K-B4 |
| 70 RxP | P-N5 |
| 71 R-B6+ | K-K5 |
| 72 B-B7 | R-N7+ |

| 73 K-B3 | R-N2 |
| 74 B-R2 | R-KR2 |
| 75 B-N8 | |

Both players continued to play at lightning speed even though the time control had been reached at move 72. Karpov now paused for a while to survey the tatters of his position.

| 75 ... | R-QN2 |

| 76 B-N3 | R-N8 |
| 77 R-B4+ | K-K6 |
| 78 R-B8 | N-K2 |
| 79 P-R6 | |

If 79 ... N-B3 80 P-R7 NxP 81 B-B2+ wins the knight. Karpov therefore **resigned** by signing the score sheet and hurrying from the stage.

(Times: 4.54—4.15)

# GAME THIRTY

**10th and 11th October**

Korchnoi's win in game twenty-eight had indicated that the challenger was not prepared simply to lie down and die. His win in the twenty-ninth game did much more. For the first time since Karpov achieved a three game lead by winning the seventeenth game, the whole result of the match really seemed in doubt.

There were suggestions that Karpov had cracked in games twenty-eight and twenty-nine but I think this is an oversimplification. His play had in fact been patchy for some time, but then so had Korchnoi's. What marked the twenty-eighth and twenty-ninth games was that Korchnoi seemed to have got his second wind and was not leaving Karpov's mistakes unpunished. If Korchnoi could keep it up Karpov needed to raise his own level of play to finish the match off.

The public had been rather spoilt by the recent rich diet of three decisive games. In game thirty they were served much humbler fare. The advantage fluctuated slightly but the game always seemed to be heading for the draw which was finally agreed after forty-two moves. Karpov must have been relieved to stop the rot, but Korchnoi could also be well satisfied with a comfortable draw with Black.

With the completion of game thirty the match reached another milestone. It equalled the number of games of the 1935 encounter between Alekhine and Euwe. In both matches the score stood at 15½—14½ but there was the important difference that this was the final score in 1935.

One more landmark beckoned — the thirty-five games of the 1927 Capablanca—Alekhine match. It is interesting that the present match had already lasted longer in terms of days than the 1927 encounter. Needing so few rest days maybe the 1927 contestants really were made of sterner stuff!

Karpov now led 5-4 with 21 draws.

**White: Karpov**
**Black: Korchnoi**

### English Opening

| | |
|---|---|
| 1 P-QB4 | N-KB3 |
| 2 N-QB3 | P-Q4 |

The game now transposes into a kind of Grunfeld Defence on which Korchnoi is a leading expert.

The first game in which the Grunfeld Defence proper was played in international chess was Alekhine-Grunfeld Vienna 1922. I

138

believe that is the game which Alekhine resigned by hurling his king across the room!

| 3 PxP | NxP |
|---|---|
| 4 P-KN3 | P-KN3 |
| 5 B-N2 | NxN |
| 6 NPxN | B-N2 |
| 7 N-B3 | 0-0 |
| 8 0-0 | P-QB4 |
| 9 R-N1 | N-B3 |
| 10 Q-R4 | N-R4 |
| 11 P-Q3 | P-N3 |
| 12 Q-R4 | B-N2 |
| 13 B-R6 | BxB |
| 14 QxB | BxN |
| 15 BxB | R-B1 |
| 16 B-N2 | Q-Q2 |
| 17 QR-K1 | P-QN4 |

**18 R-N1**

An indecisive move since the rook has only just moved to K1. After the game 18 P-KB4 was widely recommended but Korchnoi's intended 18 . . . Q-Q3 and if 19 P-B5, Q-K4 is a perfectly adequate response.

| 18 . . . | R-N1 |
|---|---|
| 19 Q-K3 | Q-Q3 |
| 20 KR-Q1 | P-QR3 |

After White's indecision, Black enjoys a slight advantage which he could have retained by playing 20 . . . R-N3 now or on the next move.

| 21 R-Q2 | KR-B1 |
|---|---|
| 22 R(Q2)-N2 | N-B3 |
| 23 Q-Q2 | N-K4 |

23 . . . R-N3 was still the right move. Now the initiative passes back to White but it is nothing serious.

| 24 Q-B4 | N-Q2 |
|---|---|
| 25 QxQ | PxQ |
| 26 B-R3 | R-Q1 |
| 27 P-R4 | PxP |
| 28 BxN | RxR |
| 29 RxR | RxB |
| 30 R-R2 | K-B1 |
| 31 RxP | R-R2 |
| 32 K-B1 | K-K2 |
| 33 K-K1 | K-Q2 |
| 34 K-Q2 | P-KR4 |

Here Korchnoi offered a draw through the Arbiter. Karpov declined by playing another move without comment. This may seem impolite but it wasn't. It is a perfectly legitimate and commonly adopted means of declining a draw.

| 35 K-B2 | R-R1 |
|---|---|
| 36 R-KB4 | K-K3 |
| 37 P-R4 | R-QN1 |
| 38 R-K4+ | K-Q2 |
| 39 R-R4 | R-QR1 |
| 40 R-KB4 | K-K3 |
| 41 R-B4 | R-R2 |
| 42 R-K4+ | |

The sealed move which strictly forms part of the game even though it was never played on the board. One and a half hours before play was due to be resumed I accepted on behalf of Korchnoi Karpov's offer of a **draw** which was relayed through the acting chief arbiter Filip.

(Times: )

139

# GAME THIRTY-ONE

12th and 13th October

Korchnoi believes that thirteen is his lucky number. This may seem perverse since he lost disastrously in the thirteenth game of the present match as he had done in the thirteenth game of the Candidates' final against Spassky. But it was on Friday the thirteenth in game 31 (the reverse of 13!?!) that he stunned the chess world by equalising the score at 5-5.

The game started quietly. Korchnoi built up a slight advantage by adopting an unusual plan in a well-known variation. He wisely refrained from forcing the issue until after the time control and Karpov made no attempt to compel him to do so. After the time control (but still in the first session) Korchnoi finally broke the position open and Karpov should probably then have adjourned to give himself time to work out how to defend. But he continued playing until move 47, by which time his position had become critical. After the game Tal claimed the adjourned position was already lost for Karpov, but our adjournment analysis had unearthed resources for Karpov against which we were unable to find a clear win. As it was Karpov failed to find the best defence and Korchnoi finished him off in ruthless style. Although the earlier stages of the game were rather tedious the ending should find its way into all the text books as a classic demonstration of the importance of active pieces and mobile pawns in rook and pawn endings.

Korchnoi's victory in this game heralded the most spectacular comeback ever witnessed in a world championship match. Steinitz had recovered from 4-1 down against Zukertort in 1886 and Euwe was twice three games down before beating Alekhine in 1935. What marked out Korchnoi's achievement was that it was performed while the sword of Damocles was poised over his head ready to end the whole match if he made a single mistake.

After the game Korchnoi declared that the chances in the match were now equal and that the result was a lottery. To observers, however, it appeared to be a lottery in which Korchnoi held most of the tickets.

The score was now 5-5 with 21 draws.

| | | |
|---|---|---|
| **White: Korchnoi** | 1 P-QB4 | P-K3 |
| **Black: Karpov** | 2 N-QB3 | P-Q4 |
| | 3 P-Q4 | N-KB3 |
| Queen's Gambit Declined | 4 PxP | |

Karpov has varied from the English Opening with which he failed to achieve equality in the twenty-ninth game. For the first time in the match Korchnoi now opts for a straight exchange variation of the Queen's Gambit.

| 4 ... | PxP |
|-------|-----|
| 5 B-N5 | B-K2 |
| 6 P-K3 | 0-0 |
| 7 B-Q3 | QN-Q2 |
| 8 N-B3 | R-K1 |
| 9 Q-B2 | P-B3 |
| 10 0-0 | N-B1 |
| 11 BxN | BxB |
| 12 P-QN4 | B-N5 |
| 13 N-Q2 | R-B1 |

It seems more sensible for Black to preserve his QB by e.g. 13 . . . B R4.

| 14 B-B5 | BxB |
|---------|-----|
| 15 QxB | Q-Q2 |

So far we have been following the game Miagmasuren-Reshevsky Sousse 1967 in which Black played 15 . . . P-KN3. Having played the opening moves quickly, Karpov stopped for a long think before offering the exchange of queens. In my opinion he made the wrong decision since the simplification gives White a freer hand and reduces Black's chances of kingside play.

Before the match the Korchnoi camp considered that Karpov was an expert in simplified positions but not so good in complications. The present game in combination with Karpov's previous two losses suggests that he is also ill at ease in complex positions without queens.

| 16 QxQ | NxQ |
|--------|-----|
| 17 P-QR4 | B-K2 |
| 18 KR-N1 | N-B3 |

**19 P-R5**

A very interesting plan. By sealing the queenside Korchnoi makes Black's QNP a permanent liability and prepares a long-term central break with P-K4. The idea is that after vast exchanges on the king's file Black's QNP will be very vulnerable to a White knight on QB5. The only drawback is the lack of mobility in White's queenside infantry.

| 19 ... | P-QR3 |
|--------|-------|
| 20 N-R4 | B-B1 |
| 21 N-B5 | R-K2 |
| 22 K-B1 | N-K1 |
| 23 K-K2 | N-Q3 |
| 24 K-Q3 | QR-K1 |
| 25 R-K1 | P-KN3 |

Hereabouts the Russians (Tal, Vasiukov, Zaitsev etc.) were claiming an advantage for Black. Euwe was very scathing about this: 'They are entitled to their opinion but I know White is better!' He obviously had in mind his win against Alekhine from Zurich 1934 in which he employed a similar strategy, but with queens on the board. He took great delight in making his point by repeatedly slaughtering Baturinsky from this position in the press room.

**26 R-K2    P-B3**

Karpov is pussyfooting about. At some stage he should have taken his life in his hands and played 26 ... P-KB4, even though it weakens his K4 square. Korchnoi said that one of Karpov's main weaknesses was in allowing himself to be taken by the throat before he truly started to fight.

| 27 QR-K1 | B-R3 |
|---|---|
| 28 N(2)-N3 | B-B1 |
| 29 N-Q2 | B-R3 |
| 30 P-R3 | K-B2 |
| 31 P-N4 | B-B1 |
| 32 P-B3 | R-Q1 |
| 33 N(2)-N3 | N-N4 |
| 34 R-KB1 | B-R3 |
| 35 P-B4 | |

White would like to play P-K4 but then Black could settle his bishop on KB5.

| 35 ... | B-B1 |
|---|---|
| 36 N-Q2 | N-Q3 |
| 37 R(1)-K1 | P-R3 |
| 38 R-KB1 | R-N1 |
| 39 R-QR1 | R(1)-K1 |
| 40 R(1)-K1 | R-N1 |
| 41 P-K4 | |

At last. Korchnoi had been in time trouble and so delayed this expected advance until after the time control.

| 41 ... | PxP |
|---|---|
| 42 N(2)xP | N-N4 |

Setting a trap. 43 P-B5 now looks very promising but Black can play 43 ... PxP 44 PxP R-Q1 45 N-K6 RxP+! 46 NxR R-Q2 with enormous counterplay.

| 43 N-B3 | RxR |
|---|---|
| 44 RxR | BxN |
| 45 NPxB | R-Q1 |
| 46 NxN | RPxN |

**47 P-B5**

Korchnoi's original idea was 47 R-QR2 but he changed his mind. Up to now Karpov had been moving with his usual speed and had taken about one hour less than Korchnoi. He now decided to adjourn and took twenty minutes on his sealed move. Since the time control he had taken two crucial decisions in exchanging both pairs of minor pieces. Both of these decisions may have been correct (I am not certain myself) but since Karpov had time in hand surely it would have been more prudent to adjourn and consider them at leisure.

A complex position. Superficially it might appear that White's weak pawns on QR5 and Q4 give Black some advantage. In reality it is White who has the chances since his powerful horns on QB5 and KB5 cramp Black and represent dangerous potential passed pawns. White's winning plans (all involving pawn sacrifices) are based on the annexation of the Black pawns on Black's QB3 and KB3. One idea is P-QR6 followed by K-B3-N4-R5-N6 and another is R-K6 followed by P-R6.

| 47 . . . | PxP |
|---|---|
| 48 PxP | R-KN1 |

If 48 . . . R-K1 white plays 49 R-QR2 not 49 P-Q5 R-Q1 50 P-Q6 R-K1 which is a draw.

**49 K-B3**

Less obvious than 49 R-QR2 with the idea of P-R6, which is also better for White but clearer to defend.

**49 . . .          R-K1?**

Better was 49 . . . R-N8 when Korchnoi intended to play the risky line 50 P-R6 PxP 51 R-K6 P-QR4 52 RxQBP R-N6+ 53 K-Q2 when both sides get connected passed pawns. White's chances are better but there is no clear cut win. Winning White's irrelevant KRP by 49 . . . R-N6+ would be suicidal after 50 K-N4 RxP 51 P-R6 PxP 52 K-R5 followed by 53 K-N6 etc. In this ending it is the quality of pawns which counts more than their quantity.

**50 R-Q2          R-K5**

We had not considered this. Stronger is 50 . . . R-K8 51 P-Q5 R-B8+ and if 52 R-B2 R-QR8! Better for White is 52 K-N2 RxP 53 PxP when White still has some chances. The text prevents P-Q5 but does not impede P-R6.

**51 K-N4          K-K1**

| 52 P-R6 | PxP |
|---|---|
| 53 K-R5 | K-Q2 |
| 54 K-N6 | |

Now Black can do nothing to prevent the crushing P-Q5, clearing the path for White's QBP.

| 54 . . . | P-N5 |
|---|---|
| 55 P-Q5 | PxP |
| 56 RxP+ | K-B1 |
| 57 R-Q3 | |

Aiming to seize the KN file.

| 57 . . . | P-QR4 |
|---|---|
| 58 R-KN3 | P-N6 |
| 59 K-B6 | |

Not at once 59 RxP??, R-N5+ and Black wins.

| 59 . . . | K-N1 |
|---|---|
| 60 RxP+ | |

The ending has now turned into a rout. White picks up Black's pawns at his leisure.

| 60 . . . | K-R2 |
|---|---|
| 61 R-N7+ | K-R3 |
| 62 R-N6+ | K-R2 |
| 63 K-N5 | P-R5 |
| 64 RxP | R-KB5 |
| 65 RxP | P-R6 |
| 66 R-R6+ | K-N1 |
| 67 RxP | RxP |
| 68 R-KN3 | R-B3 |
| 69 R-N8+ | K-B2 |
| 70 R-N7+ | K-B1 |
| 71 R-KR7 | resigns |

# GAME THIRTY-TWO

## 17th October

After the buffeting he had been receiving recently nobody was surprised when Karpov decided to postpone the thirty-second game. He spent his time relaxing in Manila while Korchnoi stayed in Baguio entertaining journalists by standing on his head and performing other yoga exercises.

The Russians pulled out all the stops for what everyone sensed would be the final game. On the morning of the game they called a meeting of the jury and demanded that the Ananda Margas should be removed from Korchnoi's *private* villa. Since they were on bail pending the result of their appeal this demand contradicted their rights under the Philippino constitution. But the jury (which had unfortunately lost the moderating influence of Euwe, who had just left Baguio) did not seem to care. When it became clear that the vote was going to go 5-2 against me I reluctantly gave way and agreed to do my best to remove the Ananda Margas from Korchnoi's villa. Since nothing had changed since the Russians had accepted the compromise whereby the Ananda Margas were to be confined to Korchnoi's villa, why did they suddenly bring the matter up again at this stage? Could the score in the match possibly have had anything to do with it?

When the thirty-second game started who should be sitting in the fourth row of the audience but our old friend Dr. Zukhar? This clear breach of the agreement that he should sit at the back of the hall at least relieved me from the undertaking which I had given, under duress, regarding the Ananda Margas.

After all the efforts which had been made to ensure he won it would have been ungrateful of Karpov not to produce his best form in the final game. He duly obliged but Korchnoi was unrecognisable as the lion who had roared in the four previous games. Karpov broke through the centre in classic style and the final stages of the game witnessed an anti-climatic mopping up operation. Korchnoi adjourned but his position was obviously hopeless and his heroic challenge ended with a whimper when he resigned without resumption. As a final gesture of defiance he refused to sign the score sheet in protest against the pressure to which he had been subjected in the final game.

So after three months and thirty-two games the match was over at last.

Final score: Karpov 6, Korchnoi 5, with 21 draws.

**White: Karpov**
**Black: Korchnoi**

### Pirc Defence

| | |
|---|---|
| 1 P-K4 | P-Q3 |
| 2 P-Q4 | N-KB3 |
| 3 N-QB3 | P-KN3 |
| 4 N-B3 | B-N2 |
| 5 B-K2 | 0-0 |
| 6 0-0 | P-B4 |

Korchnoi varies from the standard 6 . . . B-N5 which he played in the eighteenth game. The text leads to a position more commonly reached by the move order 1 P-Q4 P-QB4 2 P-Q5 N-KB3 3 N-QB3 P-Q3 4 P-K4 P-KN3 5 N-B3 B-N2 6 0-0 0-0 — an unusual and rather dubious variation championed by the chief arbiter of the present match, Lothar Schmid. This variation produces an uncompromising struggle, which is what Korchnoi wanted. In retrospect it might have been more circumspect to play a quieter defence with Black with a view to drawing this game and winning with White in game thirty-three. But after Karpov's recent collapse who can blame Korchnoi for trying to finish the match in the present game?

| | |
|---|---|
| 7 P-Q5 | N-R3 |
| 8 B-KB4 | N-B2 |
| 9 P-QR4 | P-N3 |
| 10 R-K1 | B-N2 |
| 11 B-B4 | N-R4? |
| 12 B-KN5 | N-B3 |

An admission that his last move was a mistake. If 12 . . . P-KR3 13 B-R4 P-KN4 14 N-Q2! is better for White.

| | |
|---|---|
| 13 Q-Q3 | P-QR3 |
| 14 QR-Q1 | R-N1 |
| 15 P-R3 | N-Q2 |

| | |
|---|---|
| 16 Q-K3 | B-QR1 |
| 17 B-R6 | P-QN4 |

Black has obtained his strategic objective of expanding on the queenside but it does not achieve very much. The play now revolves round White's attempt to achieve his strategic objective — the advance P-K5. If he can play this move in favourable circumstances his space advantage will guarantee him the better game.

| | |
|---|---|
| 18 BxB | KxB |
| 19 B-B1 | N-B3 |
| 20 PxP | PxP |
| 21 N-K2 | B-N2 |
| 22 N-N3 | QR-R1 |
| 23 P-B3 | R-R5 |
| 24 B-Q3 | Q-R1 |

Black is trying to prevent P-K6 by piling up on White's QP so that the advance of the KP will leave the QP too exposed. But White gets in P-K5 anyway through a tactical trick. Better, therefore, was 24 . . . K-R1 holding up the advance.

| | |
|---|---|
| 25 P-K5! | PxP |

If Black had played 24 . . . K-R1 he could now have refuted White's central thrust by 25 . . . QNxP but this now loses to 26 PxN *check*. It seams that Black could have played 25 . . . KNxP but then comes the crushing 26 N-R5+!! mating e.g. 26 . . . K-N1 27 Q-R6 or 26 . . . PxN 27 Q-N5+ K-R1 28 Q-R6 P-B4 29 N-N5. Korchnoi denies Karpov the satisfaction of finishing the match off in this elegant manner but he is now strategically lost anyway.

| | |
|---|---|
| 26 QxKP | NxP |
| 27 BxQNP | R-R2 |

27 . . . R-R4 trying to bolster up the weakling QBP may be an improvement. But White should still win by combining threats against the Black king with pressure on the Black QBP

**28 N-R4**

Threatening (either) N-B5+.

| | |
|---|---|
| 28 . . . | B-B1 |
| 29 B-K2 | B-K3 |
| 30 P-QB4 | N-N5 |
| 31 QxBP | |

White is now a pawn up with the better position. Normally Korchnoi would have resigned about now but in the circumstances he chooses to fight on to the bitter end. The final few moves represent a tragic climax to Korchnoi's bid for the world championship. Fortunately he was too short of time to consider the pathos of the situation.

| | |
|---|---|
| 31 . . . | Q-N1 |
| 32 B-B1 | R-B1 |
| 33 Q-KN5 | K-R1 |
| 34 R-Q2 | N-B3 |
| 35 Q-R6 | R-N1 |
| 36 N-KB3 | Q-KB1 |
| 37 Q-K3 | K-N2 |
| 38 N-N5 | B-Q2 |
| 39 P-N4 | Q-R1 |
| 40 P-N5 | N-R4 |
| 41 P-N6 | R-N2 |

The sealed move. **Korchnoi resigned** without resuming.

# CONCLUSION

Anatoly Karpov won the world chess championship in 1975 without playing a game, but it took him 32 gruelling games to retain his title in 1978. Here is a summary of how he did it.

|  | Karpov | Korchnoi | Opening | Number of moves |
|---|---|---|---|---|
| 1 | ½ | ½ | Queen's Gambit | 18 |
| 2 | ½ | ½ | Ruy Lopez | 29 |
| 3 | ½ | ½ | Nimzo-Indian Defence | 30 |
| 4 | ½ | ½ | Ruy Lopez | 19 |
| 5 | ½ | ½ | Nimzo-Indian Defence | 124 |
| 6 | ½ | ½ | English Opening | 23 |
| 7 | ½ | ½ | Nimzo-Indian Defence | 42 |
| 8 | 1 | 0 | Ruy Lopez | 28 |
| 9 | ½ | ½ | Queen's Gambit | 41 |
| 10 | ½ | ½ | Ruy Lopez | 44 |
| 11 | 0 | 1 | Sicilian Defence | 51 |
| 12 | ½ | ½ | Ruy Lopez | 44 |
| 13 | 1 | 0 | Queen's Gambit | 61 |
| 14 | 1 | 0 | Ruy Lopez | 50 |
| 15 | ½ | ½ | Catalan Opening | 25 |
| 16 | ½ | ½ | French Defence | 42 |
| 17 | 1 | 0 | Nimzo-Indian Defence | 39 |
| 18 | ½ | ½ | Pirc Defence | 64 |
| 19 | ½ | ½ | Catalan Opening | 39 |
| 20 | ½ | ½ | Caro Kann Defence | 63 |
| 21 | 0 | 1 | Queen's Gambit | 60 |
| 22 | ½ | ½ | French Defence | 64 |
| 23 | ½ | ½ | Queen's Gambit | 41 |
| 24 | ½ | ½ | Ruy Lopez | 45 |
| 25 | ½ | ½ | English Opening | 80 |
| 26 | ½ | ½ | English Opening | 27 |
| 27 | 1 | 0 | English Opening | 41 |
| 28 | 0 | 1 | Ruy Lopez | 61 |
| 29 | 0 | 1 | English Opening | 79 |
| 30 | ½ | ½ | English Opening | 42 |
| 31 | 0 | 1 | Queen's Gambit | 71 |
| 32 | 1 | 0 | Pirc Defence | 41 |

Final score: Karpov 6 wins, Korchnoi 5 wins, 21 draws.

The match divides naturally into four phases. During the first (Games 1-12) Korchnoi clearly had the better of the play but he was only able to convert one of his advantageous positions into a win. With the score standing at 1-1 with 10 draws Karpov had ceased to be firm favourite and the result of the match appeared to be completely open. But the second phase (Games 13-17) changed all that. Karpov won three more games without reply and the question in most people's minds became not who would win but how long Korchnoi could make the match last. The third phase (Games 18-26) was in many ways the reverse of the first. Now it was Karpov who established good positions only to throw them away. Korchnoi managed to pull back one game during this phase but this still left him trailing 4-3.

The fourth phase (Games 27-32) produced the final shoot-out. Karpov won game 27 to go 5-2 up but then appeared to run out of ammunition. Korchnoi scored 3½ points from the next four games to level the score at 5-5. It looked as though a miracle was about to occur but it was not to be. Karpov won the thirty-second game and retained his title by the narrowest possible margin, 6-5.

So Karpov remains world chess champion for at least another three years. It is curious that his chess-playing reputation should actually have suffered as a result of a match he won, but such undoubtedly is the case. During the three years before the match he bestrode the chess world like a colossus and acquired a reputation for near-invincibility. But Korchnoi changed all that by winning five games and letting Karpov off the hook in several more. During his three years in clover Karpov was renowned for doing nothing in particular but doing it very well. In this match he continued to do little but Korchnoi was able to show that much of what he did was wrong. This was partly due to Karpov's handling of the clock. He had obviously decided this was Korchnoi's Achilles' heel and he played on this weakness constantly. He played fast (superficially?) to induce Korchnoi to get into time trouble and played double-edged (rash?) moves when Korchnoi was in time trouble. In the end this unaesthetic tactic worked but it came perilously close to costing Karpov the match. It would have been a better match, and probably Karpov would have obtained a better result, if Karpov had used his full time allowance and concentrated on trying to find the best moves. For all these criticisms, one cannot take away from Karpov the fact that he won the match and so established himself as the most effective player in the world today.

Korchnoi played better than Karpov — but he also played worse. His play was generally on a higher creative plane than Karpov's. But too often his play descended briefly but decisively to the depths. Nearly always these lapses were caused by his perennial enemy, the clock. It was easy enough to spot the disease but it proved impossible to find a cure. Korchnoi failed to win the world title but he took the champion the full distance and his play at its best was worthy of any world champion. He deserves to be ranked alongside Tarrasch Rubinstein and Keres as one of the greatest players never to win the world championship.

The match was marred by some spectacular blunders which may give a misleading impression of the overall quality of the play. Blunders have occurred in all previous world championship matches, but the rose-tinted contact lenses through which those matches are now viewed have not yet been donned by the commentators on the present match. Let there be no doubt that the general quality of the play was high. In the three years before the match the contestants had not played one another but in their separate spheres of combat each had established himself as a well-nigh irresistible force. Logic required that they could not both be immovable objects and so, after sparks had flown in all directions and both players had tottered, it was Korchnoi who finally fell. But before he did the chess world had been entertained and instructed by varied and original opening play, fiercely contested middle games and skilfully conducted endings. The games will be profitably studied for many years to come.

This was not the first world championship to be conducted against a backcloth of hate but I think it was the worst. Previous matches have been soured by personal antipathy (e.g. Lasker v Tarrasch 1908 and Capablanca v Alekhine 1927) or ideological differences (e.g. Spassky v Fischer 1972). The present match was afflicted by both these problems to a greater degree than ever before and the situation was exacerbated by the fact that the cross-currents of controversy swept up not only the players themselves but also members of their delegations, the organisers and members of the jury. The bones of contention which arose in this hostile atmosphere included not only matters of genuine importance but also trivia which could have easily been buried if only the ground had been less frosty.

How this fractious atmosphere affected Karpov I find hard to judge. He maintained an unruffled exterior and may indeed have been more immune to disturbance than Korchnoi but I am sure he cannot have been totally unaffected. I know only too well how the atmosphere affected Korchnoi. Among the many disrupting factors I will single out the Zukhar Dispute. There is no doubt in my mind that this contributed substantially to Korchnoi's disastrous performance in games 13-17. Whether or not Korchnoi's fears were justified, chess matches should not be influenced by factors such as this.

The spectre of Bobby Fischer haunted the whole match. There were many who claimed that Fischer would have easily beaten either of the jerks who were presumptuously fighting for his title. The situation was similar to the match between Steinitz and Anderssen in 1866 held between the best two players in the world except the retired Paul Morphy. I regard the Fischer question as basically irrelevant. I know he was a superb player in 1972 and I would be very interested to know whether, weighed down by the accumulation of six years' mildew, he can play to anywhere near the some standard now. If so, let him come out of retirement and prove it (Morphy never did). If not, let the disputation of chess honours be left to those who are prepared to play. Fischer denied the chess world the spectacle of a world championship match in 1975. In 1978, despite all the problems, Karpov and Korchnoi laid on a thirty-two game banquet for the hungry chess world. We must all be grateful to them for this magnificent feast.

# *Part III*
## ———— Appendix ————
# DOCUMENTS
# RELATING TO THE
# MATCH

To
L. I. Brezhnev                                    V. L. Korchnoi
General Secretary of the Communist Party          Int. Chess Grandmaster
President of the Supreme Soviet of the USSR        Challenger for the World
Marshall of the USSR                                 Chess Championship
                                                Resident in Switzerland

*Open Letter*

Dear Mr. Brezhnev,

As a professional chess grandmaster, recently a citizen of the USSR, now resident in Switzerland, I turn to you.

Two years ago I emigrated to the West, since it was no longer in my power to bear the extreme and hostile attitude of Party, Soviet and Sport leaders, since I no longer had the possibility to continue my creative activity in the Soviet Union.

My family remained in the Soviet Union, my wife and son. Inspite of the fact that they are loyal Soviet citizens they submitted a request in July, 1977 to emigrate from the Soviet Union. They did this, impelled by their love for a husband and a father. November, 1977 this request was refused. In private conversation Soviet police chiefs left no doubt open that the members of my family are hostages, human beings who have been chosen to suffer penance for my escape.

About one year has passed since their request for emigration. The situation of my family is now catastrophic. They have been robbed of the means of their existence and of the possibility of working or studying. The authorities confront them with suspicion and hatred, ordinary people avoid all contact with them. For my family there has now been a severe dimunition of all the rights guaranteed by the Constitution — but there has been no reduction in their duties! My son, who already a year ago declared his intention of leaving his homeland, has nevertheless been obstinately called up for military service.

You, Marshall of the Soviet Union, praise the heroism of a Muhammed Ali, who refused to fight in Vietnam. My son also does not want to fight. He does not want to be a soldier of the state which has unscrupulously degraded his father.

Is it not curious, my dear Chairman of the Supreme Soviet, that the guilty go free while it is those who are without protection who are punished, punished for their own incapacity to work, for the appearance of unhealthy sporting relations, and finally for the professional incompetence of the Soviet leaders. The practice of punishing political hostages has, unfortunately, been common throughout the entire world, but how, my dear President, does that suit the complexion of one of the regimes which significantly helps to determine world political fashions?!

In these days a Match is beginning in the Philippines for the World Chess Championship between myself and the Soviet Grandmaster and World Champion Anatoly Karpov.

Soviet leaders have declared more than once that sport must be separated from politics. It is self-evident that those states should also adhere to this principle who will participate in the World Sport Olympiad destined for Moscow in 1980.

I appeal to your political common sense, my dear General Secretary: In order to ensure that this match for the World Chess Championship should take place under normal conditions, without political complications, I beg you to allow my family to depart from the Soviet Union.

I appeal to you to demonstrate the goodwill necessary for the fulfillment of the conditions of the Helsinki International Agreement, which prescribes the reunification of divided families.

I invoke your mercy, Mr. Chairman; I beg you to show compassion for two citizens of the USSR, whose life, by decree of fate, is no longer bound to the life of Soviet society. Permit them to leave the Soviet Union.

1-7-1978                                   Chess Grandmaster

cc: Soviet Ambassador in Manila             Viktor Korchnoi

We protest in the strongest possible terms to the tactics of blackmail and intimidation used by the Soviet delegation in negotiations over the question of the Swiss flag. By threatening to walk out of the match the Soviets placed their hosts in an impossible situation. We shall not lower ourselves to the reciprocal use of such tactics, but ask the Filipino people not again to allow the legitimate rights of an individual to be crushed on their own soil by the weight of Soviet power.

We also ask the Soviet delegation to make public one shred of documentary evidence, either in the rules of F.I.D.E. or in the independent report submitted from the University of Heidelberg, denying Viktor Korchnoi the right to play under the Swiss flag. We are bound by the rules of F.I.D.E. to accept the decision of the jury, but challenge any independent body not operating under duress to reach the same conclusion on the basis of the same evidence.

V. KORCHNOI

P. LEEUWERIK

To the chief arbiter
Herr Lothar Schmid
Thursday July 20 1978

Dear Herr Schmid,

It was observed during the second game today that at one point a yoghourt was passed to Mr Karpov from the Soviet delegation via one of the arbiters. According to the FIDE rules for the World Championship section 4.54 "an arbiter may make and receive emergency calls at the special phone in his dressing room. There shall be no other communication into or out of the restricted area." (Restricted Area is defined in Section 4.5).

Reception of Yoghourt or alternative sustenance is evidently not countenanced by this clause, and we protest most strongly against this serious infringement of the FIDE regulations. It is clear that a cunningly arranged distribution of edible items to one player during the game, emanating from one delegation or the other, could convey a kind of code message. Thus a yoghourt after move 20 could signify "we instruct you to offer a draw"; or a sliced mango could mean "we order you to decline a draw". A dish of marinated quails' eggs could mean "play Ng4 at once" and so on. The possibilities are limitless.

The player should take all his requirements onto the stage with him at the start of the game, and no extraneous food or extra equipment should be delivered during the game. We protest against this action by the Soviet delegation during game two and request the chief arbiter to suppress all further infringements of this nature.

Yours sincerely
P. Leeuwerik
Head of Korchnoi Delegation


PINES HOTEL
AUGUST 3rd 1978

Dear Florencio,

I would like to clarify the position of our delegation on the matter of the so called Dr Zukhar, which is causing difficulty at the present stage of the world championship. Many observers (including such an impeccable source as Harry Golombek) have remarked on the apparently suspicious behaviour of Dr Zukhar during recent games. Notice has been taken of his habit of riveting his gaze onto Korchnoi as if trying to hypnotise him or otherwise influence him into playing weak moves.

It would seem that Dr Zukhar's ability at chess is severely limited yet, paradoxically, he maintains his position as close as possible to the stage for the whole five hours of every game without even rising to answer simple calls of nature — a remarkable feat which argues more than humble devotion to the noble game of chess.

Anyone involved in a creative activity, such as writing, painting, or playing chess, knows how disturbing it can be to have a hostile person staring at them while they are in the act of creation. Mr Korchnoi feels deeply disturbed by the proximity of Dr Zukhar in the auditorium and we would suggest, in the interests of fair play and of the further peaceable course of the match, that Dr Zukhar should recognise Korchnoi's complaint and voluntarily remove himself to a more distant part of the spectator area. Surely this compliance would represent normal civilized behaviour on the part of any man who appreciated that his presence was causing distress to one of the participants in the world championship.

We would naturally prefer to settle the whole matter in a friendly way without recourse to official protests. If the Soviet delegation is here simply to play chess (as they have so often claimed) then they can raise no objection to accepting their compatriot Dr Zukhar amongst their own ranks at the back of the auditorium. If, on the other hand, the Soviet delegation refuses this reasonable step it will be a sign of their bad faith and we will have to resort to official remedies. Of course, we hope to solve all problems by friendly agreement between the contending parties.

Since the Soviet delegation disowns Dr Zukhar as a member and insists on regarding him simply as a member of the public then you, Florencio, as chief organiser of the match, have total jurisdiction to direct the movements of Dr Zukhar within the auditorium in the best interests of the match. If Dr Zukhar is, indeed, not a member of the Soviet delegation then that delegation has no right to dispute your placing of Dr Zukhar within the auditorium. We would prefer that Dr Zukhar should be seated along with the bona-fide members of the USSR delegation, at a proper distance from the stage, but if this step is resisted we request the total exclusion of Dr Zukhar from the entire spectating area for the duration of the match.

Raymond Keene, Chief Second of Viktor Korchnoi

August 5, 1978

ATTN:  PROF. LIM KOK ANN
       Chairman of the Match Jury
       World Chess Championship

       MR. LOTHAR SCHMID
       Chief Arbiter of the Match

       MR. FLORENCIO CAMPOMANES
       Organizer of the Match

Dear Sirs:

In connection with the letter of the Challenger's Second, Mr. R. Keene on 3 of August, 1978, which may be considered as a formal protest against the presence of Dr. Vladimir Zoukhar in the auditorium, who allegedly negatively influences Mr. Korchnoi, I consider it necessary to bring to your notice the following:

Doctor of Medicine Sciences, Professor Vladimir Zoukhar has arrived to the Republic of the Philippines as a member of the Soviet Delegation, but, as distinct from World Champion personal physician Professor Mikhail Guershanovitch, is not an official person foreseen by the regulations of the match.

Professor Zoukhar is an expert in problems of psychology and neurology with a many-years experience and impecable professional reputation. For the past several years, he has been consulting World Champion within the limits of his competence.

In modern sport, including chess, the problems of psychology are of recognized scientific significance and not a few sportsmen and teams make use of psychologists' services and advices in the course of the preparation period as well as during a competition.

Incidentally, in Mr. Korchnoi's book, published in Holland in 1977 and translated thereafter into other languages, the author says that in 1974 during the final candidates' match, he resorted to the services of some psychologist of Leningrad.

Being present at the Match in Baguio, Dr. V. Zoukhar attentively follows the general psycholigal condition of the World Champion including the course of a game and simultaneously which is quite natural, may watch, which is not prohibited by the regulations, the conduct of the rival.

Being seated in the auditorium, Dr. V. Zoukhar infringes upon none of the requirements concerning spectators of the section 7.4 of the regulations. The fact, that sometimes during the whole period of a game, he would not leave his seat, not even to answer simple calls of nature (to which Mr. R. Keene pays particular attention in his letter) cannot be regarded as criminal behaviour.

On the contrary, Dr. Zoukhar makes less noise or disturbance than those who repeatedly enter or leave the auditorium.

In his letter, Mr. Keene points out that the very presence of Dr. Zoukhar in the auditorium, his riveting gazes at Mr. Korchnoi disturb the latter. Mr. Keene also hints to Dr. Zoukhar's abilities of hypnotic influence.

These accusations are absolutely unproven both from scientifical and factual points of view. By the way, it would be appropriate to recollect, that similar groundless suspicions and accusations Mr. Korchnoi put forward earlier, in the matches, for instance with M. Tal (1968), A. Karpov (1974) B. Spassky (1977-1978).

Such complaints of the supernatural factors' influence in the course of the chess struggle, may be explained by either Mr. Korchnoi's unhealthy inclination to exageration or the desire to purposely complicate and sharpen the atmosphere around the so important sport competition.

In connection with this, we feel ourselves obliged to remind of the fact that many matches with Mr. Korchnoi's participation were accompanied by scandalous situations. For instance, 1968 matches with Mr. Reschevsky and M. Tal, 1974 matches with Mr. E. Meking, T. Petrosian, A. Karpov, 1977-1978 match with B. Spassky.

Basing on the above-mentioned, we regard the accusations and suspicions advanced against Professor Zoukhar as well as requirement to mark out his location (as distinct from other spectators) not speaking of the exclusion from the Convention Center as being groundless and unseemly.

In conclusion, I must note that the behaviour of certain official members of the challenger's delegation in the auditorium is not immaculate and sometimes evoked discontent on the part of A. Karpov. However, World Champion, manifesting his self control did not wish to resort to police methods to have some persons ejected or replaced.

With the "hypnosis" issue being widely commented on in mass media and thus having replaced the "youghourt question", we would like to clarify our position as stated in this letter in public.

Respectfully yours,

SOVIET CHESS FEDERATION

VICTOR BATURINSKY
Vice-President

## PUBLIC STATEMENT BY VIKTOR KORCHNOI
### 8th of August 1978

Viktor Korchnoi has requested me as his official representative, to inform the press of the following:

Mr. Karpov has made it known through his Press spokesman, Mr. Roshal, that Viktor Korchnoi has made some aspersions against him and his colleagues which has made it impossible for him to shake hands with Viktor Korchnoi in the future.

Mr. Karpov now departs from a point to which he himself agreed at the beginning of the match. For the rest, he has only agreed to this point out of deference to the Philippine People and in order to lend this strange match some elegance on the stage.

When Viktor Korchnoi chose the Philippines as the location of the match, he had in mind above all that this young and developing Republic was entirely independent from outside politics. He was convinced that the influence of Soviet politics was less here than in any European country. Viktor Korchnoi is still convinced of this and renders his thanks to the host country for its friendly hospitality and for the security and protection it has afforded him.

Viktor Korchnoi regrets to find that even in this beautiful and independent country the characteristic Soviet political maneuvering in chess, of which Robert Fischer has already been a victim, has produced on occasion substantial results.

Viktor Korchnoi would be glad if Mr. Campomanes, the organizer of the match, would follow the precept of President Marcos and not allow himself to be affected by the intimidation and blackmail of the Soviet delegation so that Mr. Campomanes may fulfill his official duties in honourable fashion.

Mr. Karpov is surrounded by many accomplished aides who are attempting to persuade the world that he is solely and purely a chess player whereas Viktor Korchnoi, bluntly speaking, is uniquely engaged in playing politics.

Can it be that Mr. Karpov really believes that the efforts of Viktor Korchnoi for the last two years to get his family out of the Soviet Union are only a pretense? Does Mr. Karpov think that in discarding the Soviet flag Viktor Korchnoi has also rejected the right to have any other flags in the world?

Viktor Korchnoi realizes that Mr. Karpov learnt in school that his country was the biggest in the world but Viktor Korchnoi hopes that the intellectual niveau of Mr. Karpov permits him to look around and perceive that, all the same, there exist other countries in the world.

Does Mr. Karpov really imagine that he is acting ethically in employing the help of a mysterious Zoukhar in order to obtain the title of World Champion, yet once again, without a fight — a world Champion of a so-called Soviet world empire?

So far as the handshaking is concerned Viktor Korchnoi declares that the reason he emigrated from the Soviet Union was precisely because he wanted to be liberated from the distasteful task of clasping hands with such people as Karpov and his crew.

Viktor Korchnoi had made the decision, at the beginning of the 9th game to cut off all friendly communication with Mr. Karpov. The offer of a draw will only be made through the Chief Arbiter, Dr. Lothar Schmid.

Viktor Korchnoi has requested me to say that from now on, until the end of the match, he will be animated by a special feeling when playing the games — he will hear, resounding in the pockets of his adversary, the clank of the chains that fetter his family in the prison camp that is the Soviet Union.

Perhaps the key of these fetters is to be found in the pockets of the innocent and honourable learned gentleman Mr. Zoukhar or of Mr. Viktor Davidowitsch Baturinsky who were professional jailers and still are such and no doubt always be.

Viktor Korchnoi would be very glad if all the journalists, in those countries where free speech is allowed, would inform their readers of this decision.

### CHESS MATCH IN THE PHILIPPINES
### IS NOT A TRAINING GROUND
### FOR COLD WAR

Statement of the Soviet Chess Delegation at the World Chess Championship Match.

On August 8, 1978, Mrs. Leeuwerik who calls herself the head of "Swiss Chess Delegation" (no chess player of which by the way, is a citizen of Switzerland) in behalf of Mr. Korchnoi issued an official public statement.

This unprecedented document in the history of World Chess is from beginning to the end replete with crude personal insults and provocative political insinuations.

It continues and extends the tactics launched by the Challenger's group at the press conference held in Manila on July 4, 1978, when an attempt was made to insult and slander World Champion, Anatoly Karpov, some other famous grandmasters and chess representatives.

As far as the World Champion and all the persons who have arrived to the Match from the Soviet Union are concerned, none of them during their stay in the Philippines, neither orally nor in press, has allowed any insult or tactless remark in respect to the members of the Challenger's delegation or issued any political statement.

All disputes and discussions that had taken place before the beginning of the match and have been in the course of the games, including the question of the right to use national flag, all of them had sport and technical nature and dealt with the interpretations of certain points of the Regulations of the Match.

The fact, that so far the Jury of Appeals considered and decided all the problems not in favor of the Challenger, easily can be explained. His requirements and protests have been unfounded and sometimes, just ridiculous.

Members of the Jury have repeatedly been accused by the Challenger and Mrs. Leeuwerik of acting unobjectively and not being neutral. The question is that the decisions have been made by world known and respected chess leaders, FIDE Bureau and Central Committee member, Mr. E. Edmonson (USA), 10th Zone President and FIDE Central Committee member, Professor Lim Kok Ann (Singapore) FIDE Qualification Committee member, Mr. A. Malchev (Bulgaria). The Challenger did not get embarrassed to name members of the Jury "children" for their having not agreed to his claims.

Talking about this, Mr. Korchnoi's unceremoniousness and ill-bredness are well-known. Thus, in 1974, he publicly insulted the Final candidates' Match Chief Arbiter, Count Alberico O'Kelly (Belgium).

World Ex-Champion, Mikhail Tal is a popular and respected figure all the world over for his outstanding talent and sporting gentlemanness and Mr. Korchnoi dared to name him a slanderer.

In the letter of Aug. 6, 1978, addressed to the Match Jury, he called Professor, Doctor of Medicine Sciences, V. Zoukhar "hooligan pseudo-scholar", although, in the book published in Holland in 1978 he referred to him as one of the prominent scientists.

In the statement of August 8, 1978, it is asserted that FIDE Vice President, Mr. Florencio Campomanes, allegedly fulfills his duties as the Match Organizer in an unhonourable fashion, and the authors edify him of proper behaviour.

World Champion's refusal to shake hands with his rival beginning with the 8th game, appeared to be the immediate pretext that was chosen for the statement of August 8.

In connection with this, one should be reminded of the fact that the request of shaking hands before each game, stemmed from the Challenger and was stated in his telegram to FIDE President on March 3, 1978. This prudence accounted for the fact that some of Mr. Korchnoi's rivals in previous competitions refused to shake hands with him.

Exclusively out of respect for the organizers and audience, World Champion, Anatoly Karpov agreed, however, to the traditional handshake procedure.

Now, in the light of the statement where it is pointed out that Mr. Korchnoi had defected from the USSR "to be liberated from distasteful task of clasping hands with such people as Karpov and his crew" especially obvious seems to have been the rightfulness of the World Champion's rejection to shake hands with Mr. Korchnoi.

Now, it is appropriate to mark here that the Challenger's second, grandmaster, Mr. R. Keene has lost the traits characterizing the English gentleman, apparently as a result of contacts with the kind of people Mrs. Leeuwerik and Mr. Korchnoi are, and allowed uncrupulous, insulting retort, which to our regret, was quoted in the Press.

Analizing the statement of August 8, 1978, in the agregate with other actions of the Challenger's side, one should come to the conclusion that its principal "spring" is not so much Mr. Korchnoi himself as the above-mentioned Mrs. Leeuwerik.

This woman, who never had anything to do with chess and the international chess movement, who openly declares of her spiteful hatred to the USSR, is trying to convert the distinguished sporting competition, that the World Chess Championship Match is, into the training ground of the Cold War and impede the consolidation of friendship and cultural cooperation, to which admittedly serve chess, between countries.

USSR CHESS DELEGATION
Republic of the Philippines
Baguio City
August 10, 1978